FOR

ELISE

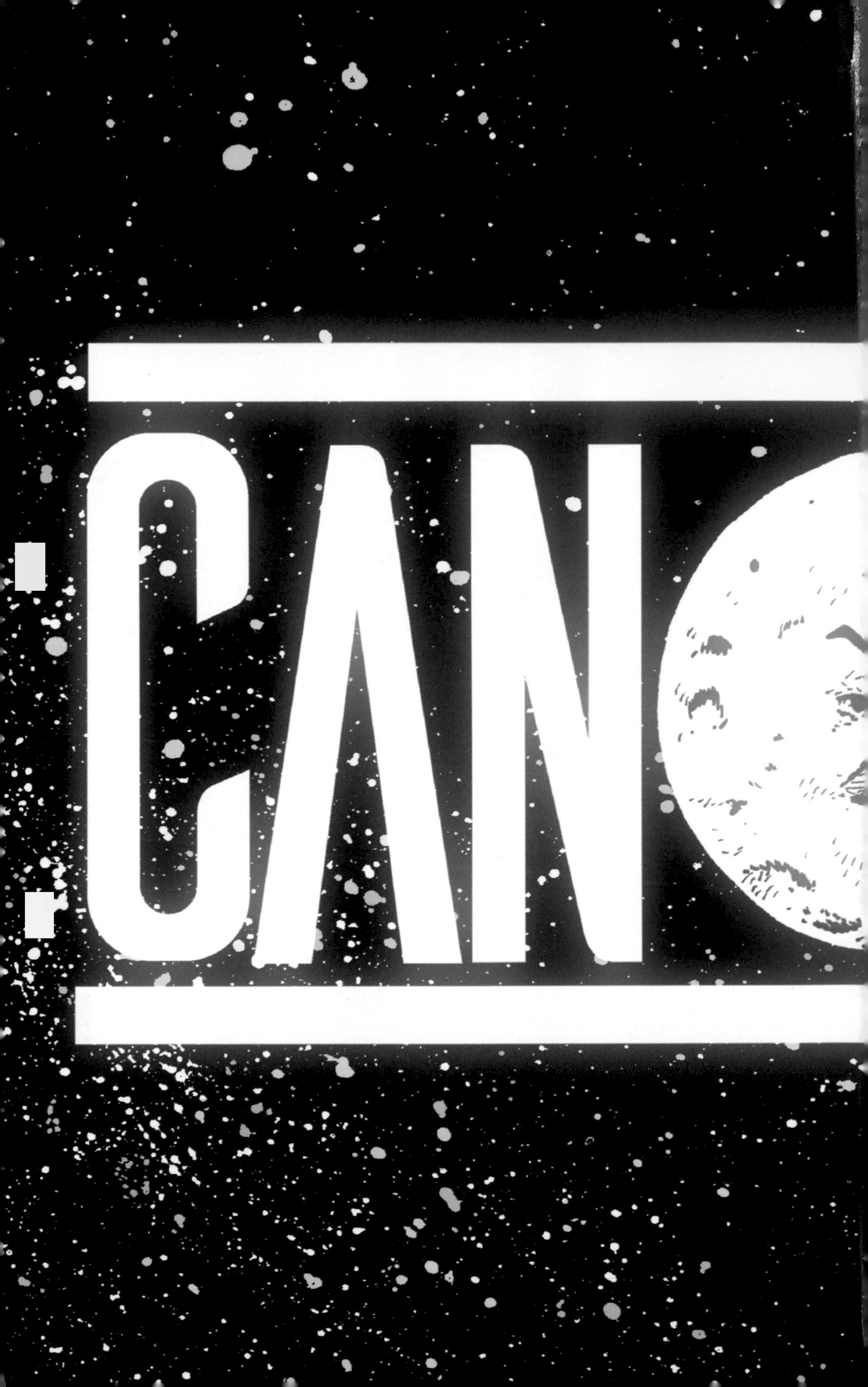
CAN

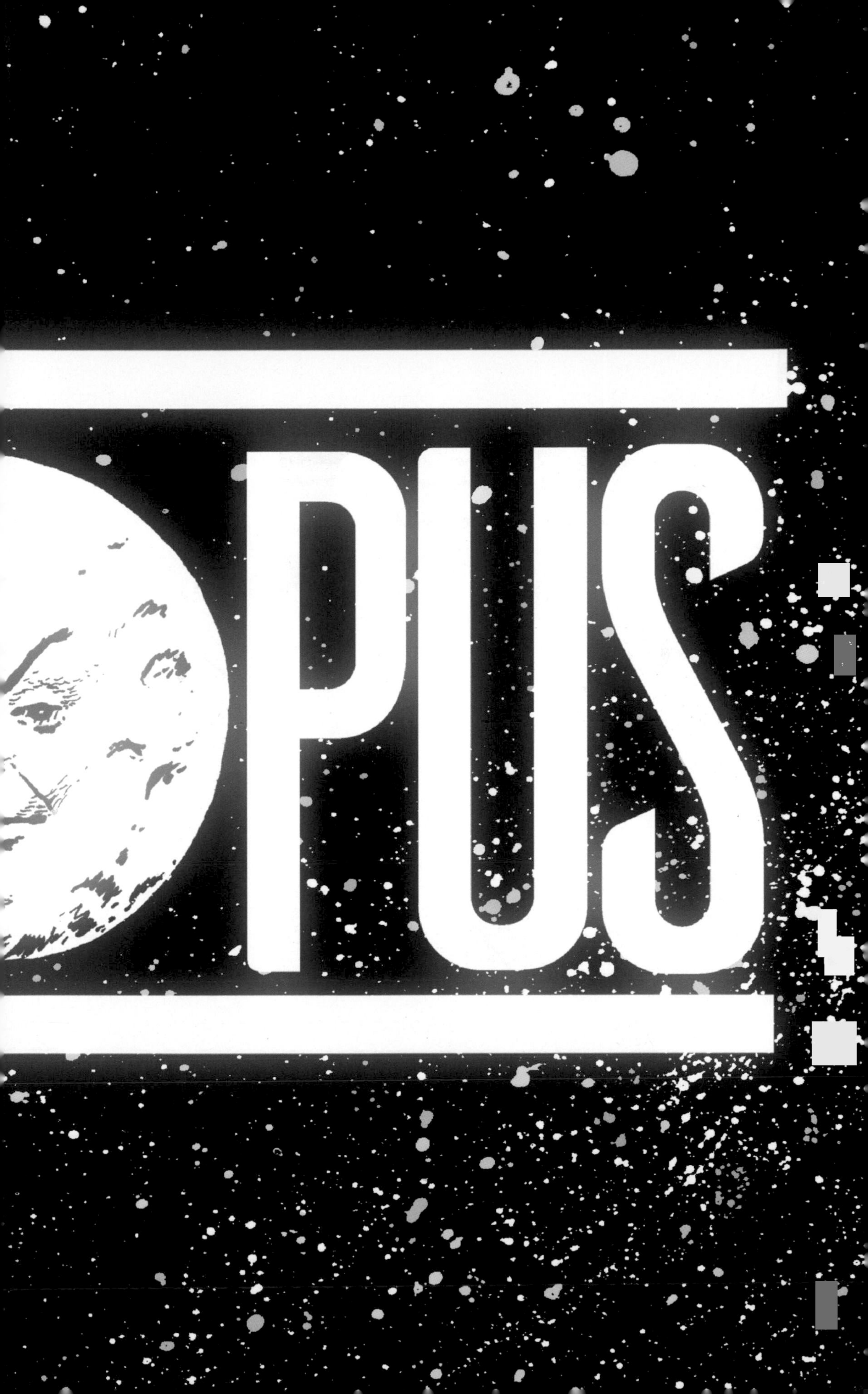
PUS

CREATED BY:
DAVE CHISHOLM

COLOR FLATS BY:
DUSTYN PAYETTE

PRODUCTION BY:
JOEL RODRIGUEZ

SCOUT COMICS

Brendan Deneen, *CEO*
James Haick III, *President*
Tennessee Edwards, *CSO*
Don Handfield, *CMO*
James Pruett, *CCO*
David Byrne, *Co-Publisher*
Charlie Stickney, *Co-Publisher*
Joel Rodriguez, *Head of Design*

FB / TW / IG:
@SCOUTCOMICS

LEARN MORE AT:
WWW.SCOUTCOMICS.COM

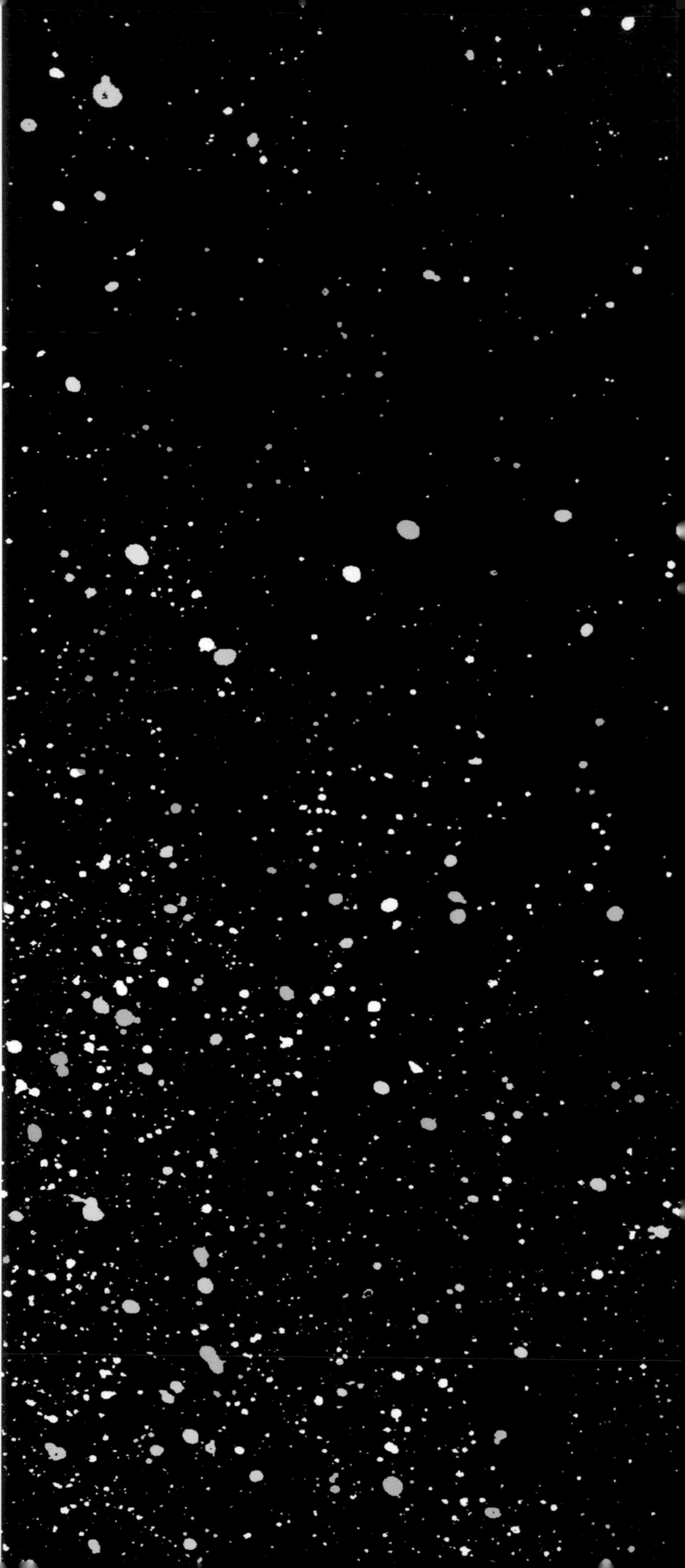

CHAPTER 1

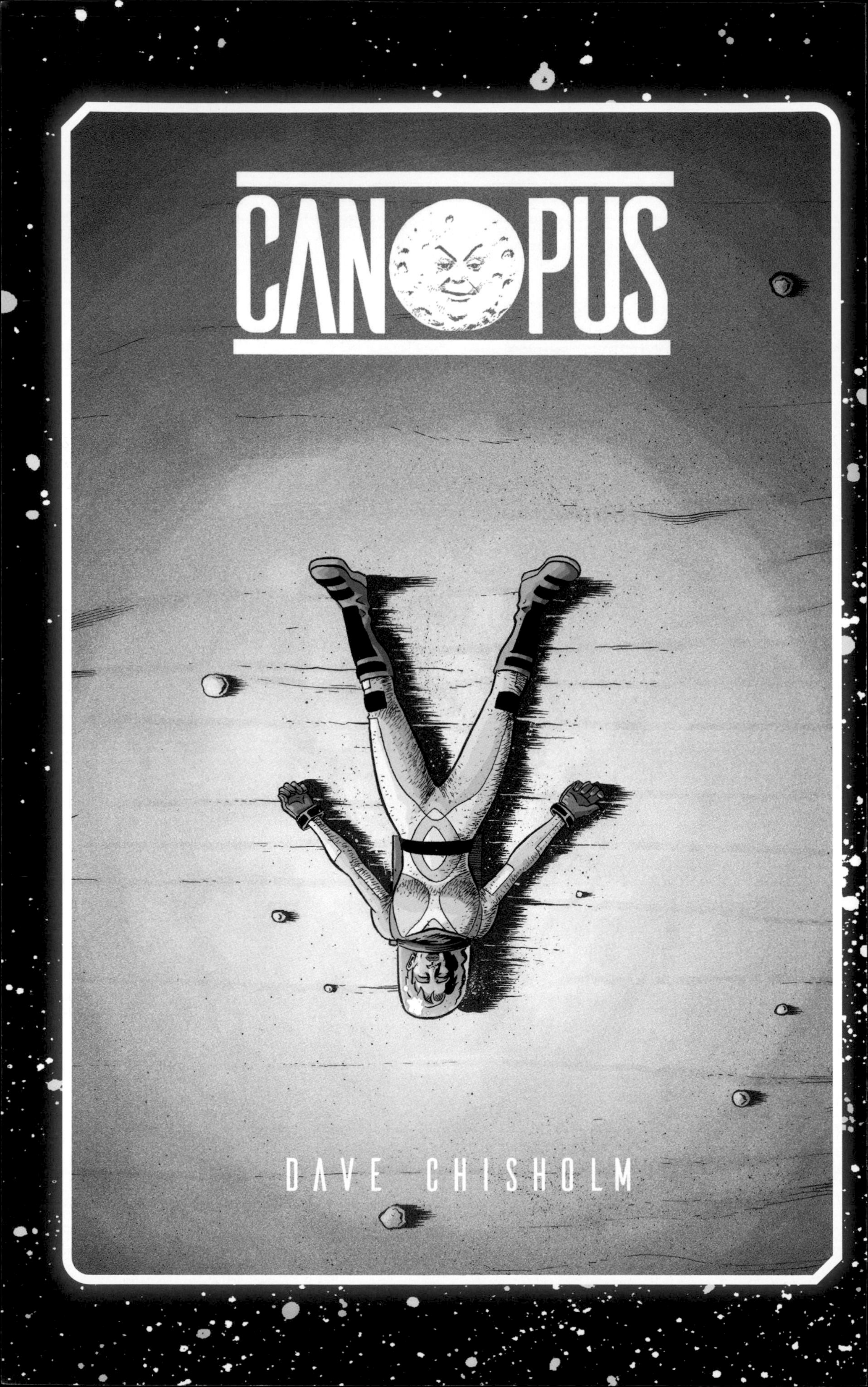
CANOPUS
DAVE CHISHOLM

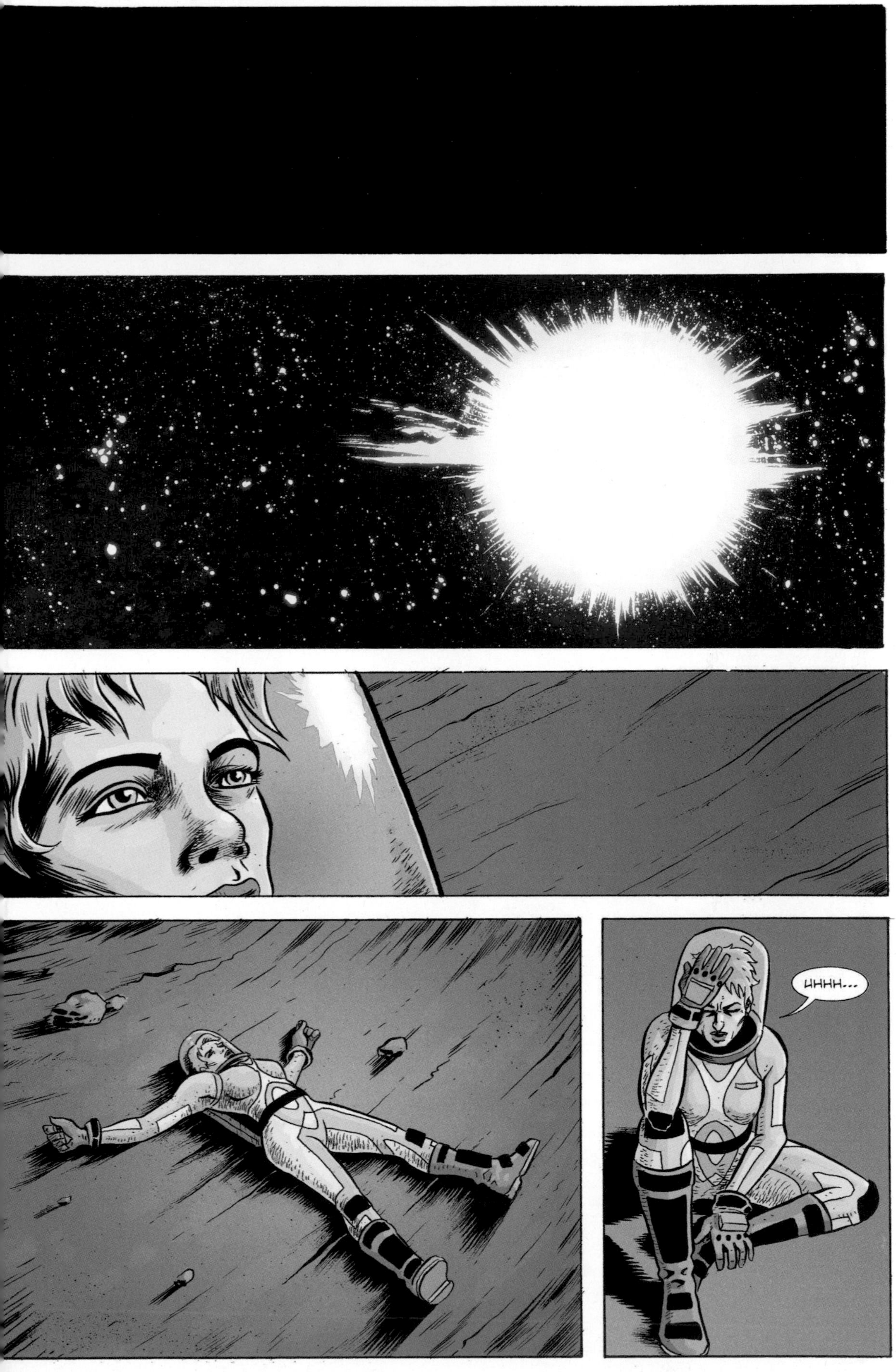
UHHH...

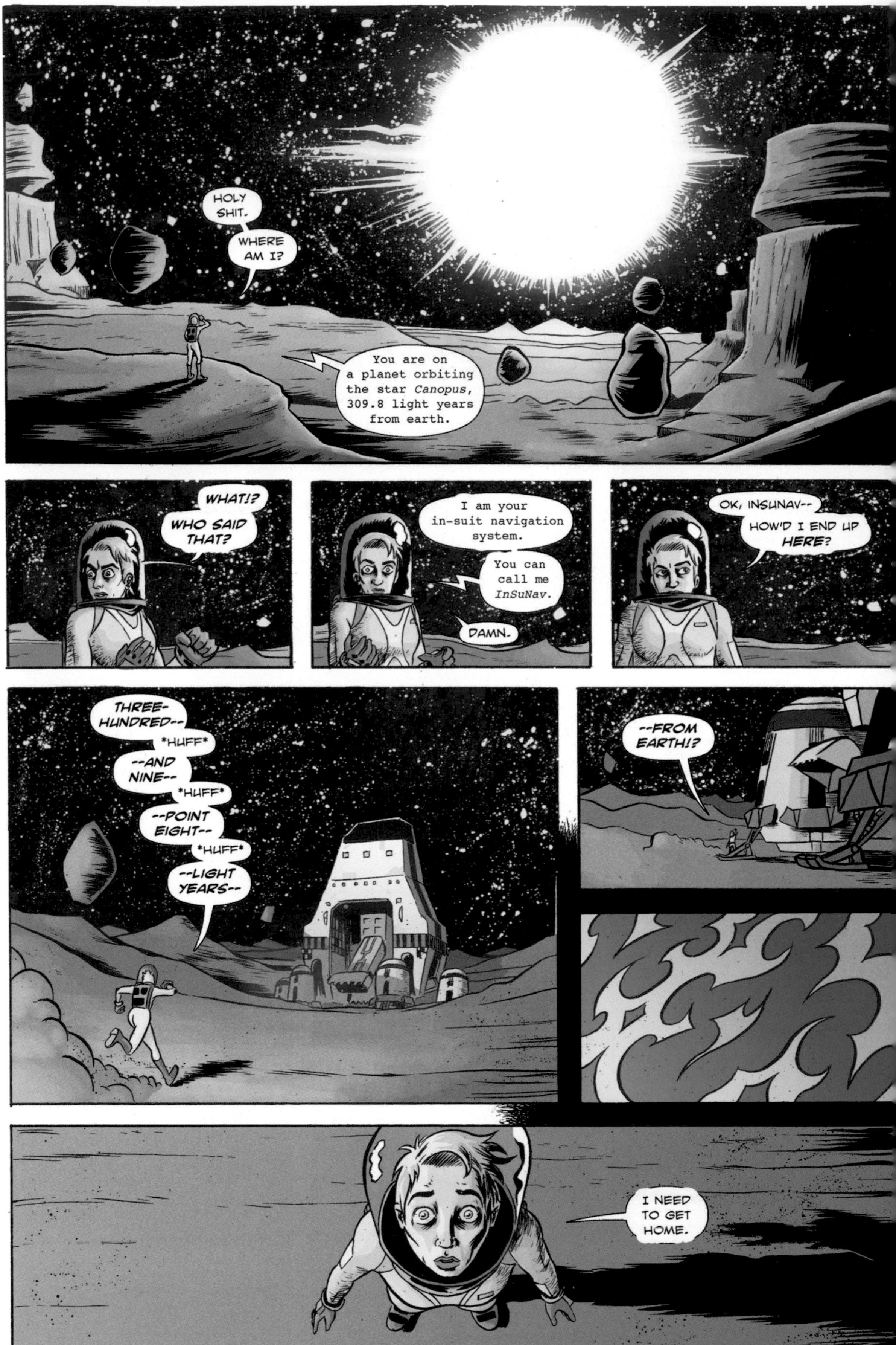
HOLY SHIT.
WHERE AM I?
You are on a planet orbiting the star *Canopus*, 309.8 light years from earth.
WHAT!? WHO SAID THAT?
I am your in-suit navigation system.
You can call me *InSuNav*.
DAMN.
OK, INSUNAV--
HOW'D I END UP HERE?
THREE-HUNDRED--
HUFF
--AND NINE--
HUFF
--POINT EIGHT--
HUFF
--LIGHT YEARS--
--FROM EARTH!?
I NEED TO GET HOME.

HELLO? IS ANYBODY HERE?

Hello, Dr. Helen Sterling. How can I help you?

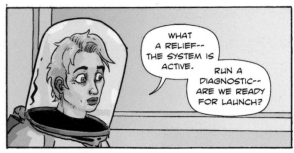

WHAT A RELIEF-- THE SYSTEM IS ACTIVE.

RUN A DIAGNOSTIC-- ARE WE READY FOR LAUNCH?

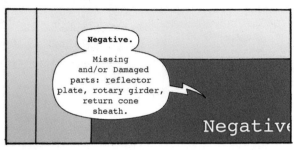

Negative.

Missing and/or Damaged parts: reflector plate, rotary girder, return cone sheath.

Negative

PRINT NECESSARY PARTS.

Negative. Need materials to print: silicate and titanium.

5 kilograms each.

DAMN. CONTACT EARTH--CONTACT MISSION CONTROL.

Negative. No signal from Earth.

NO SIGNAL? WHAT--?

SCAN THE SURFACE OF THIS PLANET FOR SILICATE AND TITANIUM.

Just a moment...

THIS BETTER WORK.

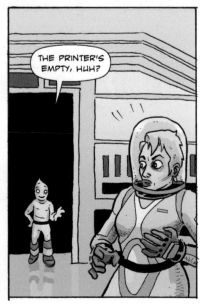

THE PRINTER'S EMPTY, HUH?

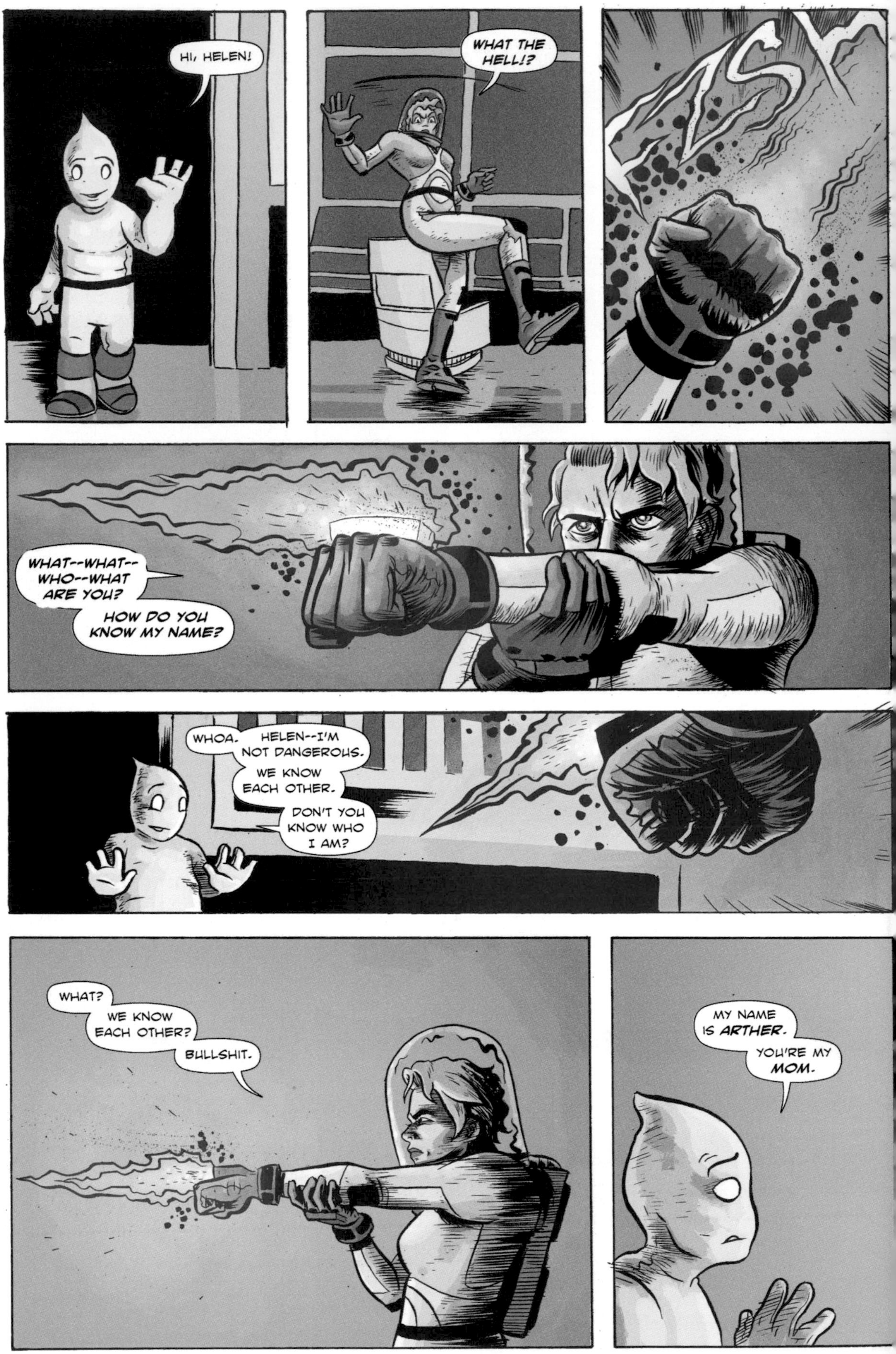
HI, HELEN!
WHAT THE HELL!?
WHAT--WHAT-- WHO--WHAT ARE YOU?
HOW DO YOU KNOW MY NAME?
WHOA.
HELEN--I'M NOT DANGEROUS.
WE KNOW EACH OTHER.
DON'T YOU KNOW WHO I AM?
WHAT?
WE KNOW EACH OTHER?
BULLSHIT.
MY NAME IS ARTHER.
YOU'RE MY MOM.

ARTHER?

ARTHER...

I'M NOT YOUR-- YOUR MOM.

YOU'RE NOT EVEN HUMAN.

YOU'RE SOME KIND OF-- --OF ROBOT.

FZT

AM I LOSING MY MIND?

NAH, YOU'RE NOT LOSING YOUR MIND.

WE CAME HERE TOGETHER ON THIS SHIP-- REMEMBER?

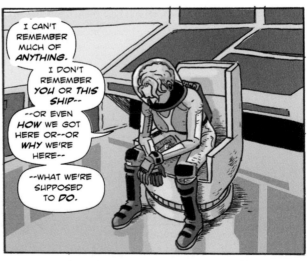

I CAN'T REMEMBER MUCH OF ANYTHING.

I DON'T REMEMBER YOU OR THIS SHIP--

--OR EVEN HOW WE GOT HERE OR--OR WHY WE'RE HERE--

--WHAT WE'RE SUPPOSED TO DO.

JESUS.

AMNESIA.

COULD THIS BE ANY MORE CLICHE?

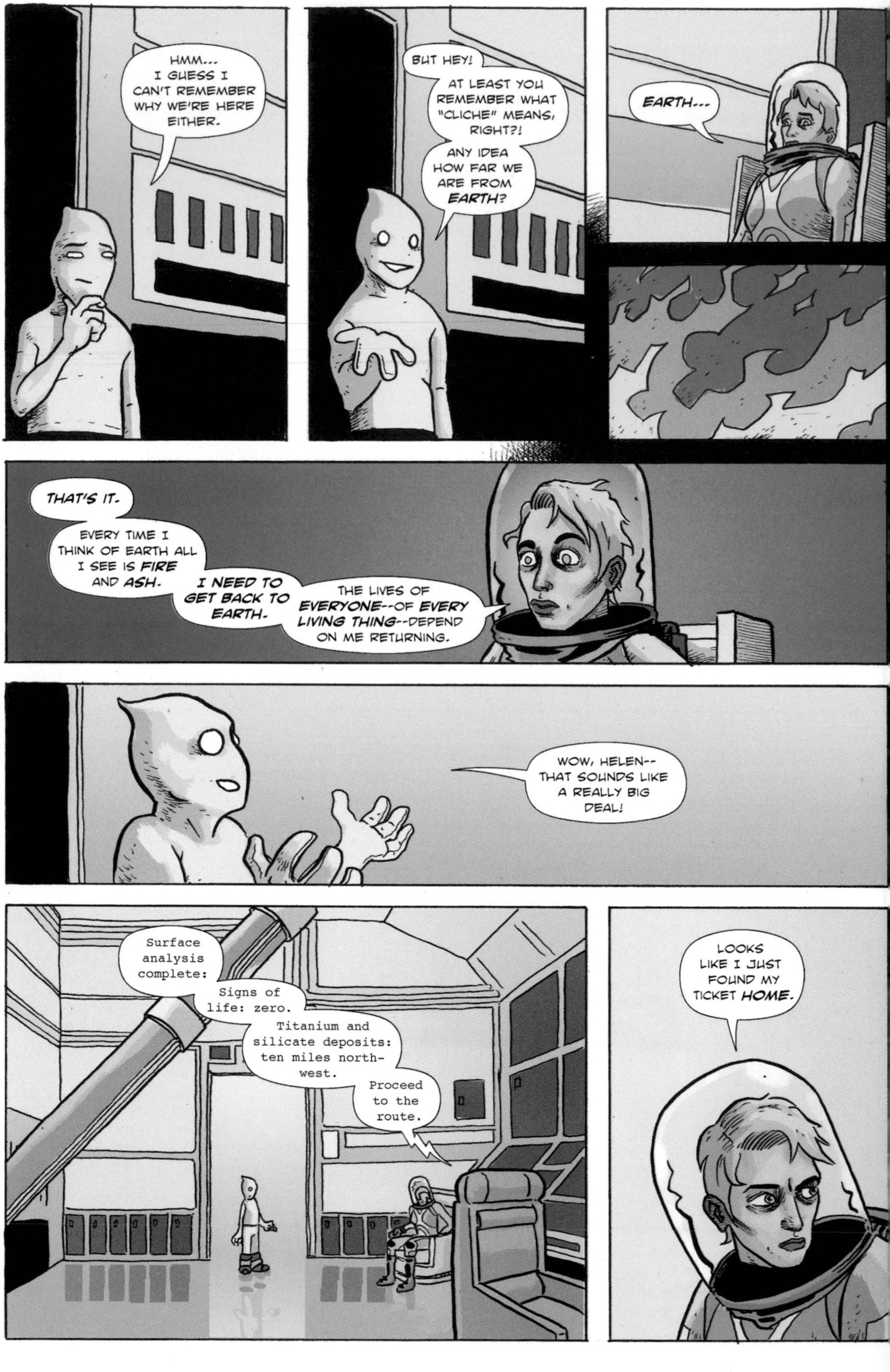
HMM... I GUESS I CAN'T REMEMBER WHY WE'RE HERE EITHER.
BUT HEY!
AT LEAST YOU REMEMBER WHAT "CLICHE" MEANS, RIGHT?!
ANY IDEA HOW FAR WE ARE FROM EARTH?
EARTH...
THAT'S IT.
EVERY TIME I THINK OF EARTH ALL I SEE IS FIRE AND ASH.
I NEED TO GET BACK TO EARTH.
THE LIVES OF EVERYONE--OF EVERY LIVING THING--DEPEND ON ME RETURNING.
WOW, HELEN--THAT SOUNDS LIKE A REALLY BIG DEAL!
Surface analysis complete:
Signs of life: zero.
Titanium and silicate deposits: ten miles north-west.
Proceed to the route.
LOOKS LIKE I JUST FOUND MY TICKET HOME.

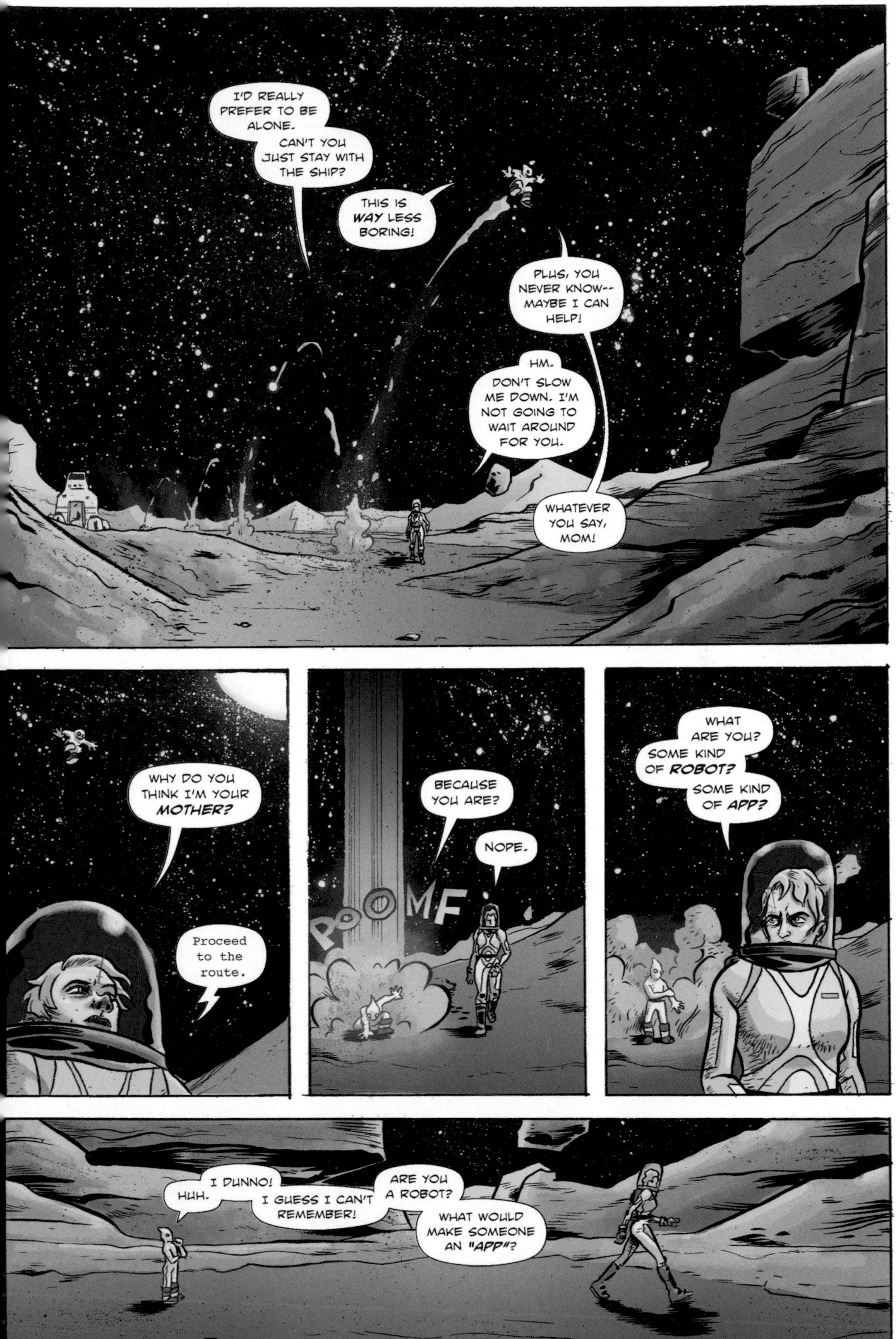
I'D REALLY PREFER TO BE ALONE.
CAN'T YOU JUST STAY WITH THE SHIP?
THIS IS WAY LESS BORING!
PLUS, YOU NEVER KNOW-- MAYBE I CAN HELP!
HM.
DON'T SLOW ME DOWN. I'M NOT GOING TO WAIT AROUND FOR YOU.
WHATEVER YOU SAY, MOM!
WHY DO YOU THINK I'M YOUR MOTHER?
Proceed to the route.
BECAUSE YOU ARE?
NOPE.
POOMF
WHAT ARE YOU?
SOME KIND OF ROBOT?
SOME KIND OF APP?
HUH.
I DUNNO!
I GUESS I CAN'T REMEMBER!
ARE YOU A ROBOT?
WHAT WOULD MAKE SOMEONE AN "APP"?

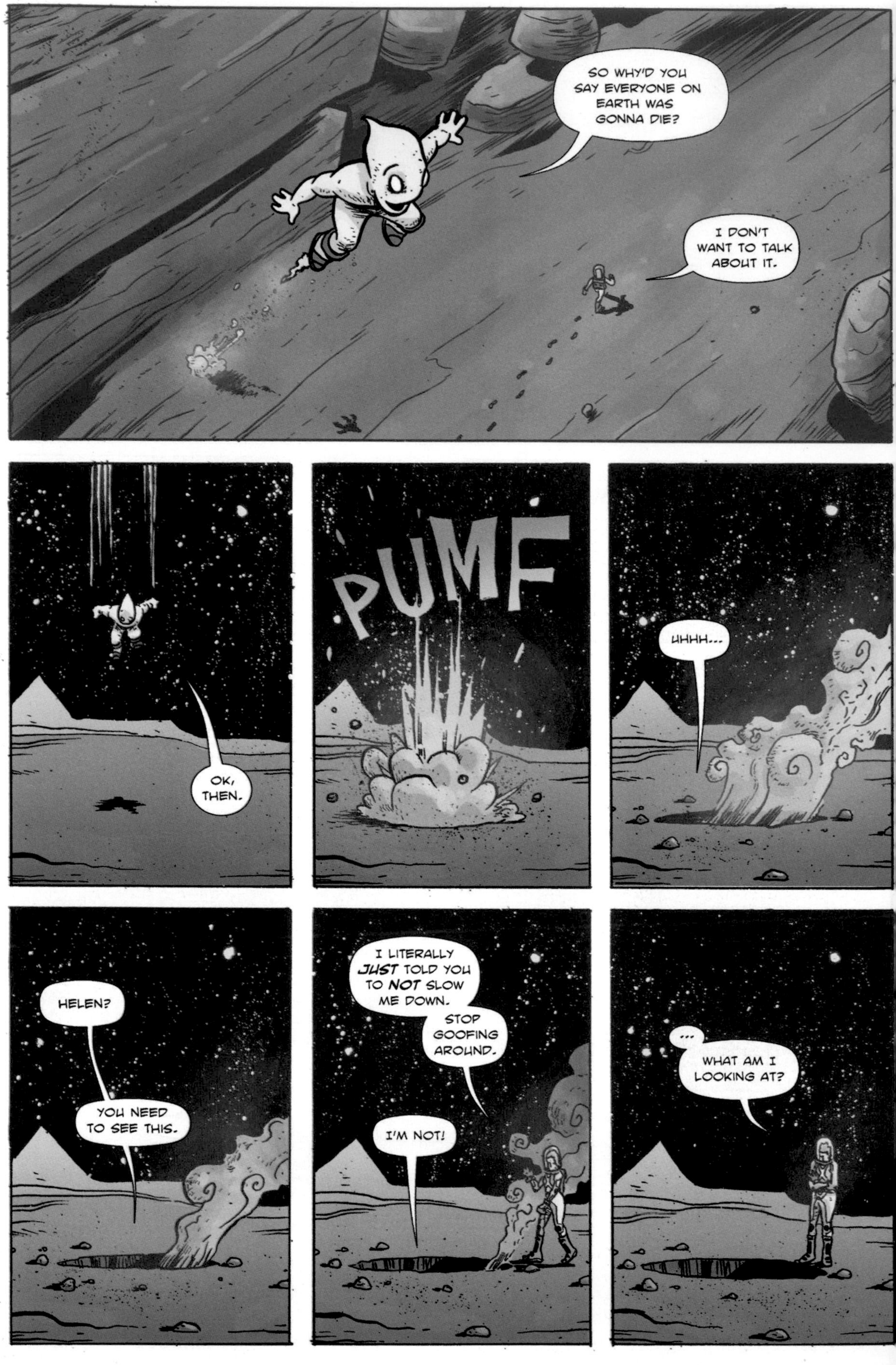
SO WHY'D YOU SAY EVERYONE ON EARTH WAS GONNA DIE?
I DON'T WANT TO TALK ABOUT IT.
OK, THEN.
PUMF
UHHH...
HELEN?
YOU NEED TO SEE THIS.
I LITERALLY JUST TOLD YOU TO NOT SLOW ME DOWN.
STOP GOOFING AROUND.
I'M NOT!
...
WHAT AM I LOOKING AT?

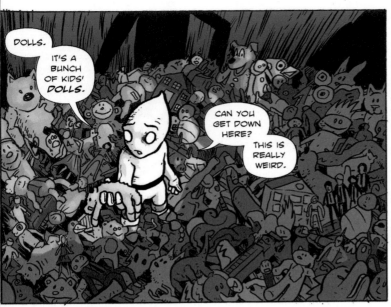

DOLLS.

IT'S A BUNCH OF KIDS' DOLLS.

CAN YOU GET DOWN HERE? THIS IS REALLY WEIRD.

WHAT THE--?

WEIRD, RIGHT?

WHAT DO YOU THINK IT MEANS?

CRNCH

IT MEANS--

--IT MEANS THAT HUMANS HAVE BEEN HERE BEFORE--

--SOMEHOW.

INSUNAV-- PLEASE CONFIRM: THERE ARE NO SIGNS OF LIFE ON THIS PLANET, CORRECT?

Correct.

HOW--?!

IMPOSSIBLE.

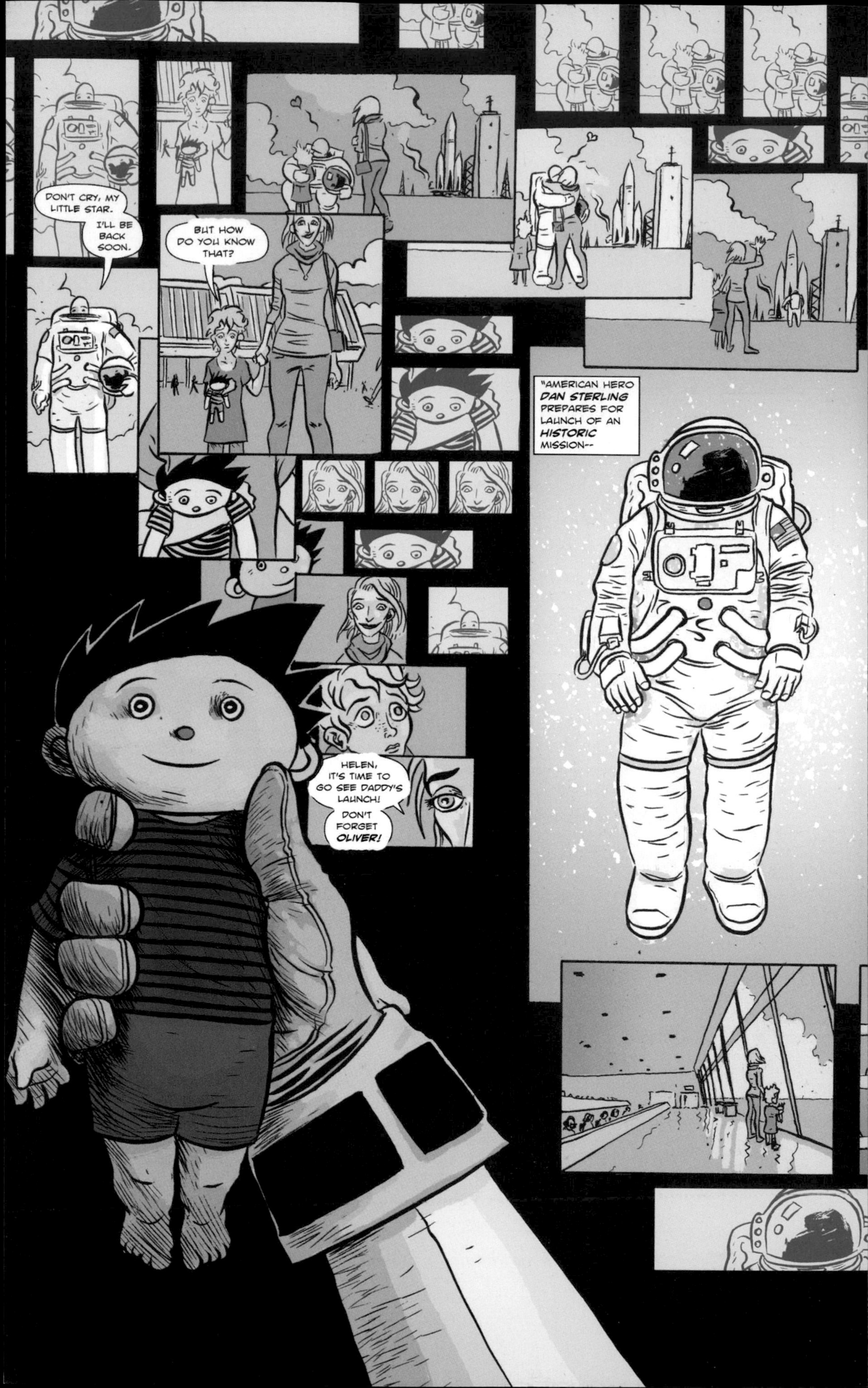
DON'T CRY, MY LITTLE STAR.
I'LL BE BACK SOON.
BUT HOW DO YOU KNOW THAT?
"AMERICAN HERO DAN STERLING PREPARES FOR LAUNCH OF AN HISTORIC MISSION--
HELEN, IT'S TIME TO GO SEE DADDY'S LAUNCH!
DON'T FORGET OLIVER!

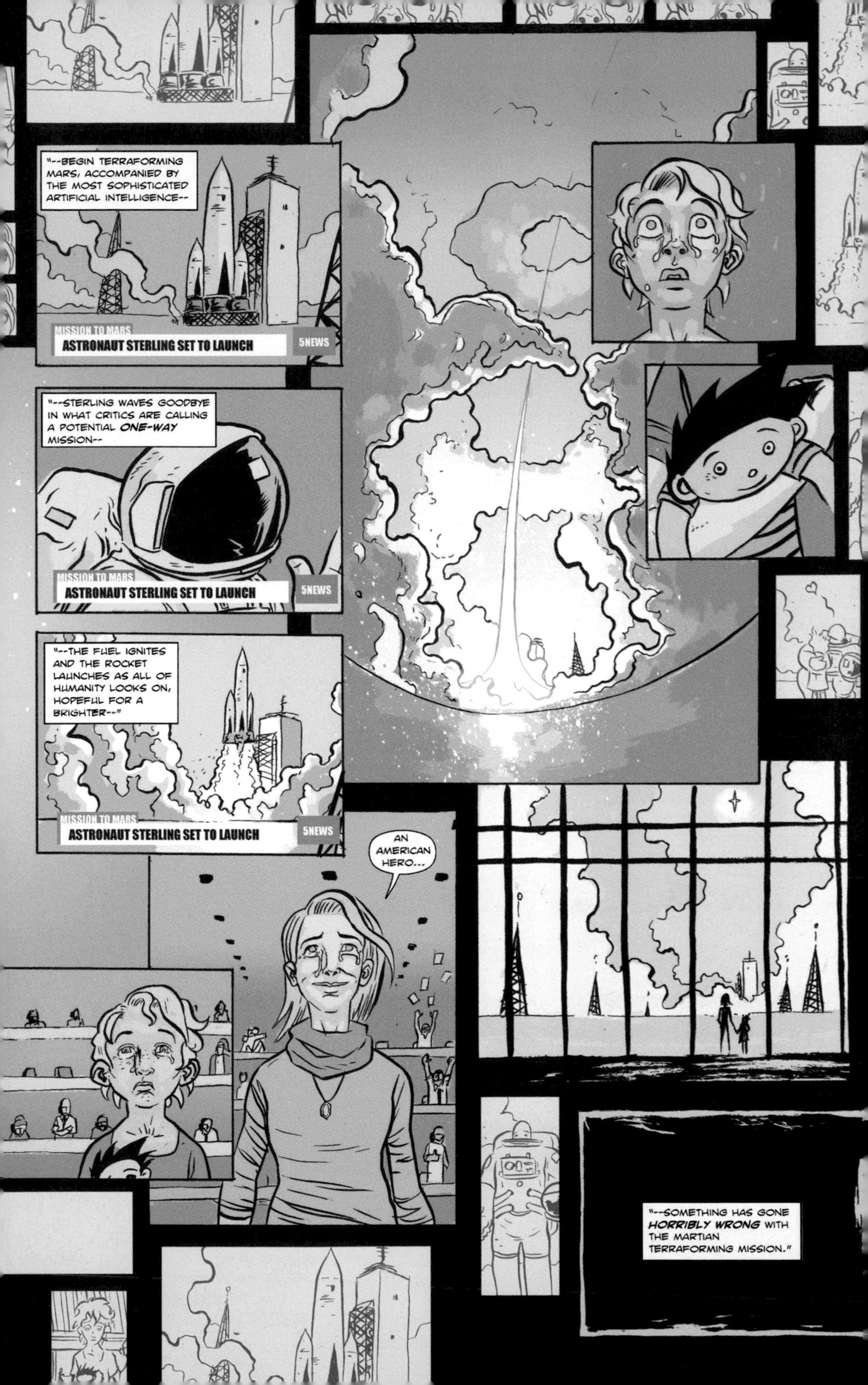
"--BEGIN TERRAFORMING MARS, ACCOMPANIED BY THE MOST SOPHISTICATED ARTIFICIAL INTELLIGENCE--
MISSION TO MARS
ASTRONAUT STERLING SET TO LAUNCH
5NEWS
"--STERLING WAVES GOODBYE IN WHAT CRITICS ARE CALLING A POTENTIAL ONE-WAY MISSION--
MISSION TO MARS
ASTRONAUT STERLING SET TO LAUNCH
5NEWS
"--THE FUEL IGNITES AND THE ROCKET LAUNCHES AS ALL OF HUMANITY LOOKS ON, HOPEFUL FOR A BRIGHTER--"
MISSION TO MARS
ASTRONAUT STERLING SET TO LAUNCH
5NEWS
AN AMERICAN HERO...
"--SOMETHING HAS GONE HORRIBLY WRONG WITH THE MARTIAN TERRAFORMING MISSION."

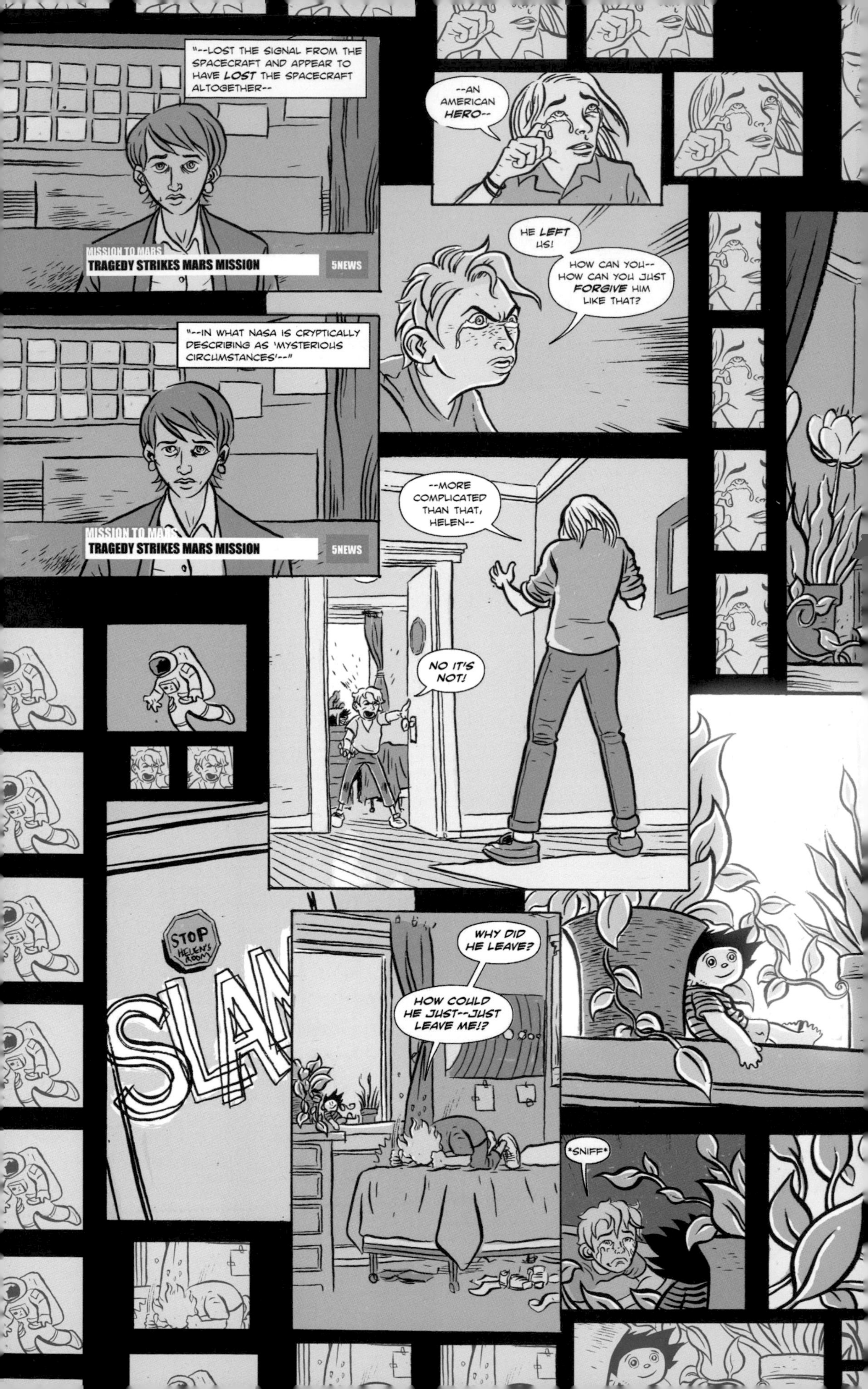
"--LOST THE SIGNAL FROM THE SPACECRAFT AND APPEAR TO HAVE LOST THE SPACECRAFT ALTOGETHER--
MISSION TO MARS
TRAGEDY STRIKES MARS MISSION
5NEWS
--AN AMERICAN HERO--
HE LEFT US!
HOW CAN YOU-- HOW CAN YOU JUST FORGIVE HIM LIKE THAT?
"--IN WHAT NASA IS CRYPTICALLY DESCRIBING AS 'MYSTERIOUS CIRCUMSTANCES'--"
MISSION TO MARS
TRAGEDY STRIKES MARS MISSION
5NEWS
--MORE COMPLICATED THAN THAT, HELEN--
NO IT'S NOT!
STOP HELEN'S ROOM
SLAM
WHY DID HE LEAVE?
HOW COULD HE JUST--JUST LEAVE ME!?
SNIFF

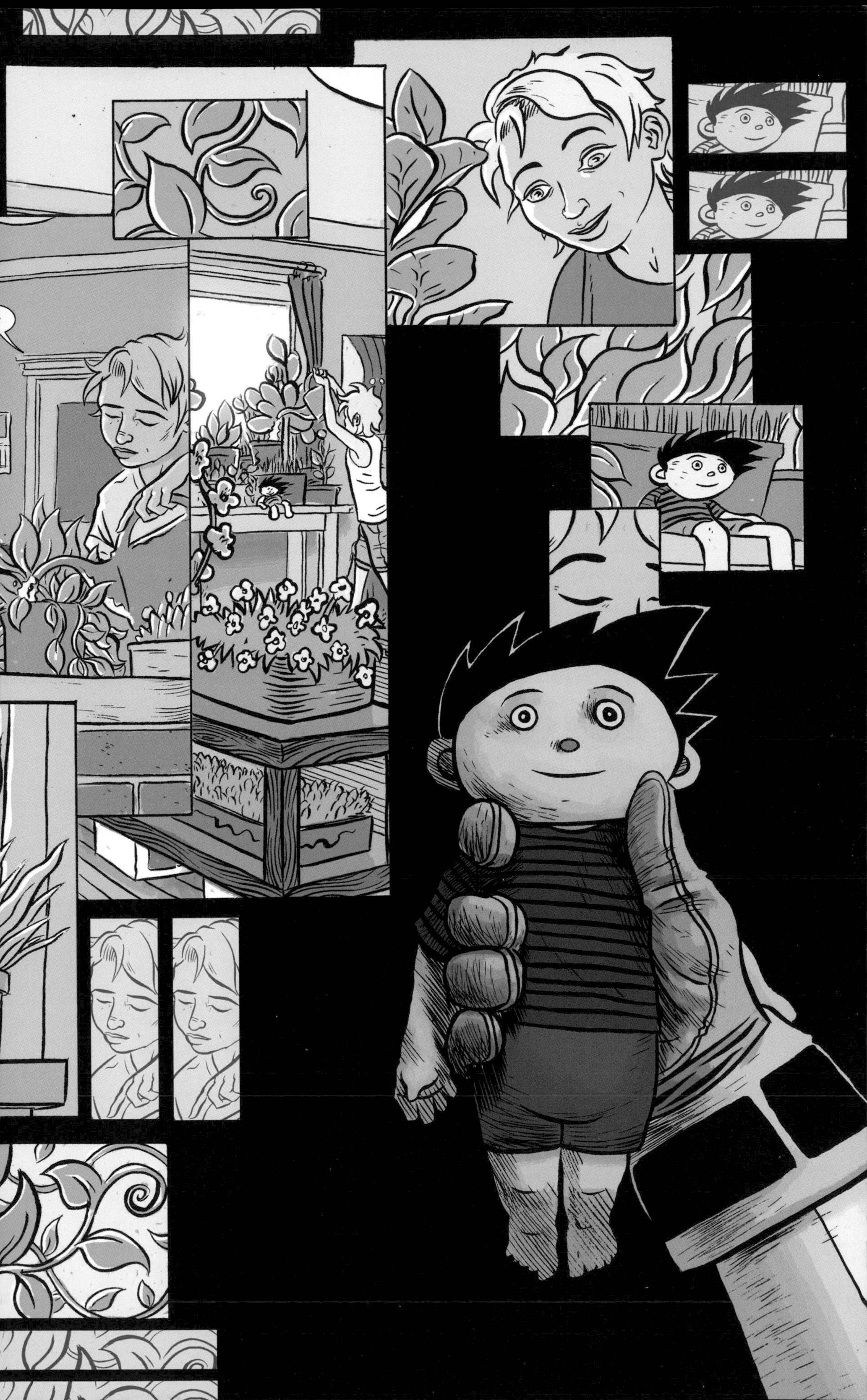

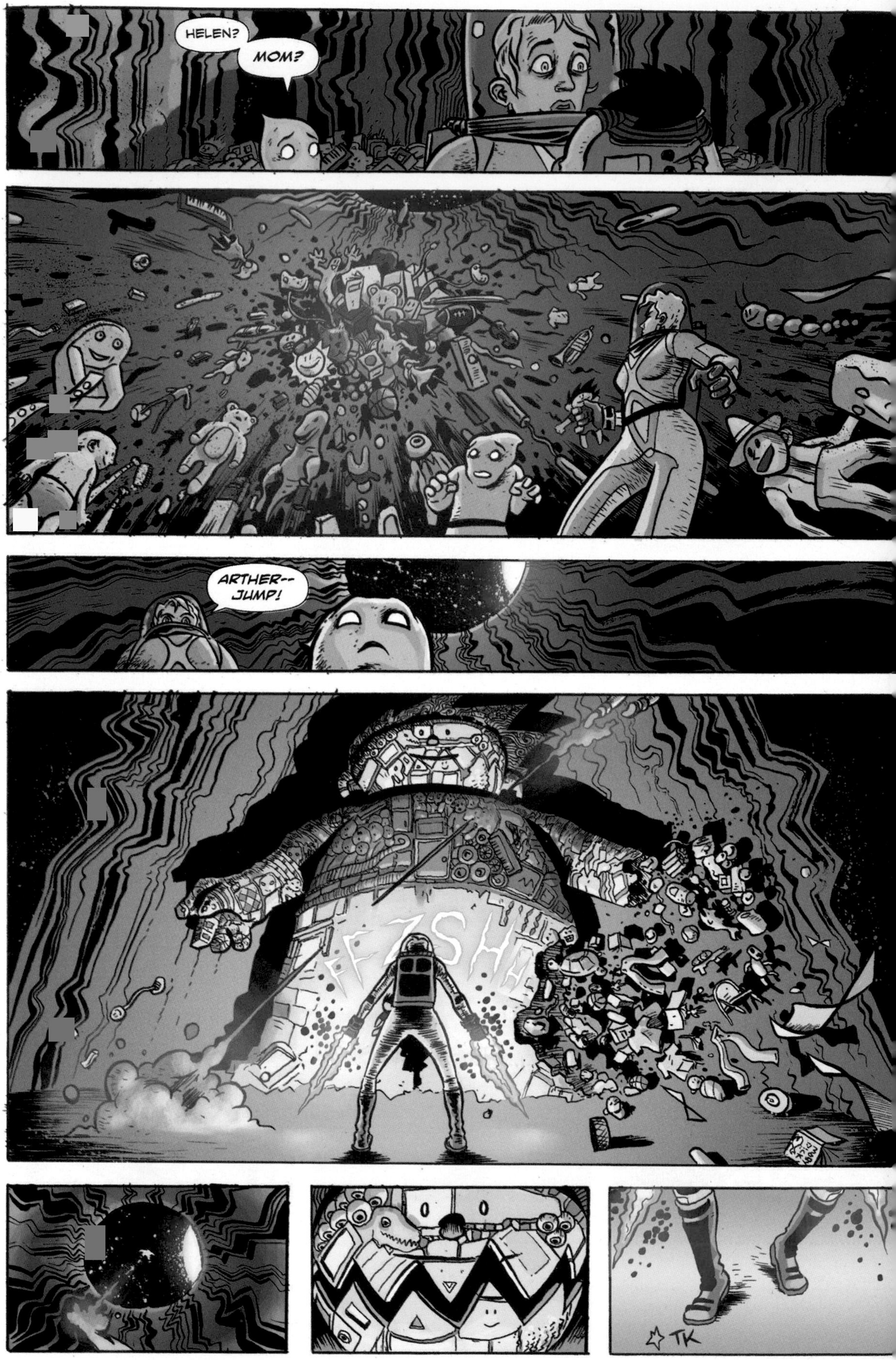
HELEN?
MOM?
ARTHER-- JUMP!
FFZSH
TK

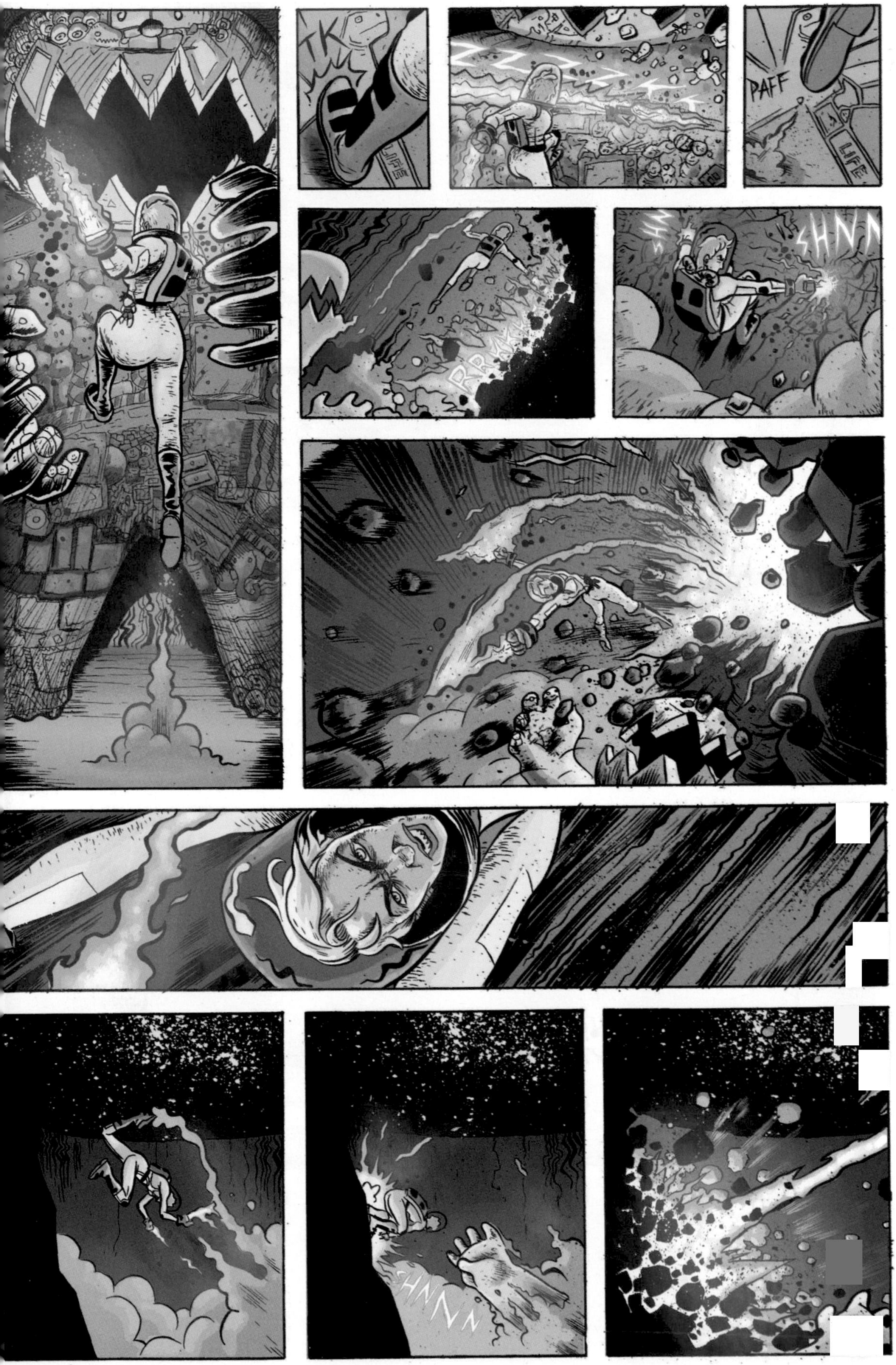
TK
PAFF
LIFE
SHN
SHNN
SHNNN

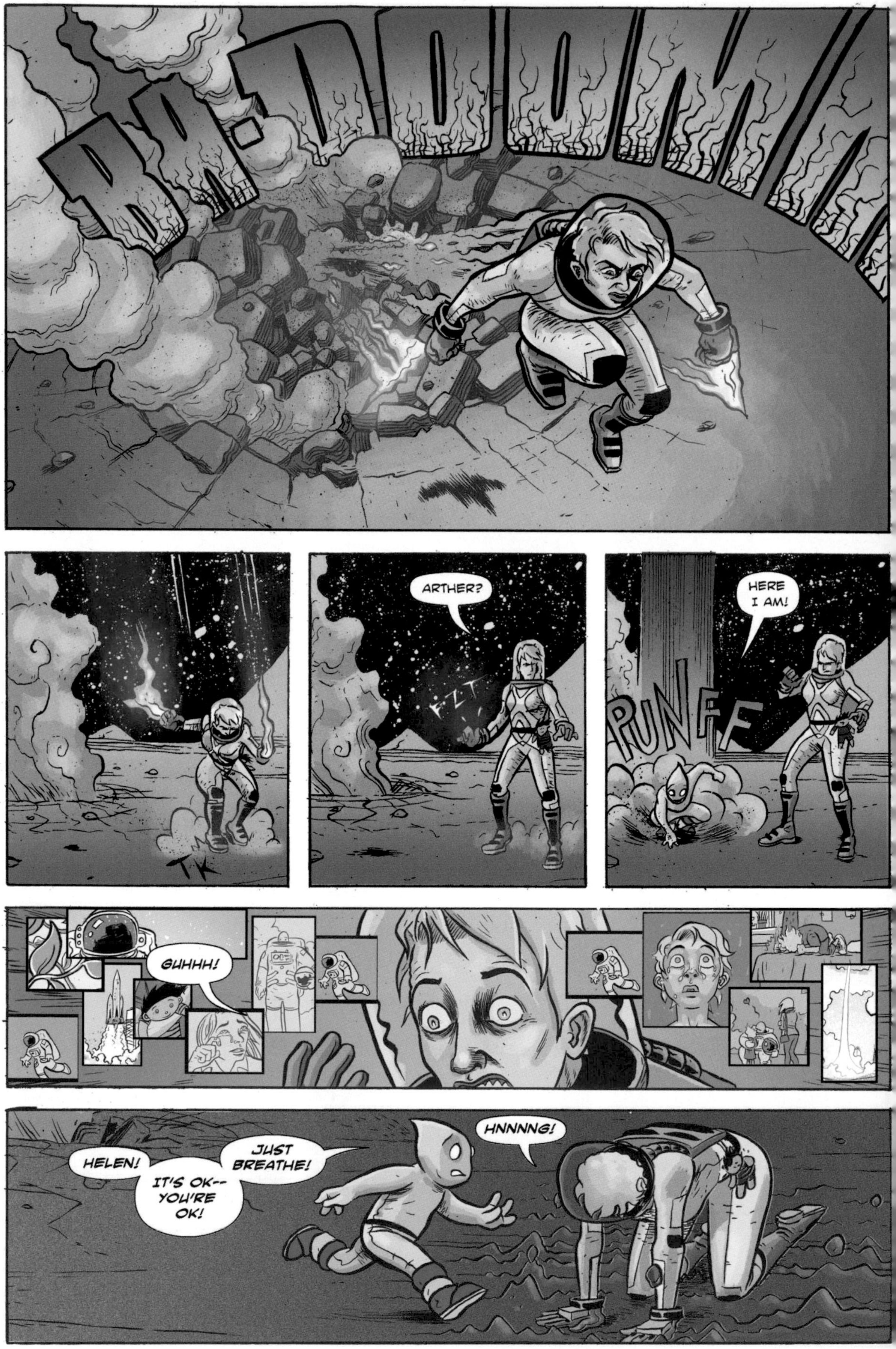
BA-DOOM!
ARTHER?
FZT
HERE I AM!
PUNFF
GUHHH!
HNNNNG!
HELEN!
IT'S OK-- YOU'RE OK!
JUST BREATHE!

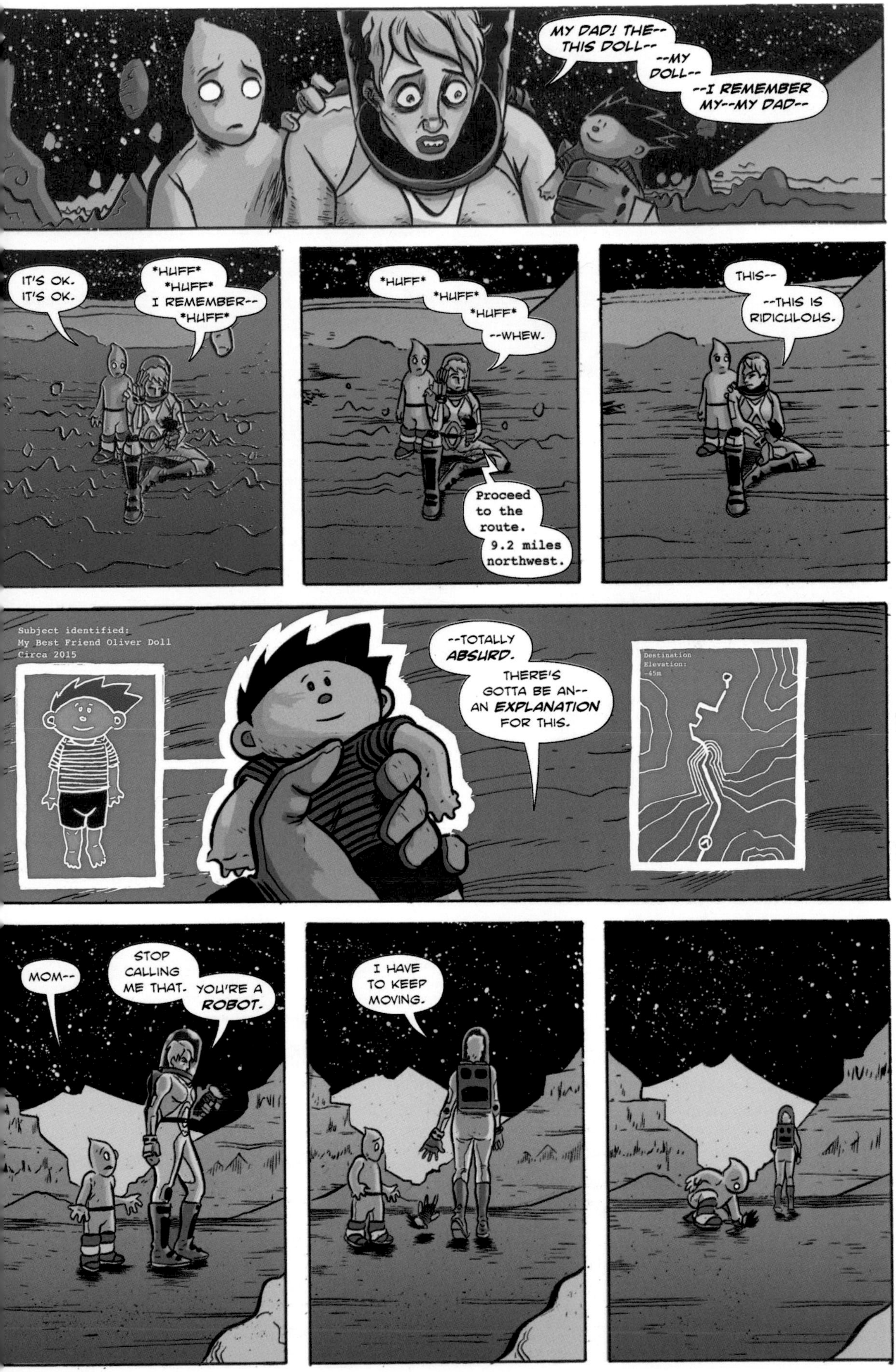
MY DAD! THE-- THIS DOLL--
--MY DOLL--
--I REMEMBER MY--MY DAD--
IT'S OK. IT'S OK.
HUFF *HUFF* I REMEMBER-- *HUFF*
HUFF
HUFF
HUFF
--WHEW.
Proceed to the route.
9.2 miles northwest.
THIS--
--THIS IS RIDICULOUS.
Subject identified:
My Best Friend Oliver Doll
Circa 2015
--TOTALLY ABSURD.
THERE'S GOTTA BE AN-- AN EXPLANATION FOR THIS.
Destination
Elevation:
-45m
MOM--
STOP CALLING ME THAT.
YOU'RE A ROBOT.
I HAVE TO KEEP MOVING.

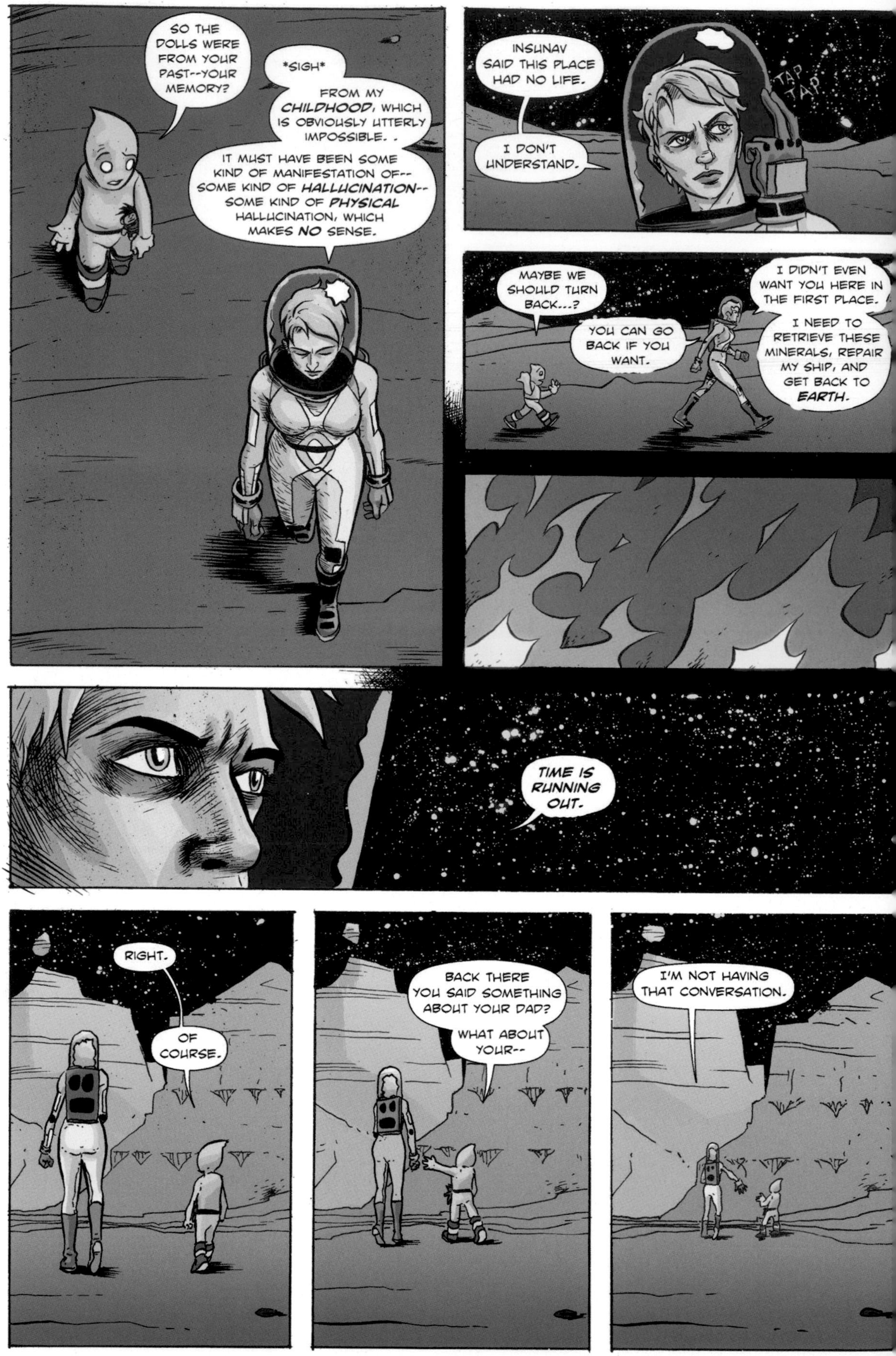
SO THE DOLLS WERE FROM YOUR PAST--YOUR MEMORY?
SIGH
FROM MY CHILDHOOD, WHICH IS OBVIOUSLY UTTERLY IMPOSSIBLE. .
IT MUST HAVE BEEN SOME KIND OF MANIFESTATION OF-- SOME KIND OF HALLUCINATION-- SOME KIND OF PHYSICAL HALLUCINATION, WHICH MAKES NO SENSE.
INSUNAV SAID THIS PLACE HAD NO LIFE.
TAP TAP
I DON'T UNDERSTAND.
MAYBE WE SHOULD TURN BACK...?
YOU CAN GO BACK IF YOU WANT.
I DIDN'T EVEN WANT YOU HERE IN THE FIRST PLACE.
I NEED TO RETRIEVE THESE MINERALS, REPAIR MY SHIP, AND GET BACK TO EARTH.
TIME IS RUNNING OUT.
RIGHT.
OF COURSE.
BACK THERE YOU SAID SOMETHING ABOUT YOUR DAD?
WHAT ABOUT YOUR--
I'M NOT HAVING THAT CONVERSATION.

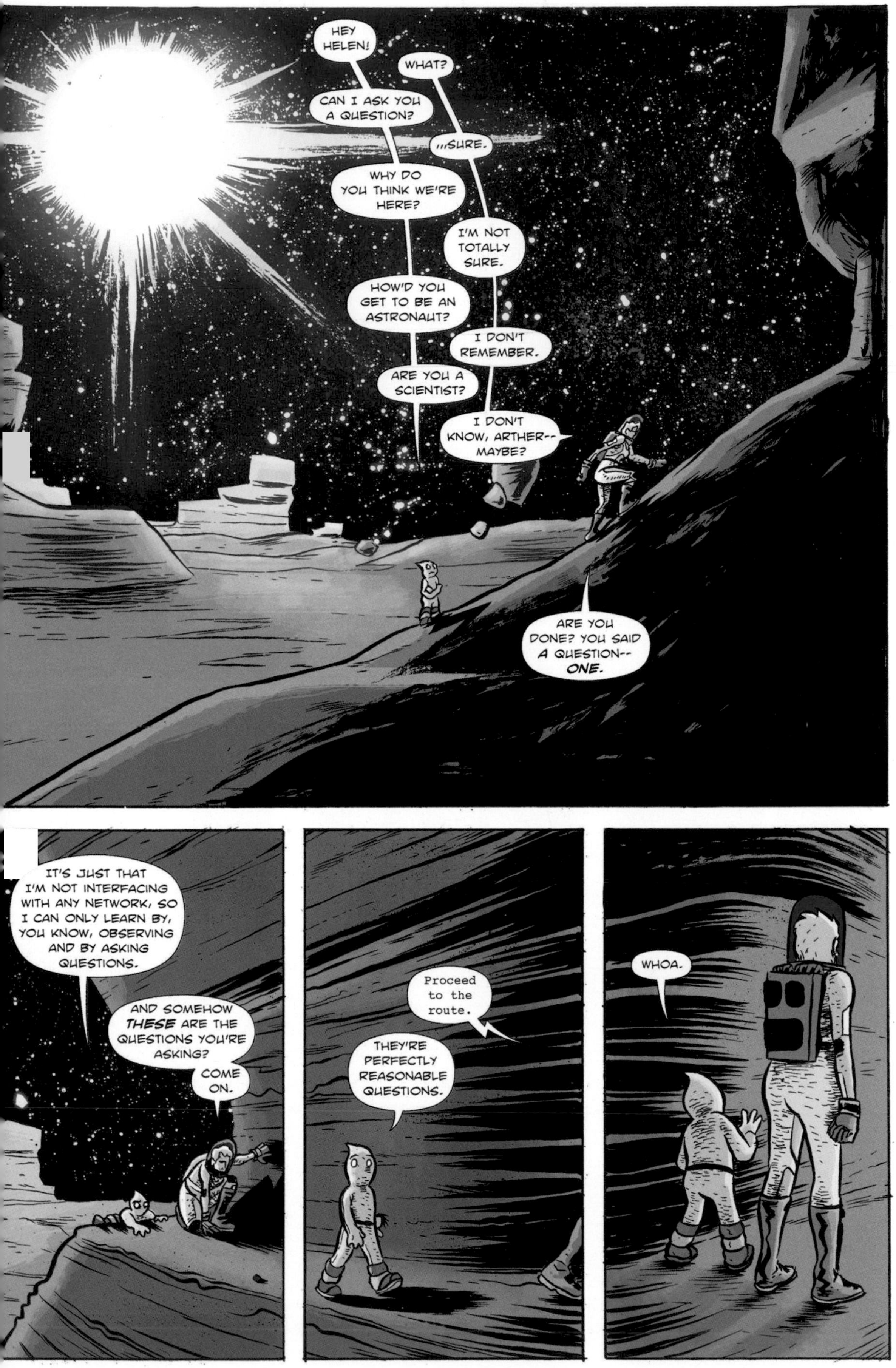
HEY HELEN!
WHAT?
CAN I ASK YOU A QUESTION?
...SURE.
WHY DO YOU THINK WE'RE HERE?
I'M NOT TOTALLY SURE.
HOW'D YOU GET TO BE AN ASTRONAUT?
I DON'T REMEMBER.
ARE YOU A SCIENTIST?
I DON'T KNOW, ARTHER-- MAYBE?
ARE YOU DONE? YOU SAID A QUESTION-- ONE.
IT'S JUST THAT I'M NOT INTERFACING WITH ANY NETWORK, SO I CAN ONLY LEARN BY, YOU KNOW, OBSERVING AND BY ASKING QUESTIONS.
AND SOMEHOW THESE ARE THE QUESTIONS YOU'RE ASKING?
COME ON.
Proceed to the route.
THEY'RE PERFECTLY REASONABLE QUESTIONS.
WHOA.

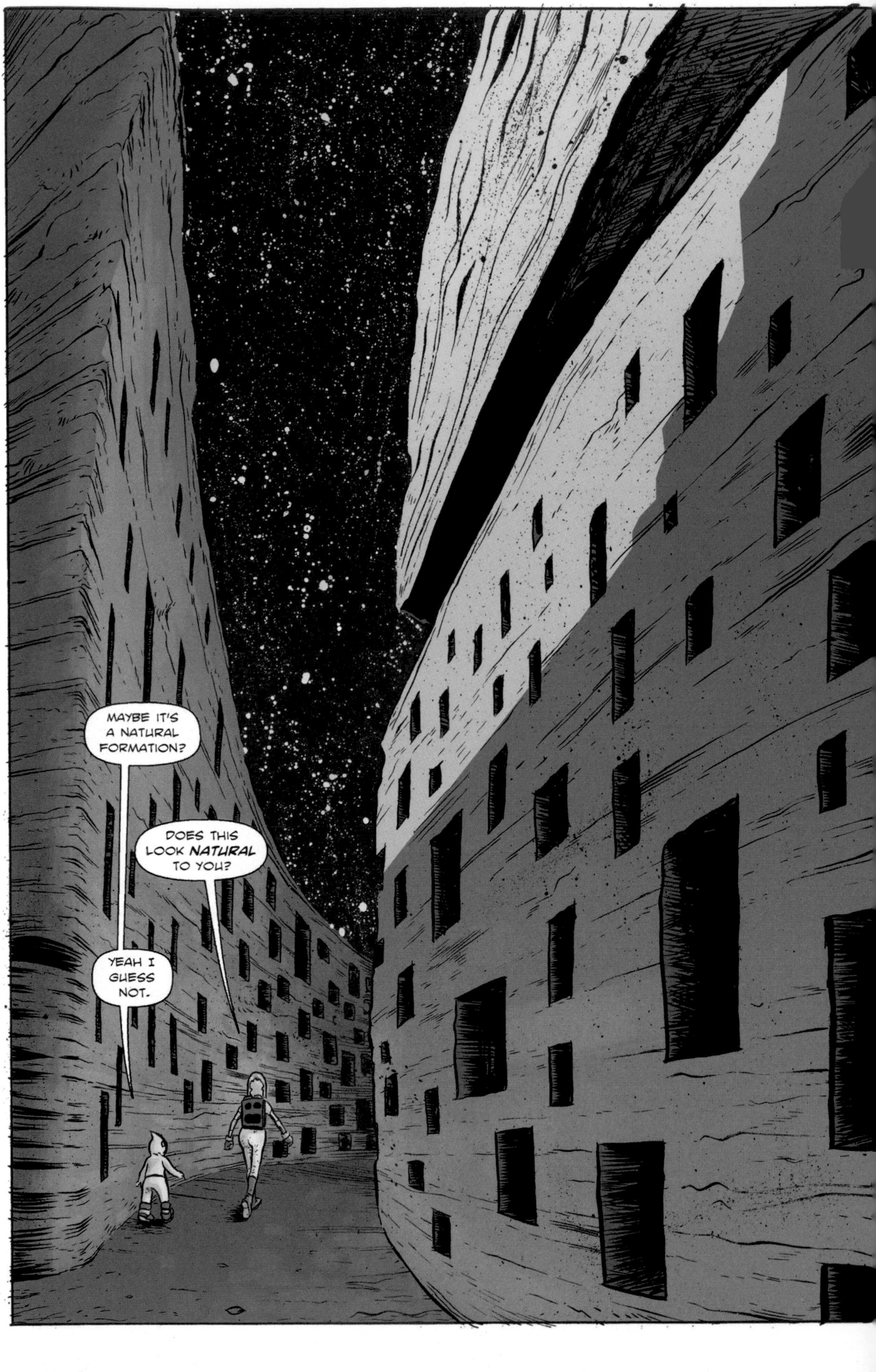
MAYBE IT'S A NATURAL FORMATION?
DOES THIS LOOK NATURAL TO YOU?
YEAH I GUESS NOT.

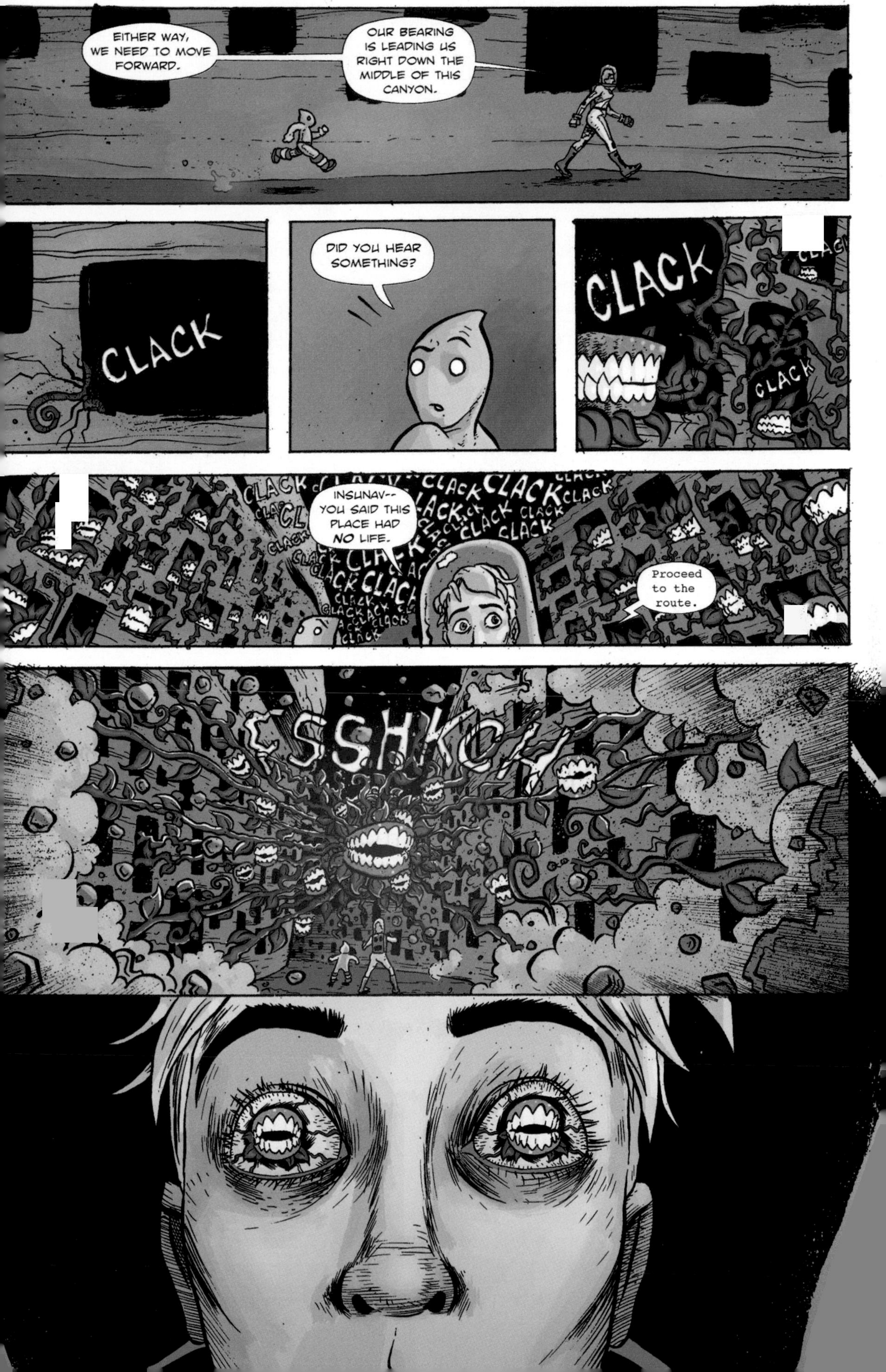
EITHER WAY, WE NEED TO MOVE FORWARD.
OUR BEARING IS LEADING US RIGHT DOWN THE MIDDLE OF THIS CANYON.
CLACK
DID YOU HEAR SOMETHING?
CLACK
CLACK
INSUNAV-- YOU SAID THIS PLACE HAD NO LIFE.
Proceed to the route.
SSHKOH

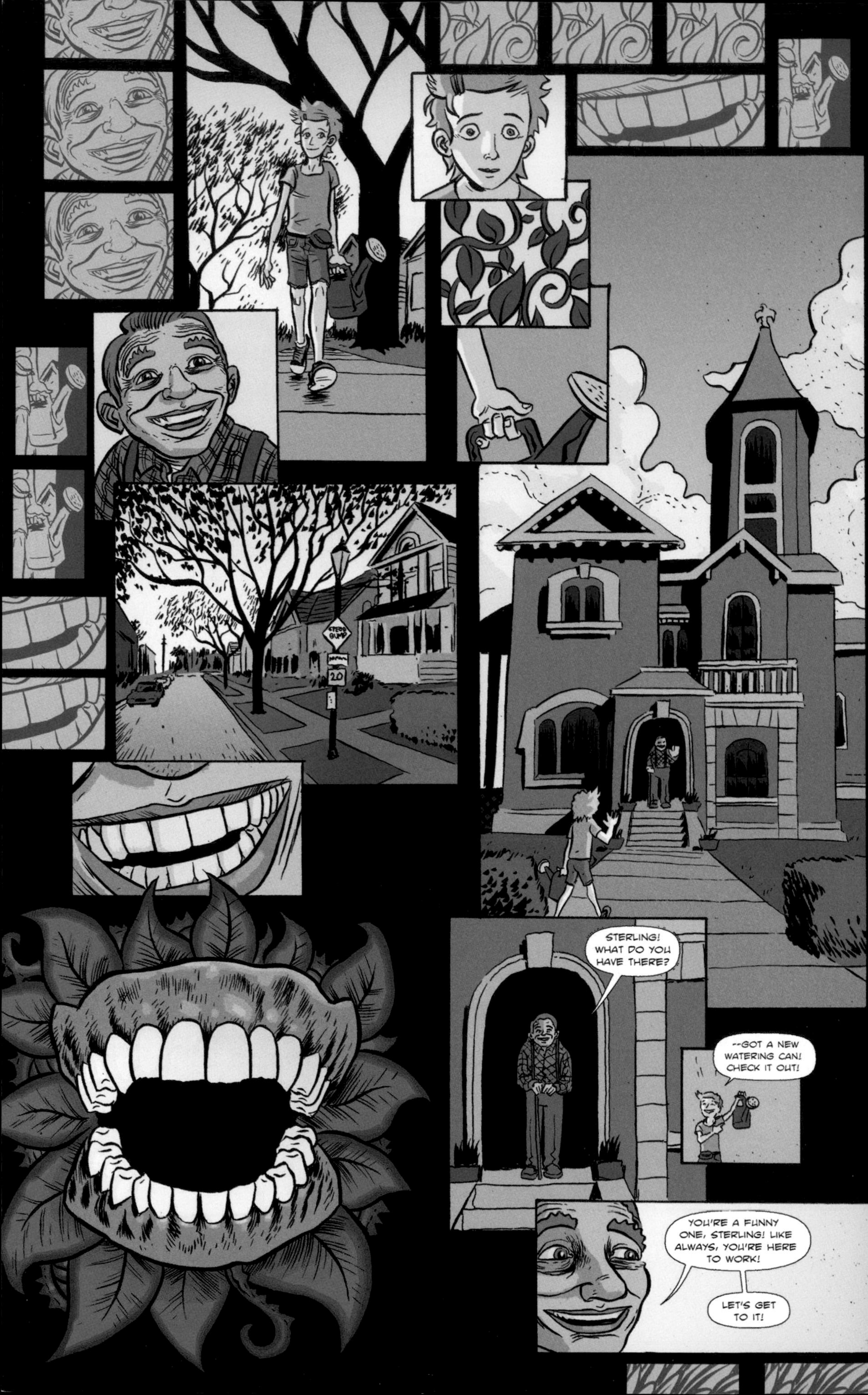
SPEED BUMP
20
STERLING! WHAT DO YOU HAVE THERE?
--GOT A NEW WATERING CAN! CHECK IT OUT!
YOU'RE A FUNNY ONE, STERLING! LIKE ALWAYS, YOU'RE HERE TO WORK!
LET'S GET TO IT!

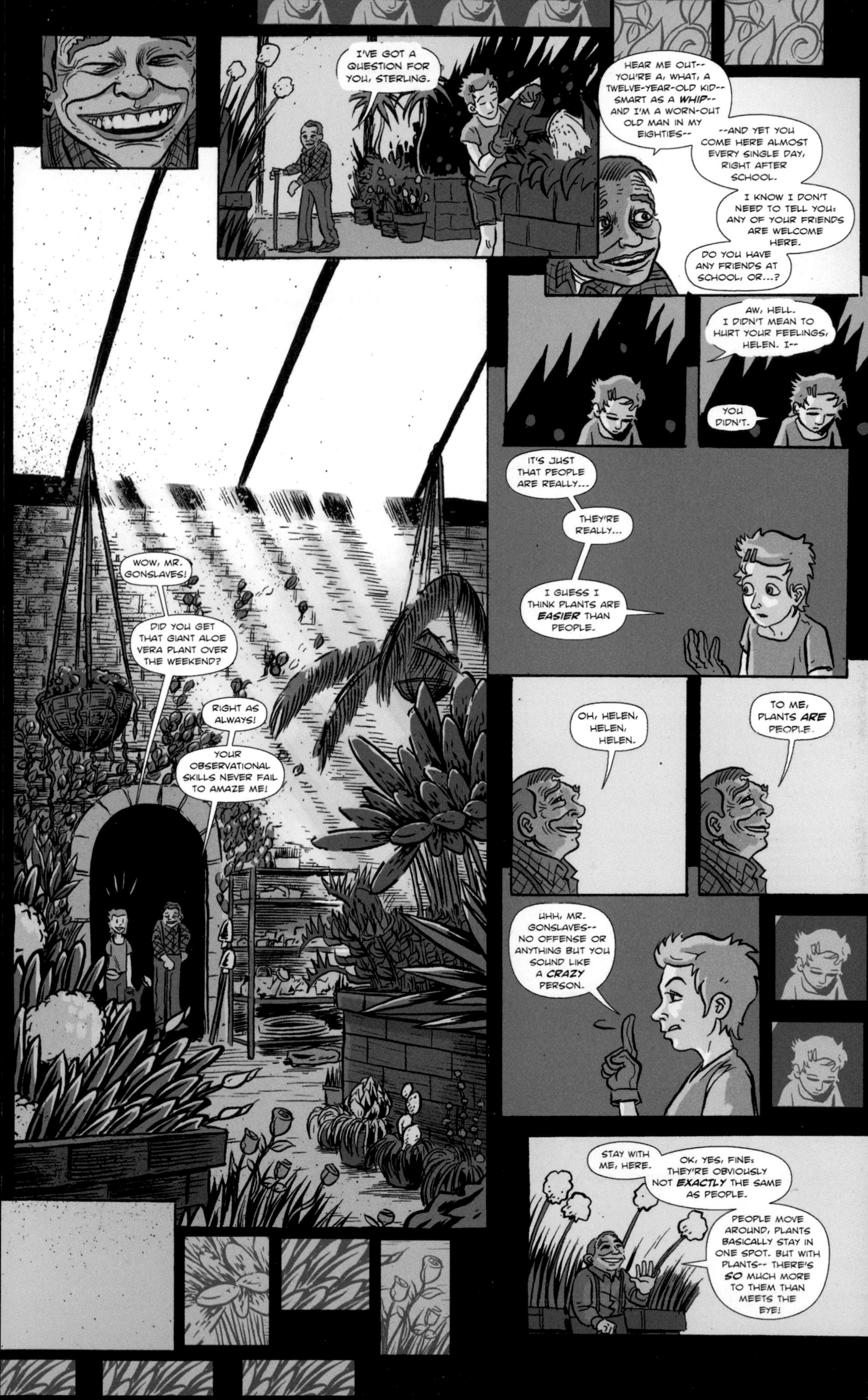

I'VE GOT A QUESTION FOR YOU, STERLING.
HEAR ME OUT-- YOU'RE A, WHAT, A TWELVE-YEAR-OLD KID-- SMART AS A **WHIP**-- AND I'M A WORN-OUT OLD MAN IN MY EIGHTIES--
--AND YET YOU COME HERE ALMOST EVERY SINGLE DAY, RIGHT AFTER SCHOOL.
I KNOW I DON'T NEED TO TELL YOU: ANY OF YOUR FRIENDS ARE WELCOME HERE.
DO YOU HAVE ANY FRIENDS AT SCHOOL, OR...?
AW, HELL. I DIDN'T MEAN TO HURT YOUR FEELINGS, HELEN. I--
YOU DIDN'T.
IT'S JUST THAT PEOPLE ARE REALLY...
THEY'RE REALLY...
I GUESS I THINK PLANTS ARE **EASIER** THAN PEOPLE.
OH, HELEN, HELEN, HELEN.
TO ME, PLANTS **ARE** PEOPLE.
UHH, MR. GONSLAVES-- NO OFFENSE OR ANYTHING BUT YOU SOUND LIKE A **CRAZY** PERSON.
STAY WITH ME, HERE.
OK, YES, FINE: THEY'RE OBVIOUSLY NOT **EXACTLY** THE SAME AS PEOPLE.
PEOPLE MOVE AROUND, PLANTS BASICALLY STAY IN ONE SPOT. BUT WITH PLANTS-- THERE'S **SO** MUCH MORE TO THEM THAN MEETS THE EYE!
WOW, MR. GONSLAVES!
DID YOU GET THAT GIANT ALOE VERA PLANT OVER THE WEEKEND?
RIGHT AS ALWAYS!
YOUR OBSERVATIONAL SKILLS NEVER FAIL TO AMAZE ME!

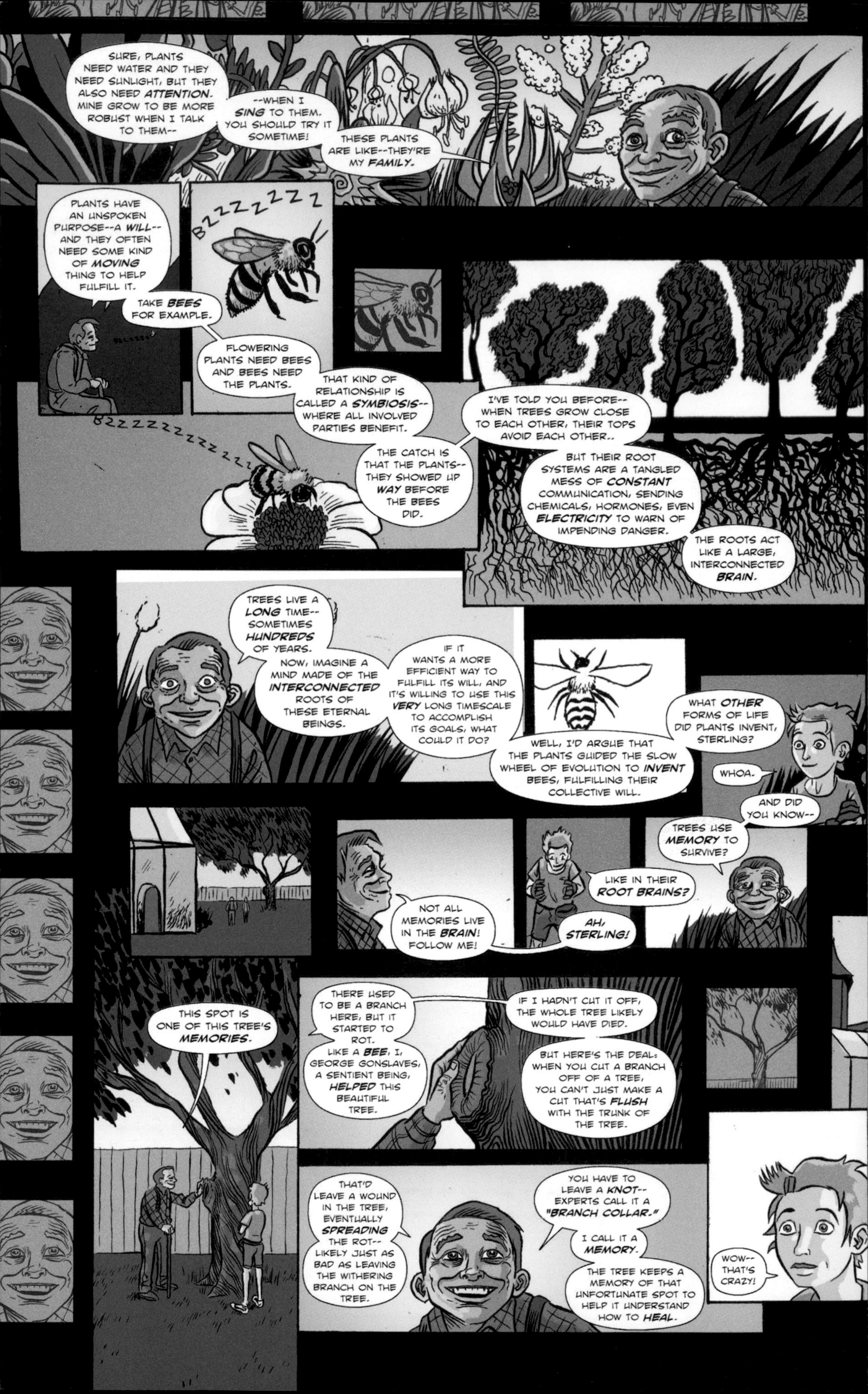
SURE, PLANTS NEED WATER AND THEY NEED SUNLIGHT, BUT THEY ALSO NEED ATTENTION. MINE GROW TO BE MORE ROBUST WHEN I TALK TO THEM--
--WHEN I SING TO THEM. YOU SHOULD TRY IT SOMETIME!
THESE PLANTS ARE LIKE--THEY'RE MY FAMILY.
PLANTS HAVE AN UNSPOKEN PURPOSE--A WILL--AND THEY OFTEN NEED SOME KIND OF MOVING THING TO HELP FULFILL IT.
TAKE BEES FOR EXAMPLE.
BZZZZZZZ Z
FLOWERING PLANTS NEED BEES AND BEES NEED THE PLANTS.
THAT KIND OF RELATIONSHIP IS CALLED A SYMBIOSIS--WHERE ALL INVOLVED PARTIES BENEFIT.
BZZZZZZZZZZZZ
THE CATCH IS THAT THE PLANTS--THEY SHOWED UP WAY BEFORE THE BEES DID.
I'VE TOLD YOU BEFORE--WHEN TREES GROW CLOSE TO EACH OTHER, THEIR TOPS AVOID EACH OTHER..
BUT THEIR ROOT SYSTEMS ARE A TANGLED MESS OF CONSTANT COMMUNICATION, SENDING CHEMICALS, HORMONES, EVEN ELECTRICITY TO WARN OF IMPENDING DANGER.
THE ROOTS ACT LIKE A LARGE, INTERCONNECTED BRAIN.
TREES LIVE A LONG TIME--SOMETIMES HUNDREDS OF YEARS.
NOW, IMAGINE A MIND MADE OF THE INTERCONNECTED ROOTS OF THESE ETERNAL BEINGS.
IF IT WANTS A MORE EFFICIENT WAY TO FULFILL ITS WILL, AND IT'S WILLING TO USE THIS VERY LONG TIMESCALE TO ACCOMPLISH ITS GOALS, WHAT COULD IT DO?
WHAT OTHER FORMS OF LIFE DID PLANTS INVENT, STERLING?
WELL, I'D ARGUE THAT THE PLANTS GUIDED THE SLOW WHEEL OF EVOLUTION TO INVENT BEES, FULFILLING THEIR COLLECTIVE WILL.
WHOA.
AND DID YOU KNOW--
TREES USE MEMORY TO SURVIVE?
LIKE IN THEIR ROOT BRAINS?
AH, STERLING!
NOT ALL MEMORIES LIVE IN THE BRAIN! FOLLOW ME!
THIS SPOT IS ONE OF THIS TREE'S MEMORIES.
THERE USED TO BE A BRANCH HERE, BUT IT STARTED TO ROT.
LIKE A BEE, I, GEORGE GONSLAVES, A SENTIENT BEING, HELPED THIS BEAUTIFUL TREE.
IF I HADN'T CUT IT OFF, THE WHOLE TREE LIKELY WOULD HAVE DIED.
BUT HERE'S THE DEAL: WHEN YOU CUT A BRANCH OFF OF A TREE, YOU CAN'T JUST MAKE A CUT THAT'S FLUSH WITH THE TRUNK OF THE TREE.
THAT'D LEAVE A WOUND IN THE TREE, EVENTUALLY SPREADING THE ROT--LIKELY JUST AS BAD AS LEAVING THE WITHERING BRANCH ON THE TREE.
YOU HAVE TO LEAVE A KNOT--EXPERTS CALL IT A "BRANCH COLLAR."
I CALL IT A MEMORY.
THE TREE KEEPS A MEMORY OF THAT UNFORTUNATE SPOT TO HELP IT UNDERSTAND HOW TO HEAL.
WOW--THAT'S CRAZY!

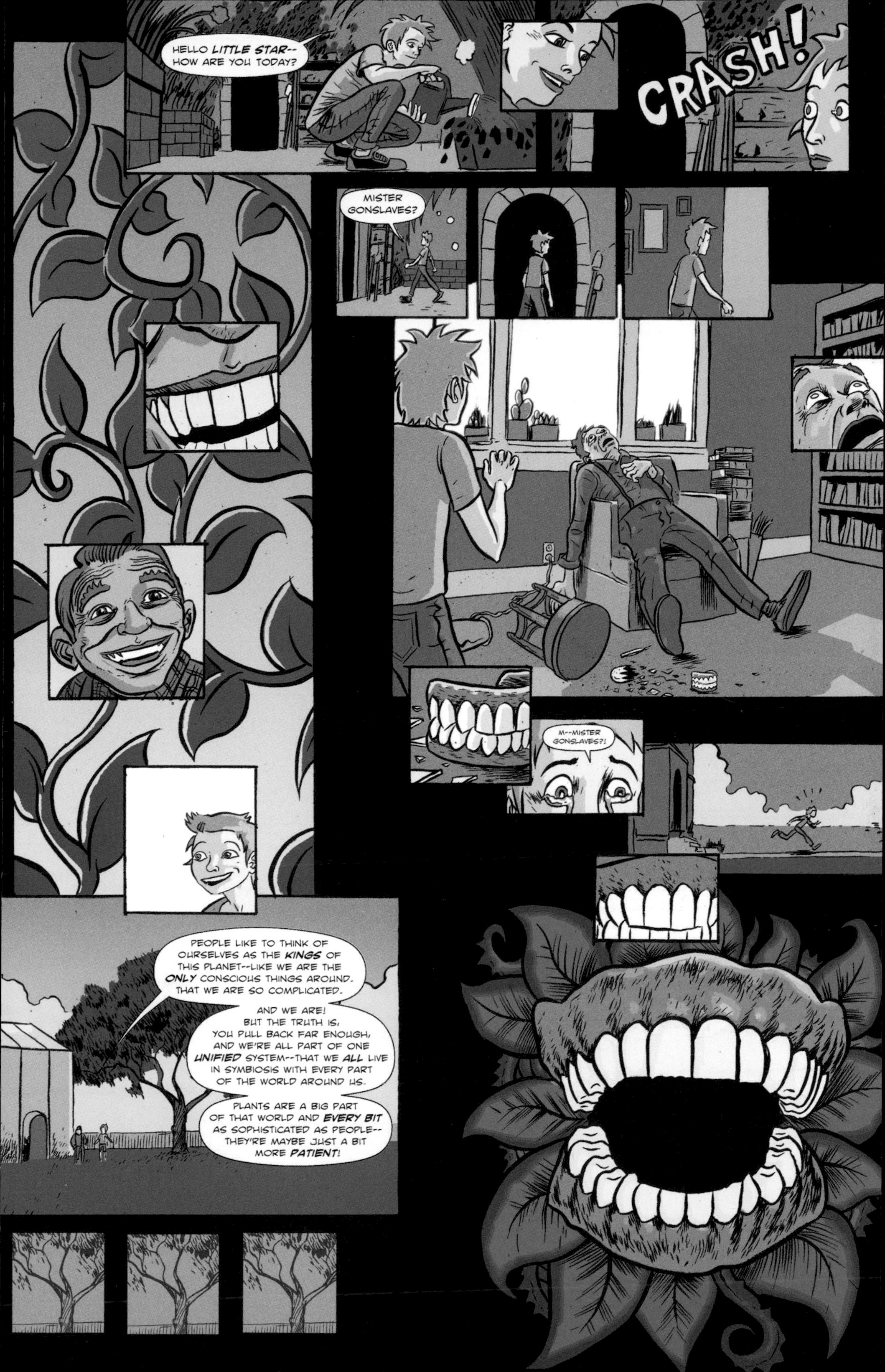
HELLO LITTLE STAR--
HOW ARE YOU TODAY?
CRASH!
MISTER GONSLAVES?
M--MISTER GONSLAVES?!
PEOPLE LIKE TO THINK OF OURSELVES AS THE KINGS OF THIS PLANET--LIKE WE ARE THE ONLY CONSCIOUS THINGS AROUND. THAT WE ARE SO COMPLICATED.
AND WE ARE! BUT THE TRUTH IS, YOU PULL BACK FAR ENOUGH, AND WE'RE ALL PART OF ONE UNIFIED SYSTEM--THAT WE ALL LIVE IN SYMBIOSIS WITH EVERY PART OF THE WORLD AROUND US.
PLANTS ARE A BIG PART OF THAT WORLD AND EVERY BIT AS SOPHISTICATED AS PEOPLE--THEY'RE MAYBE JUST A BIT MORE PATIENT!

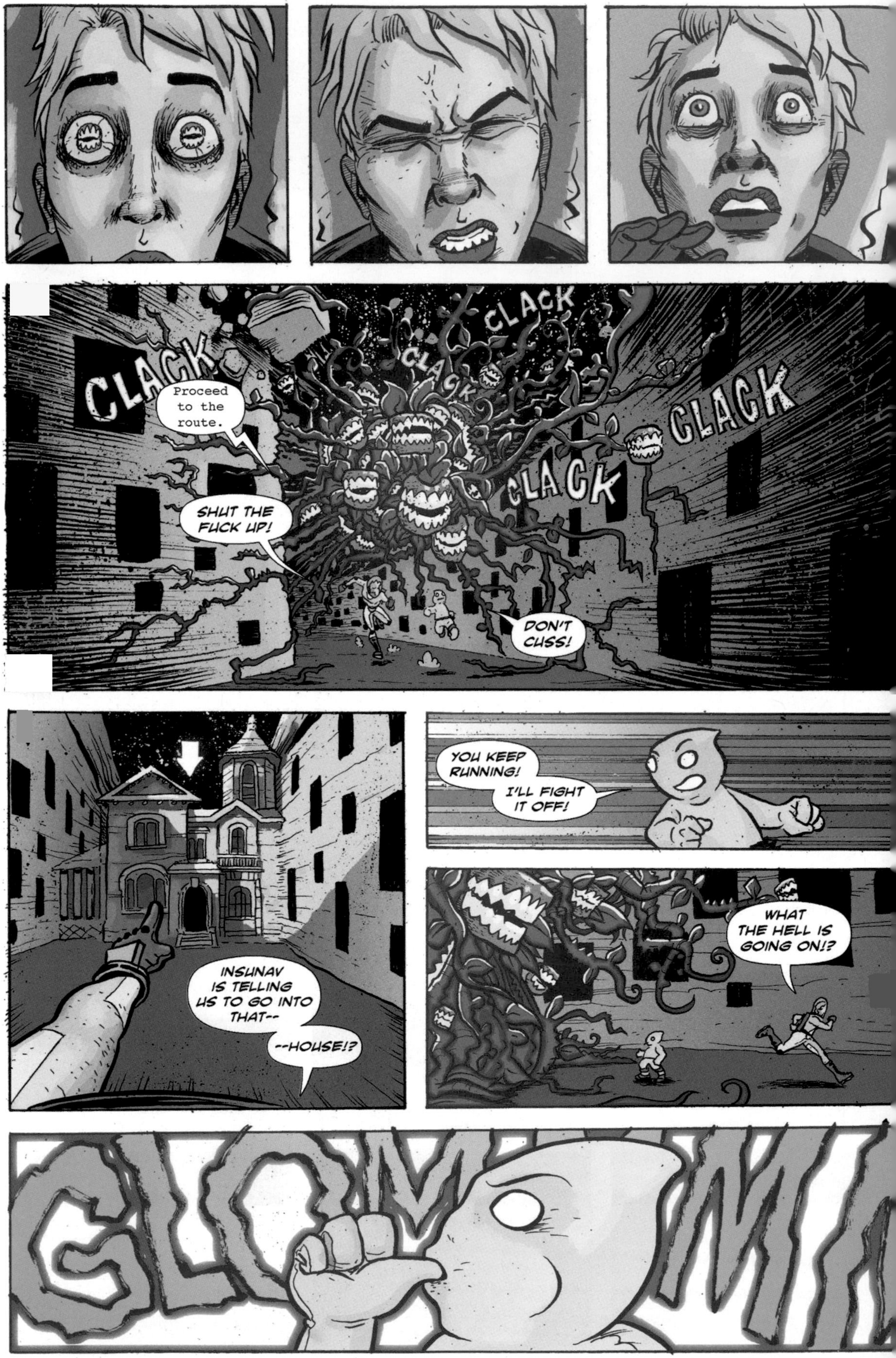
CLACK
CLACK
CLACK
CLACK
CLACK
Proceed to the route.
CLACK
SHUT THE FUCK UP!
DON'T CUSS!
INSUNAV IS TELLING US TO GO INTO THAT--
--HOUSE!?
YOU KEEP RUNNING!
I'LL FIGHT IT OFF!
WHAT THE HELL IS GOING ON!?

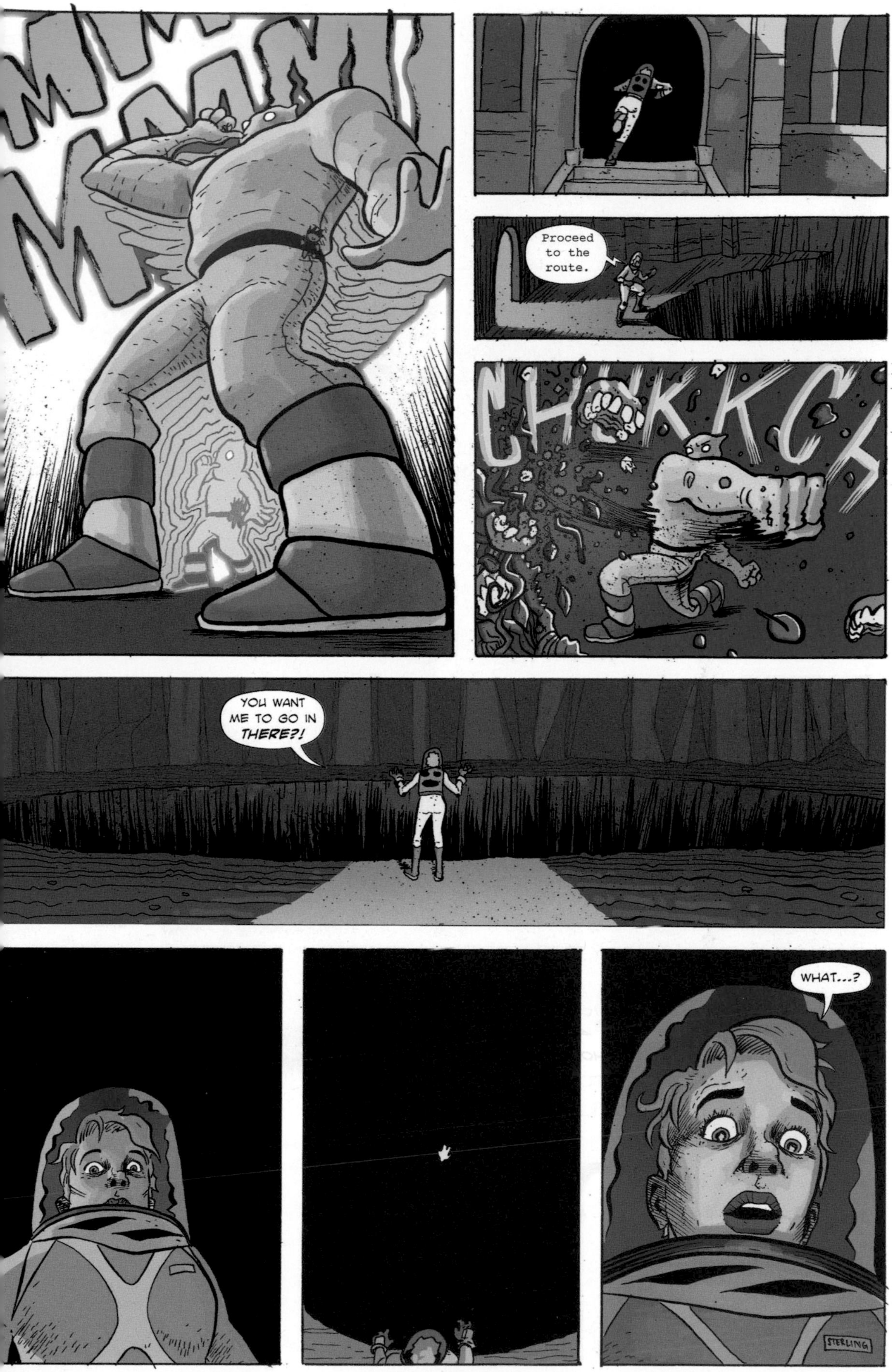

MMMMMMM
Proceed to the route.
CHKKCH
YOU WANT ME TO GO IN THERE?!
WHAT...?
STERLING

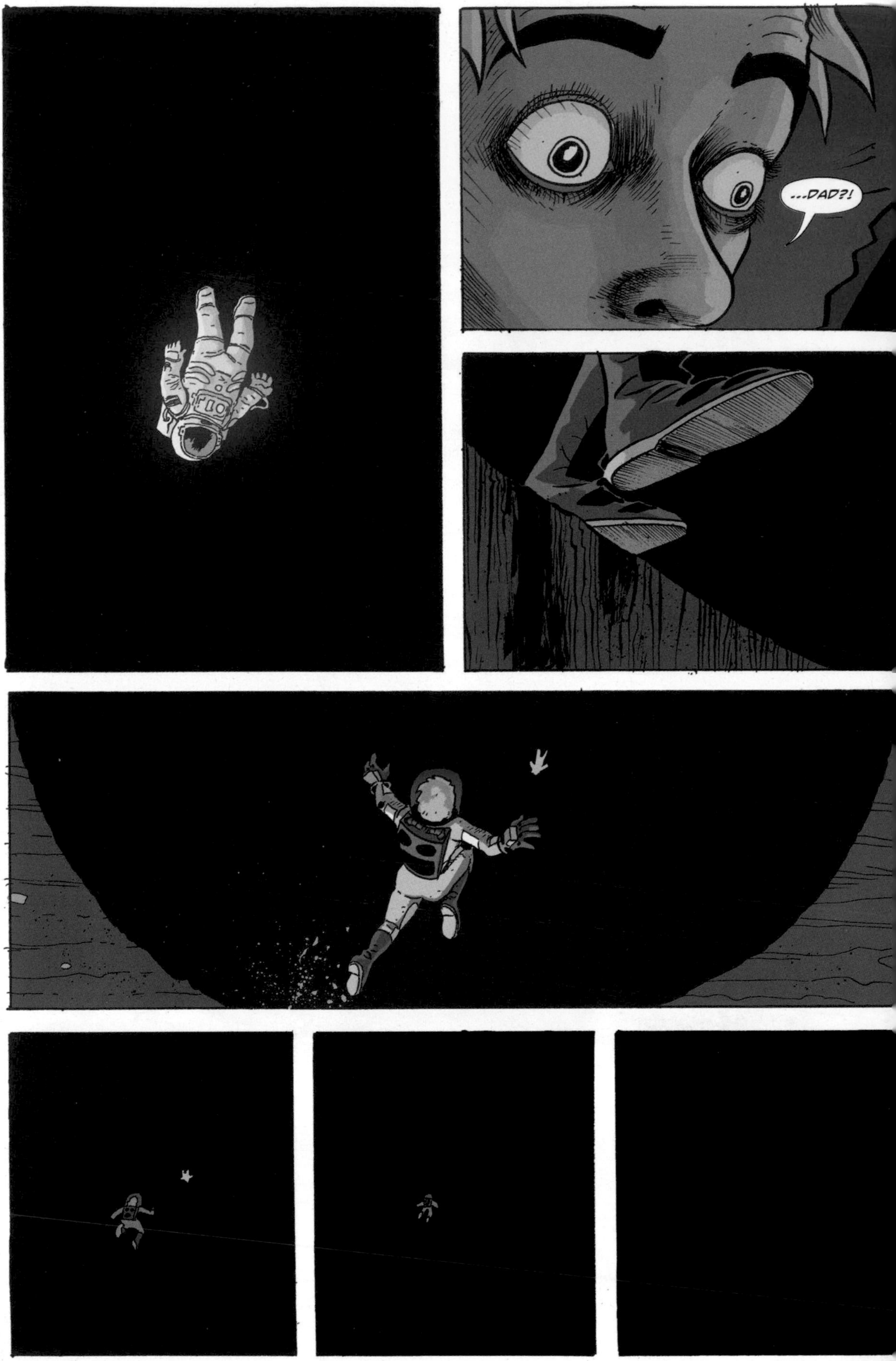
...DAD?!

CHAPTER 2

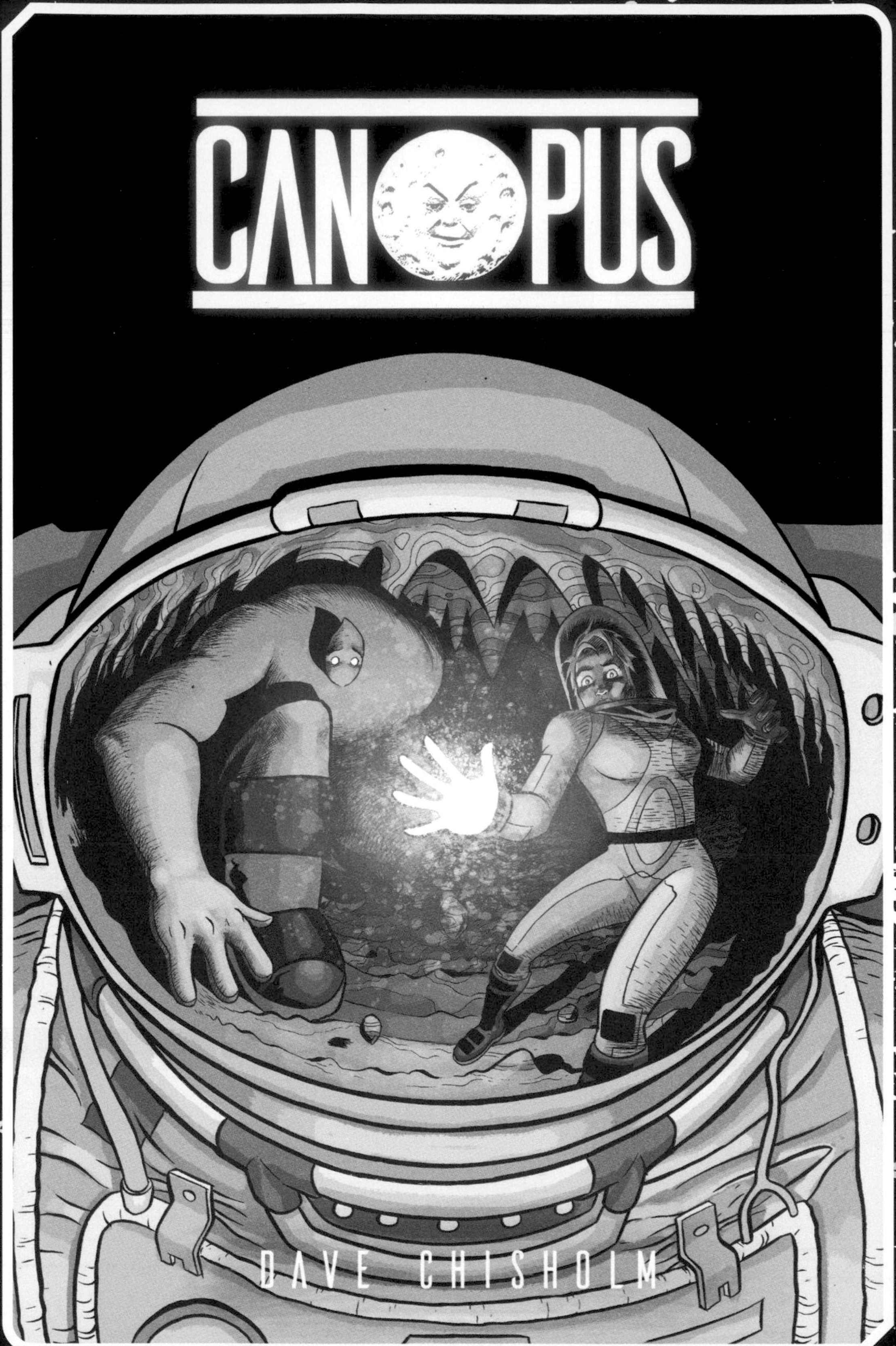
CANOPUS
DAVE CHISHOLM

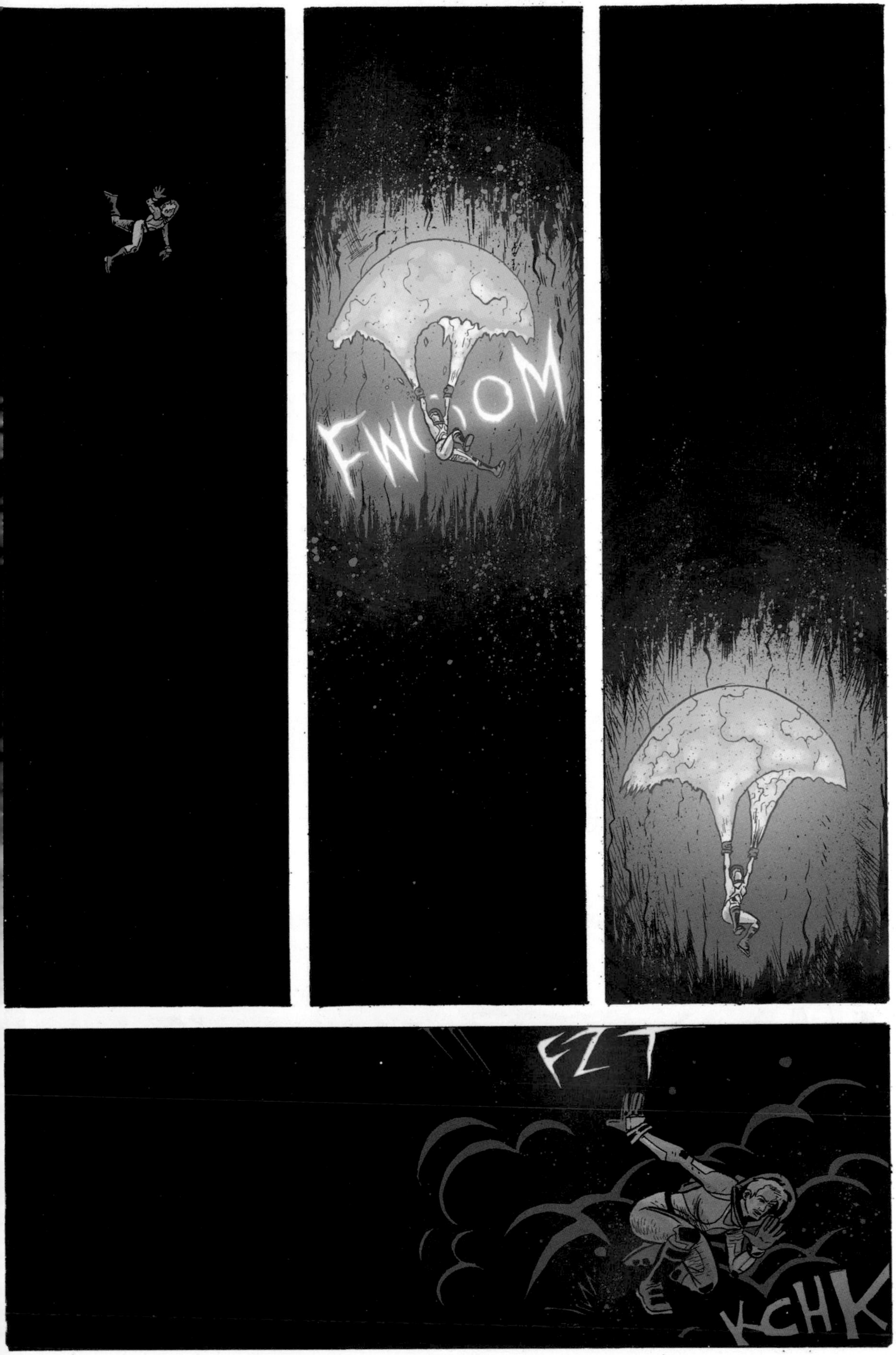
FWOOM
FZT
KCHK

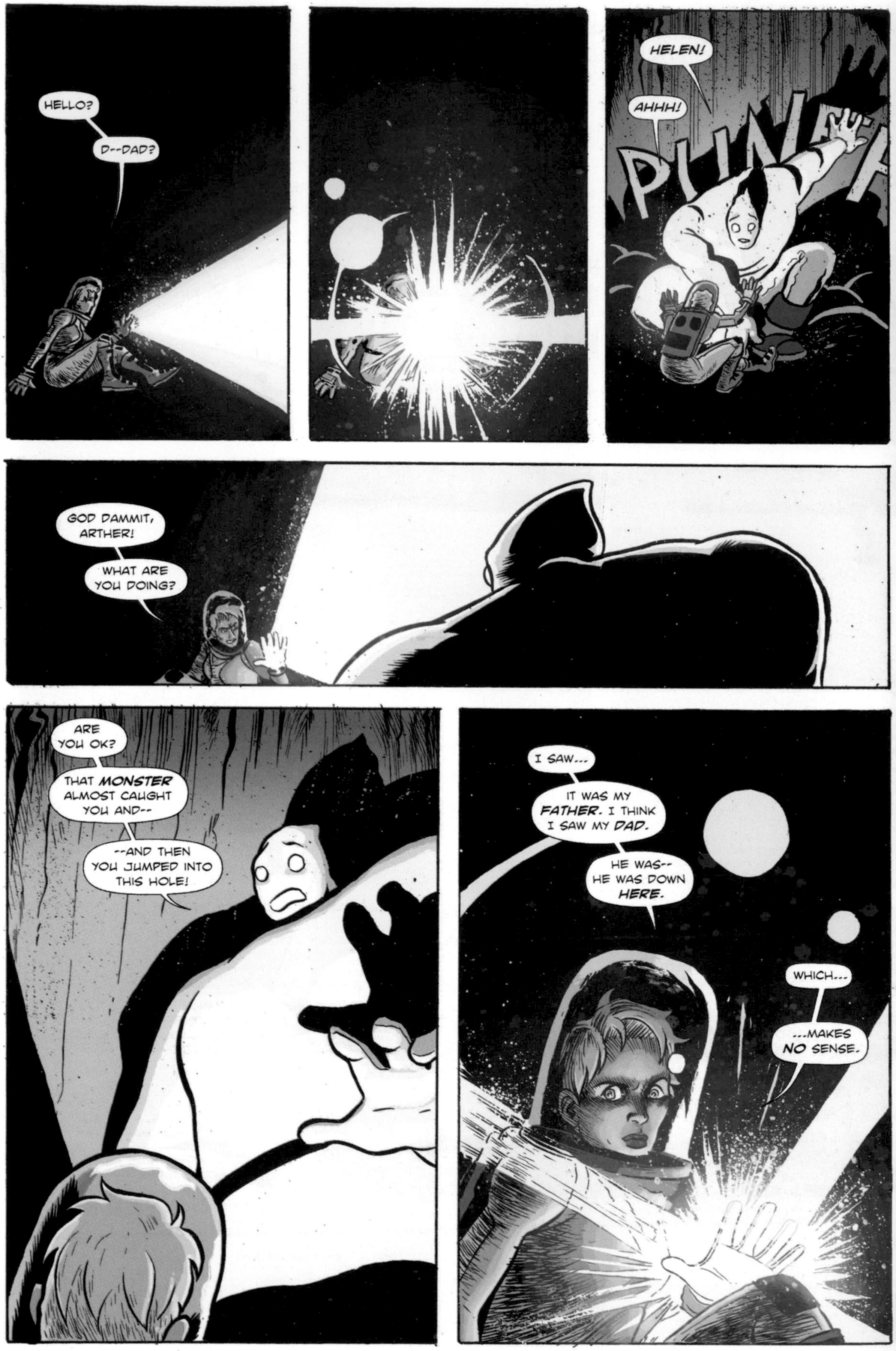
HELLO?
D--DAD?
HELEN!
AHHH!
PLINK
GOD DAMMIT, ARTHER!
WHAT ARE YOU DOING?
ARE YOU OK?
THAT MONSTER ALMOST CAUGHT YOU AND--
--AND THEN YOU JUMPED INTO THIS HOLE!
I SAW...
IT WAS MY FATHER. I THINK I SAW MY DAD.
HE WAS-- HE WAS DOWN HERE.
WHICH...
...MAKES NO SENSE.

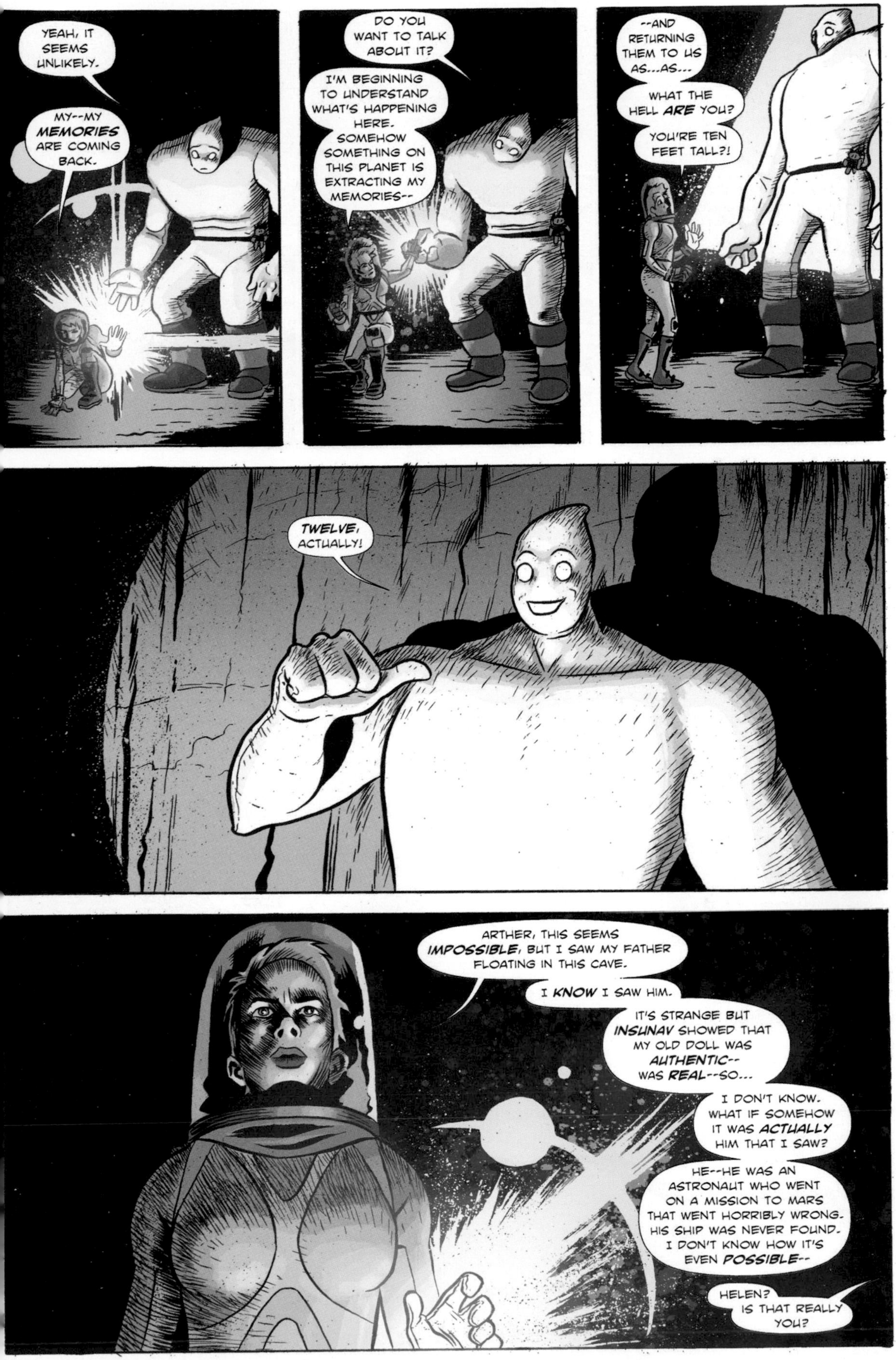
YEAH, IT SEEMS UNLIKELY.
MY--MY MEMORIES ARE COMING BACK.
DO YOU WANT TO TALK ABOUT IT?
I'M BEGINNING TO UNDERSTAND WHAT'S HAPPENING HERE. SOMEHOW SOMETHING ON THIS PLANET IS EXTRACTING MY MEMORIES--
--AND RETURNING THEM TO US AS...AS...
WHAT THE HELL ARE YOU?
YOU'RE TEN FEET TALL?!
TWELVE, ACTUALLY!
ARTHER, THIS SEEMS IMPOSSIBLE, BUT I SAW MY FATHER FLOATING IN THIS CAVE.
I KNOW I SAW HIM.
IT'S STRANGE BUT INSUNAV SHOWED THAT MY OLD DOLL WAS AUTHENTIC-- WAS REAL--SO...
I DON'T KNOW. WHAT IF SOMEHOW IT WAS ACTUALLY HIM THAT I SAW?
HE--HE WAS AN ASTRONAUT WHO WENT ON A MISSION TO MARS THAT WENT HORRIBLY WRONG. HIS SHIP WAS NEVER FOUND. I DON'T KNOW HOW IT'S EVEN POSSIBLE--
HELEN? IS THAT REALLY YOU?

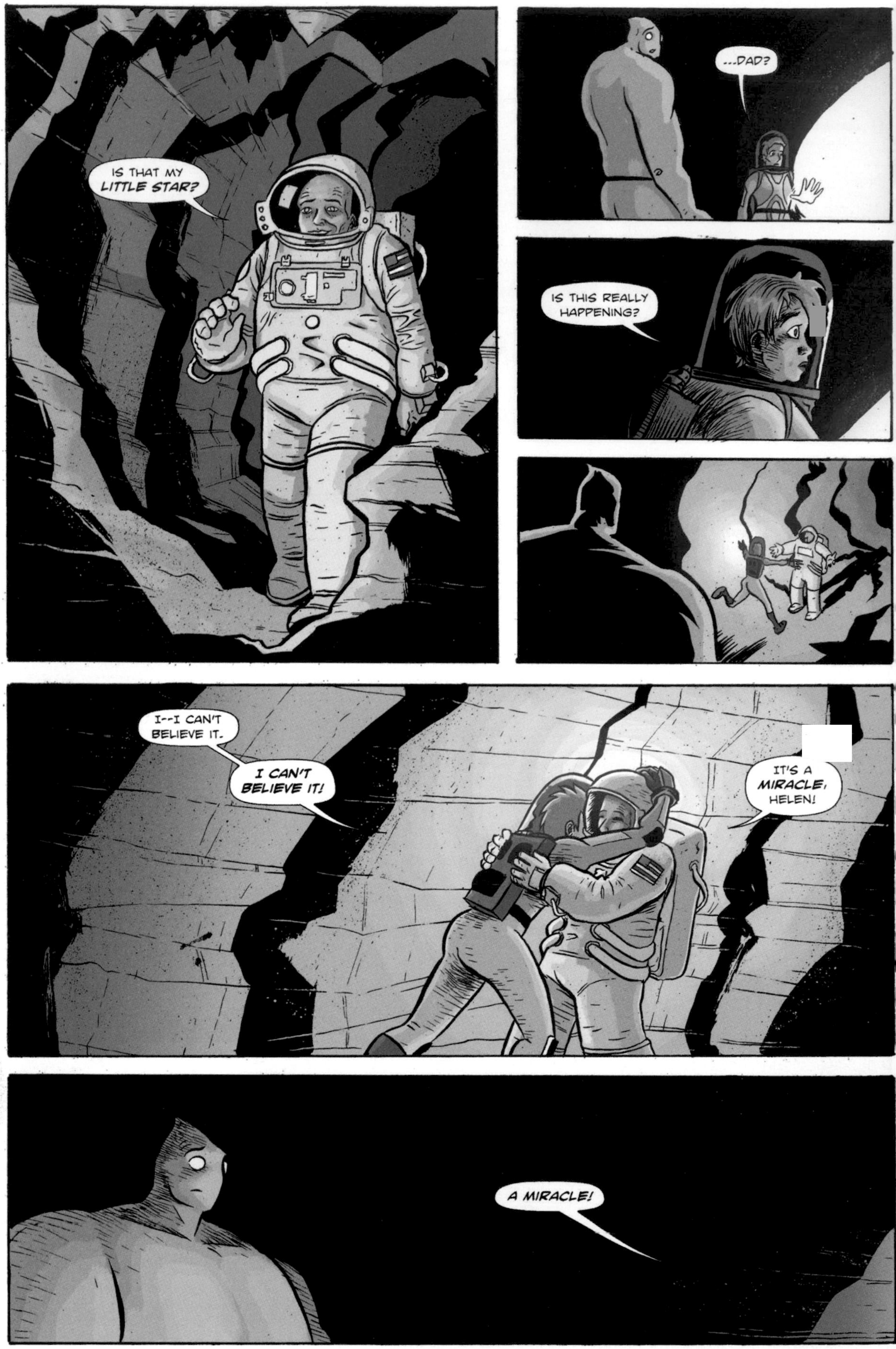
IS THAT MY LITTLE STAR?
...DAD?
IS THIS REALLY HAPPENING?
I--I CAN'T BELIEVE IT.
I CAN'T BELIEVE IT!
IT'S A MIRACLE, HELEN!
A MIRACLE!

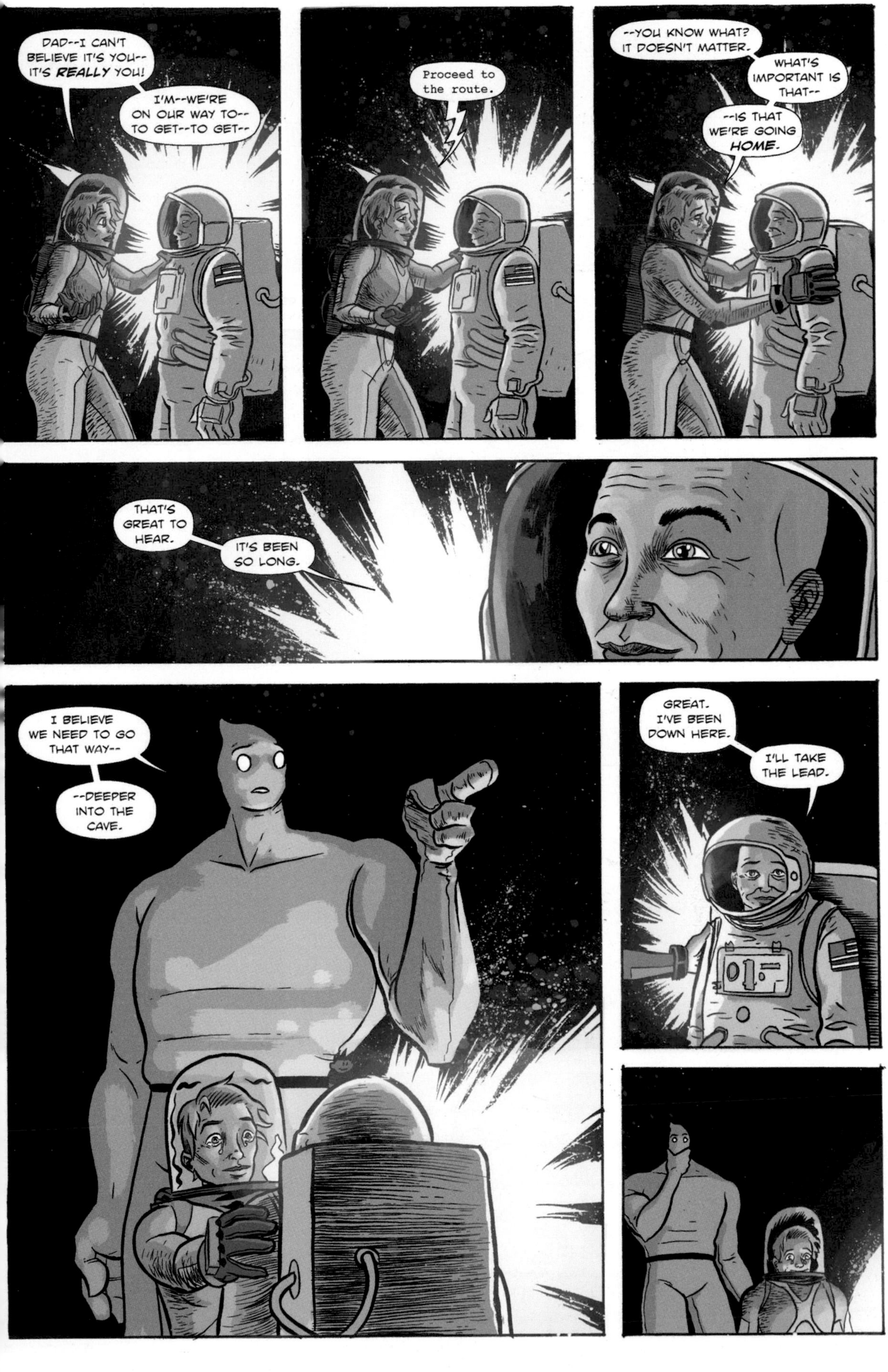

DAD--I CAN'T BELIEVE IT'S YOU-- IT'S REALLY YOU!
I'M--WE'RE ON OUR WAY TO-- TO GET--TO GET--
Proceed to the route.
--YOU KNOW WHAT? IT DOESN'T MATTER.
WHAT'S IMPORTANT IS THAT--
--IS THAT WE'RE GOING HOME.
THAT'S GREAT TO HEAR.
IT'S BEEN SO LONG.
I BELIEVE WE NEED TO GO THAT WAY--
--DEEPER INTO THE CAVE.
GREAT. I'VE BEEN DOWN HERE.
I'LL TAKE THE LEAD.

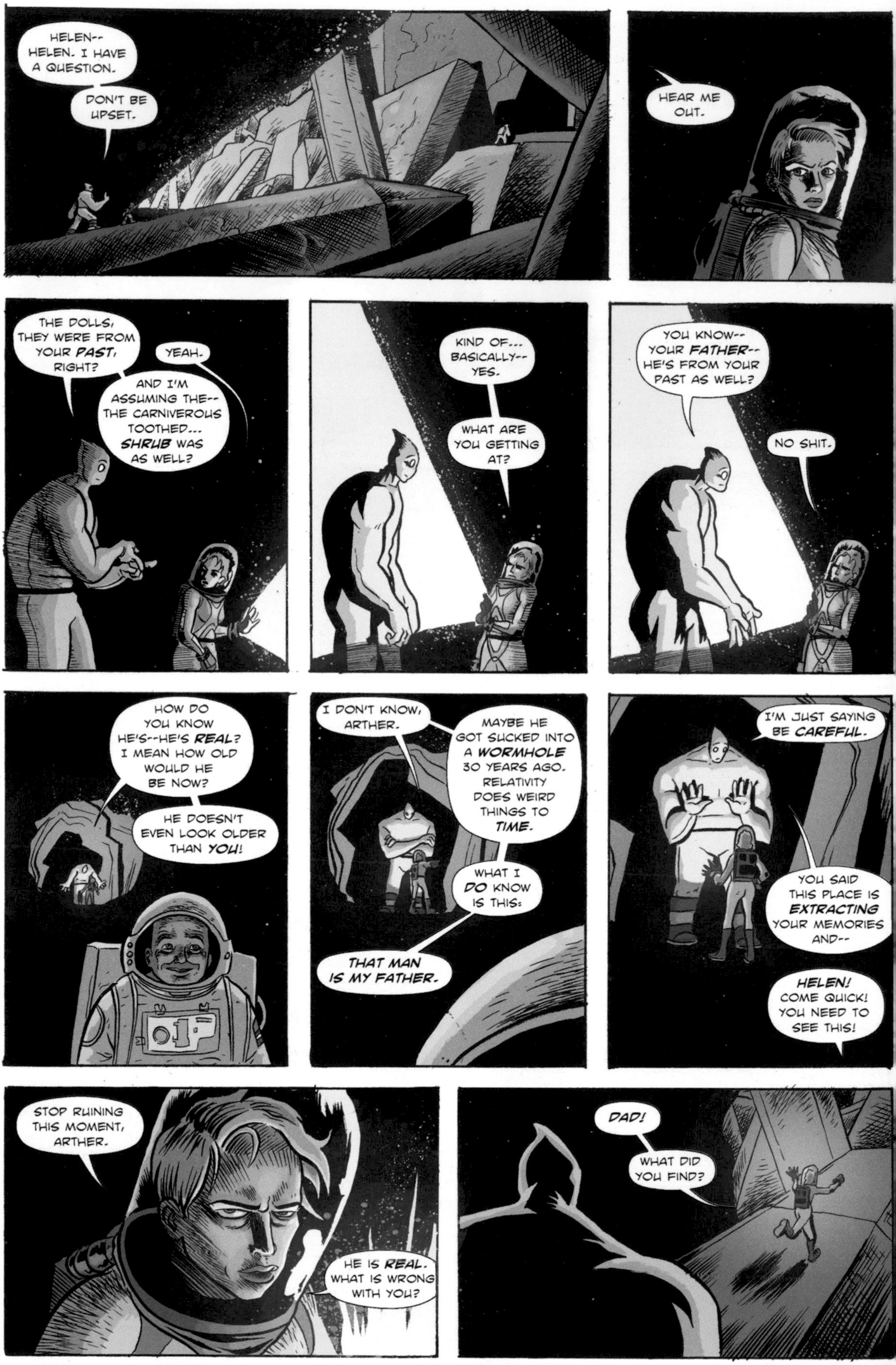
HELEN-- HELEN. I HAVE A QUESTION.
DON'T BE UPSET.
HEAR ME OUT.
THE DOLLS, THEY WERE FROM YOUR PAST, RIGHT?
YEAH.
AND I'M ASSUMING THE-- THE CARNIVEROUS TOOTHED... SHRUB WAS AS WELL?
KIND OF... BASICALLY-- YES.
WHAT ARE YOU GETTING AT?
YOU KNOW-- YOUR FATHER-- HE'S FROM YOUR PAST AS WELL?
NO SHIT.
HOW DO YOU KNOW HE'S--HE'S REAL? I MEAN HOW OLD WOULD HE BE NOW?
HE DOESN'T EVEN LOOK OLDER THAN YOU!
I DON'T KNOW, ARTHER.
MAYBE HE GOT SUCKED INTO A WORMHOLE 30 YEARS AGO. RELATIVITY DOES WEIRD THINGS TO TIME.
WHAT I DO KNOW IS THIS:
THAT MAN IS MY FATHER.
I'M JUST SAYING BE CAREFUL.
YOU SAID THIS PLACE IS EXTRACTING YOUR MEMORIES AND--
HELEN! COME QUICK! YOU NEED TO SEE THIS!
STOP RUINING THIS MOMENT, ARTHER.
HE IS REAL. WHAT IS WRONG WITH YOU?
DAD!
WHAT DID YOU FIND?

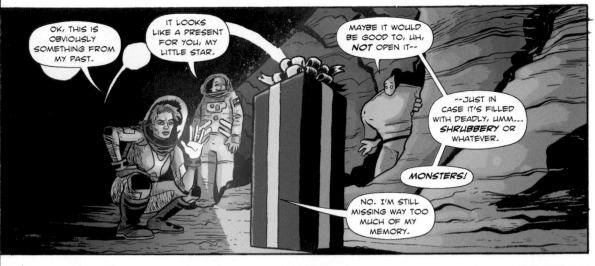

OK, THIS IS OBVIOUSLY SOMETHING FROM MY PAST.

IT LOOKS LIKE A PRESENT FOR YOU, MY LITTLE STAR.

MAYBE IT WOULD BE GOOD TO, UH, *NOT* OPEN IT--

--JUST IN CASE IT'S FILLED WITH DEADLY, UMM... *SHRUBBERY* OR WHATEVER.

MONSTERS!

NO. I'M STILL MISSING WAY TOO MUCH OF MY MEMORY.

BOTH TIMES THIS HAS HAPPENED, I'VE GAINED SOMETHING BACK-- *MY MEMORIES.*

I FEEL THIS URGENCY TO COMPLETE THIS MISSION BUT HOW CAN I FINISH IF I DON'T EVEN REMEMBER WHY I'M HERE IN THE *FIRST* PLACE?

DO YOU KNOW HOW WEIRD AND UNSETTLING IT IS TO NOT REMEMBER YOUR PAST?

POP

PLUS, THERE ARE THREE OF US NOW--

--AND, ARTHER, YOU'RE *TWELVE FEET* TALL!

I THINK YOU CAN HANDLE WHATEVER KINDS OF "MONSTERS" ARE...

RRRIPPP

...ARE...

...IN...

...THIS...

...BOX...?

ARTHER
PERSONAL ASSISTANT

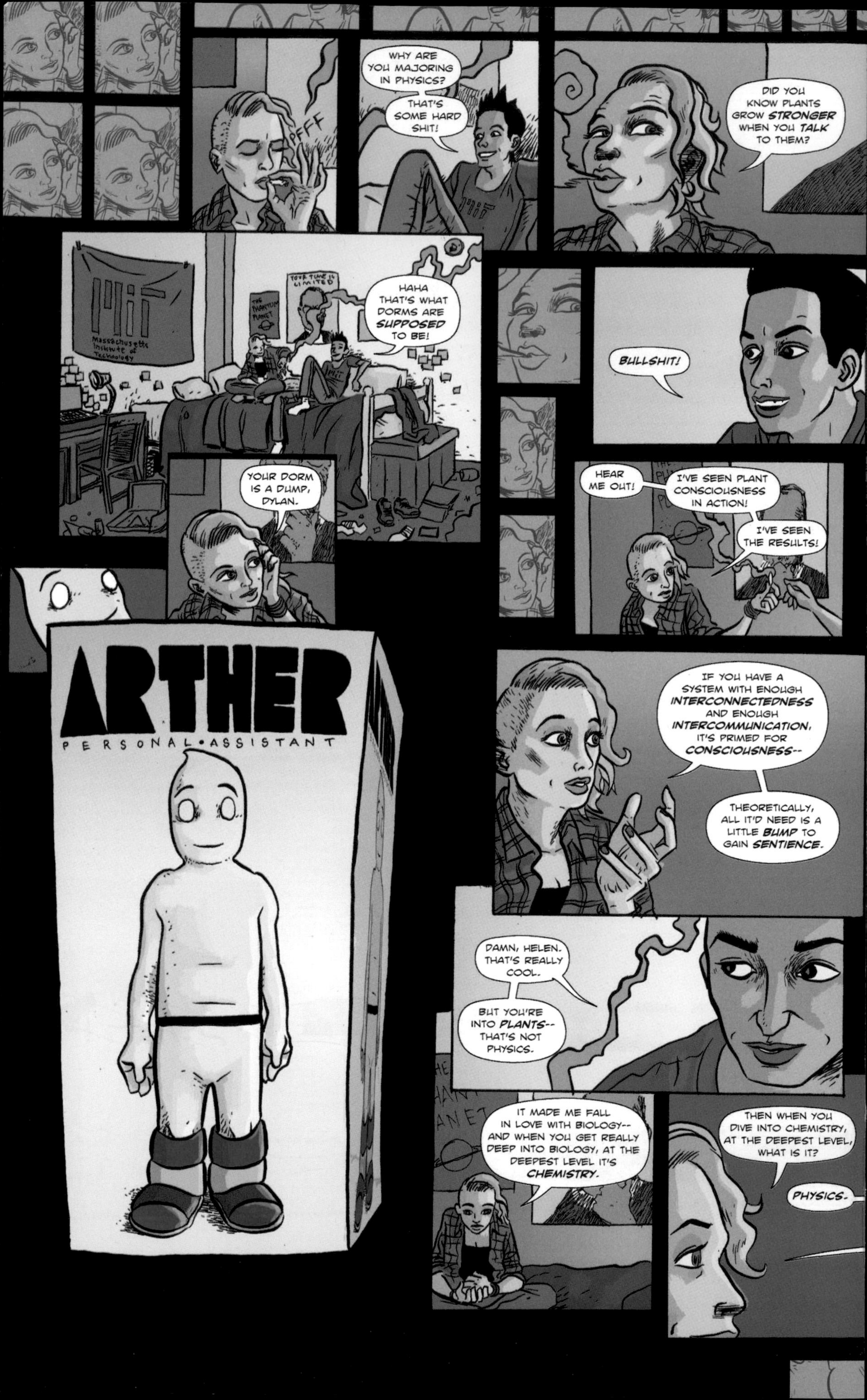
PFFF
WHY ARE YOU MAJORING IN PHYSICS?
THAT'S SOME HARD SHIT!
DID YOU KNOW PLANTS GROW STRONGER WHEN YOU TALK TO THEM?
Massachusetts Institute of Technology
THE PHANTOM PLANET
YOUR TIME IS LIMITED
HAHA THAT'S WHAT DORMS ARE SUPPOSED TO BE!
BULLSHIT!
YOUR DORM IS A DUMP, DYLAN.
HEAR ME OUT!
I'VE SEEN PLANT CONSCIOUSNESS IN ACTION!
I'VE SEEN THE RESULTS!
ARTHER
PERSONAL•ASSISTANT
IF YOU HAVE A SYSTEM WITH ENOUGH INTERCONNECTEDNESS AND ENOUGH INTERCOMMUNICATION, IT'S PRIMED FOR CONSCIOUSNESS--
THEORETICALLY, ALL IT'D NEED IS A LITTLE BUMP TO GAIN SENTIENCE.
DAMN, HELEN. THAT'S REALLY COOL.
BUT YOU'RE INTO PLANTS-- THAT'S NOT PHYSICS.
IT MADE ME FALL IN LOVE WITH BIOLOGY-- AND WHEN YOU GET REALLY DEEP INTO BIOLOGY, AT THE DEEPEST LEVEL IT'S CHEMISTRY.
THEN WHEN YOU DIVE INTO CHEMISTRY, AT THE DEEPEST LEVEL, WHAT IS IT?
PHYSICS.

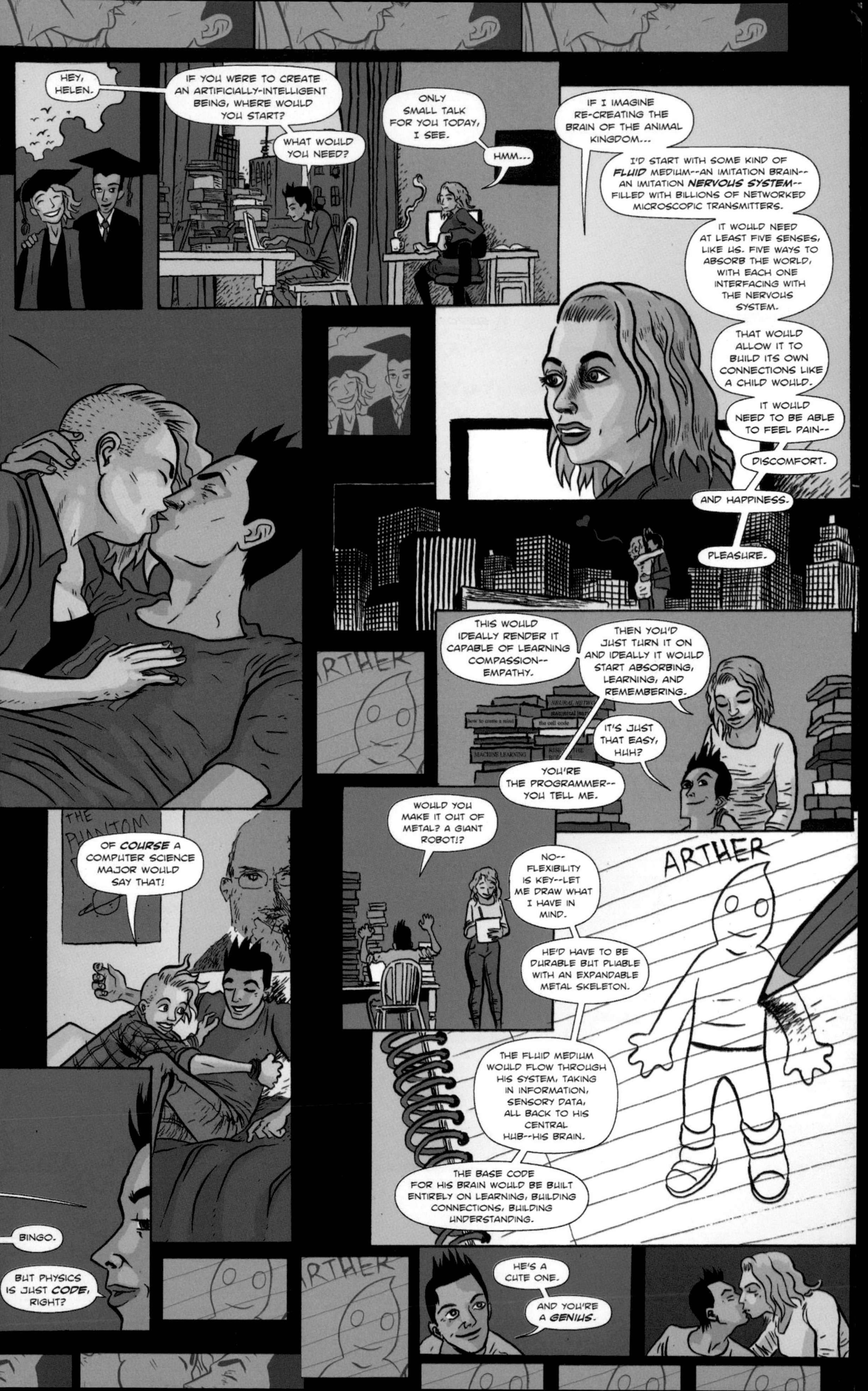
HEY, HELEN.
IF YOU WERE TO CREATE AN ARTIFICIALLY-INTELLIGENT BEING, WHERE WOULD YOU START?
WHAT WOULD YOU NEED?
ONLY SMALL TALK FOR YOU TODAY, I SEE.
HMM...
IF I IMAGINE RE-CREATING THE BRAIN OF THE ANIMAL KINGDOM...
I'D START WITH SOME KIND OF FLUID MEDIUM--AN IMITATION BRAIN--AN IMITATION NERVOUS SYSTEM--FILLED WITH BILLIONS OF NETWORKED MICROSCOPIC TRANSMITTERS.
IT WOULD NEED AT LEAST FIVE SENSES, LIKE US. FIVE WAYS TO ABSORB THE WORLD, WITH EACH ONE INTERFACING WITH THE NERVOUS SYSTEM.
THAT WOULD ALLOW IT TO BUILD ITS OWN CONNECTIONS LIKE A CHILD WOULD.
IT WOULD NEED TO BE ABLE TO FEEL PAIN--
DISCOMFORT.
AND HAPPINESS.
PLEASURE.
THIS WOULD IDEALLY RENDER IT CAPABLE OF LEARNING COMPASSION--EMPATHY.
THEN YOU'D JUST TURN IT ON AND IDEALLY IT WOULD START ABSORBING, LEARNING, AND REMEMBERING.
IT'S JUST THAT EASY, HUH?
YOU'RE THE PROGRAMMER--YOU TELL ME.
ARTHER
THE PHANTOM
OF COURSE A COMPUTER SCIENCE MAJOR WOULD SAY THAT!
WOULD YOU MAKE IT OUT OF METAL? A GIANT ROBOT!?
NO--FLEXIBILITY IS KEY--LET ME DRAW WHAT I HAVE IN MIND.
HE'D HAVE TO BE DURABLE BUT PLIABLE WITH AN EXPANDABLE METAL SKELETON.
ARTHER
THE FLUID MEDIUM WOULD FLOW THROUGH HIS SYSTEM, TAKING IN INFORMATION, SENSORY DATA, ALL BACK TO HIS CENTRAL HUB--HIS BRAIN.
THE BASE CODE FOR HIS BRAIN WOULD BE BUILT ENTIRELY ON LEARNING, BUILDING CONNECTIONS, BUILDING UNDERSTANDING.
BINGO.
BUT PHYSICS IS JUST CODE, RIGHT?
ARTHER
HE'S A CUTE ONE.
AND YOU'RE A GENIUS.

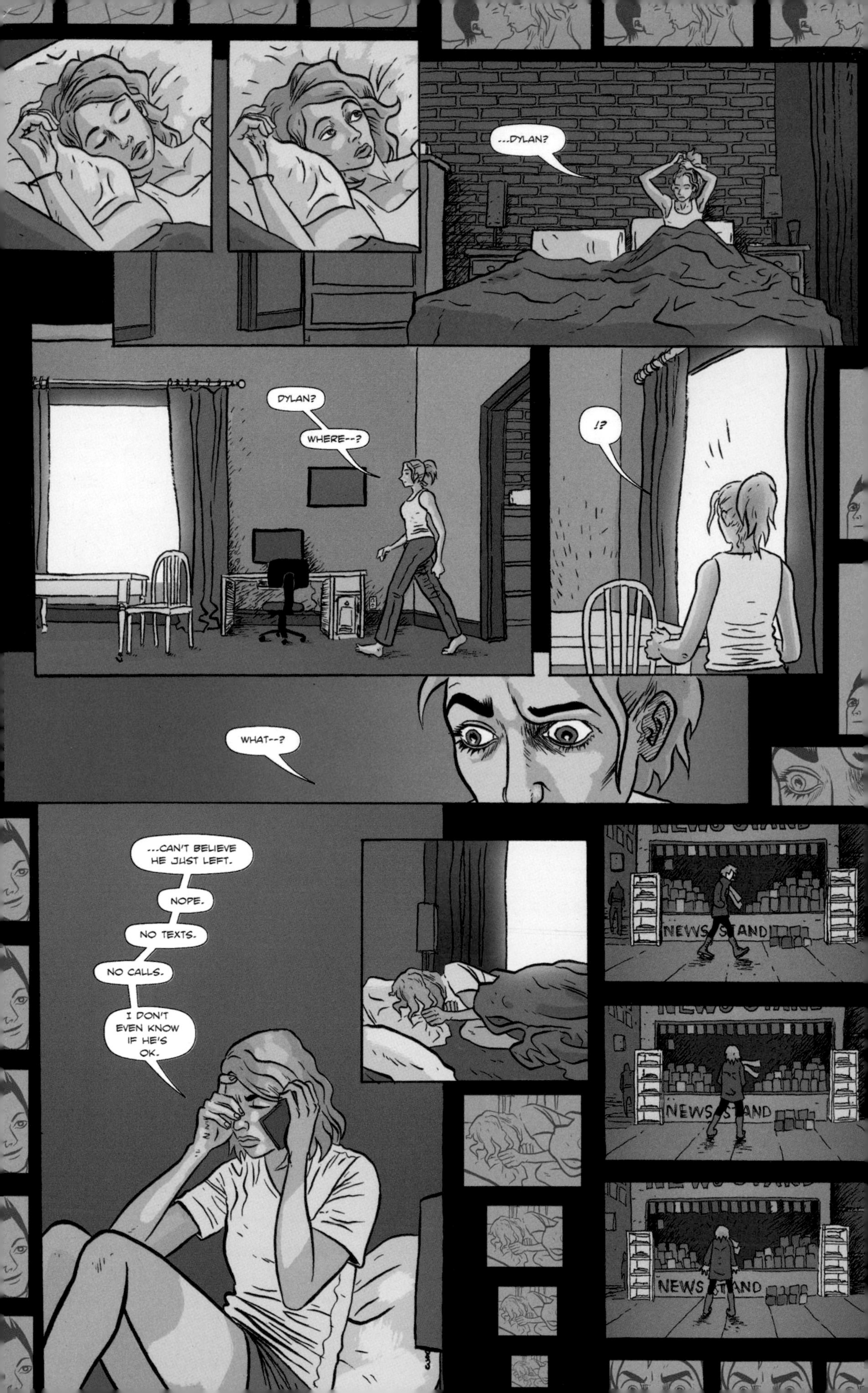
...DYLAN?
DYLAN?
WHERE--?
!?
WHAT--?
...CAN'T BELIEVE HE JUST LEFT.
NOPE.
NO TEXTS.
NO CALLS.
I DON'T EVEN KNOW IF HE'S OK.
NEWS STAND
NEWS STAND
NEWS STAND

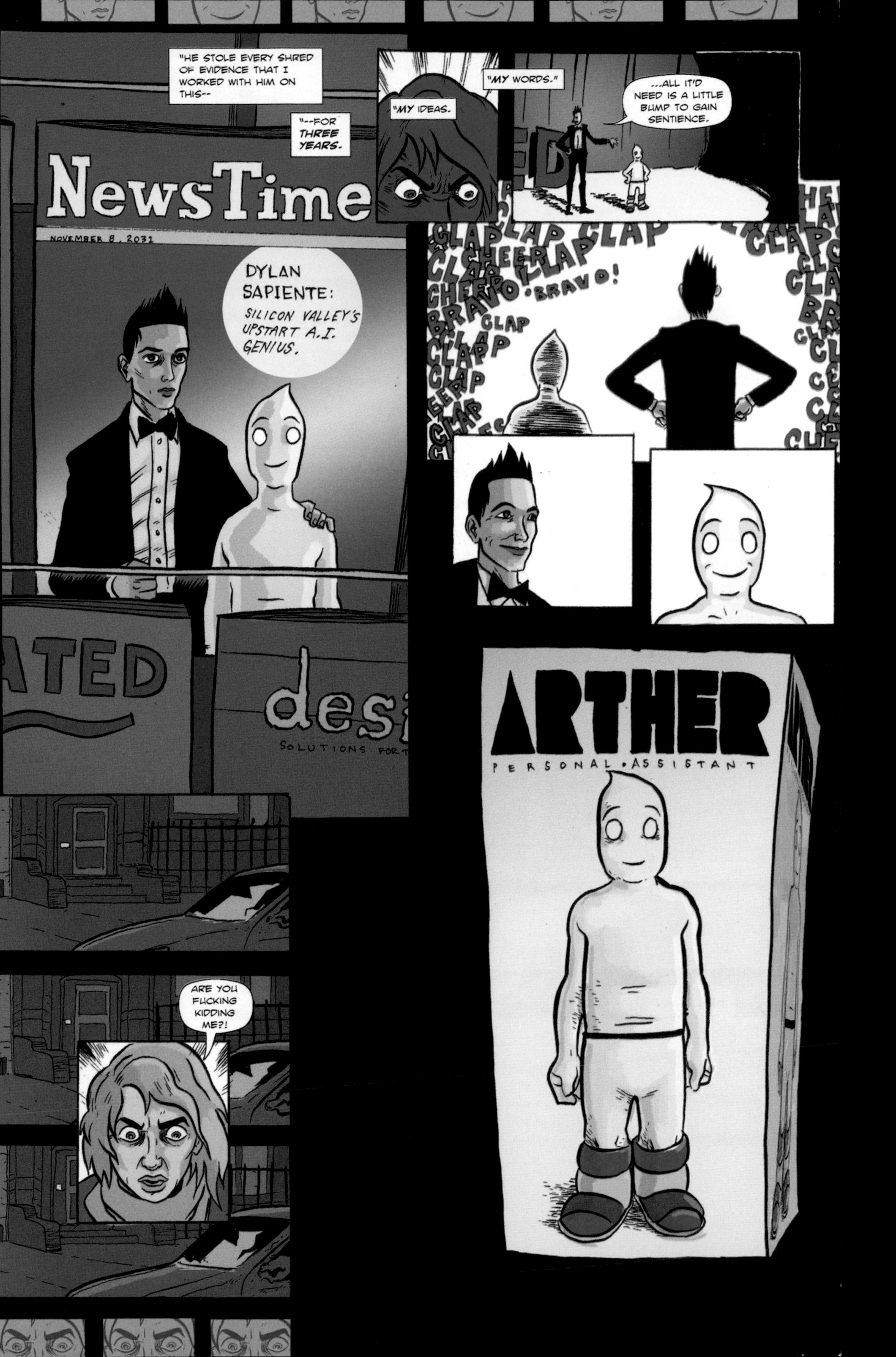

"HE STOLE EVERY SHRED OF EVIDENCE THAT I WORKED WITH HIM ON THIS--
"--FOR THREE YEARS.
"MY IDEAS.
"MY WORDS."
...ALL IT'D NEED IS A LITTLE BUMP TO GAIN SENTIENCE.
NewsTime
NOVEMBER 8, 2031
DYLAN SAPIENTE:
SILICON VALLEY'S UPSTART A.I. GENIUS.
CLAP CLAP CLAP CHEER CLAP BRAVO! BRAVO!
ATED
desi
SOLUTIONS FOR
ARTHER
PERSONAL • ASSISTANT
ARE YOU FUCKING KIDDING ME?!

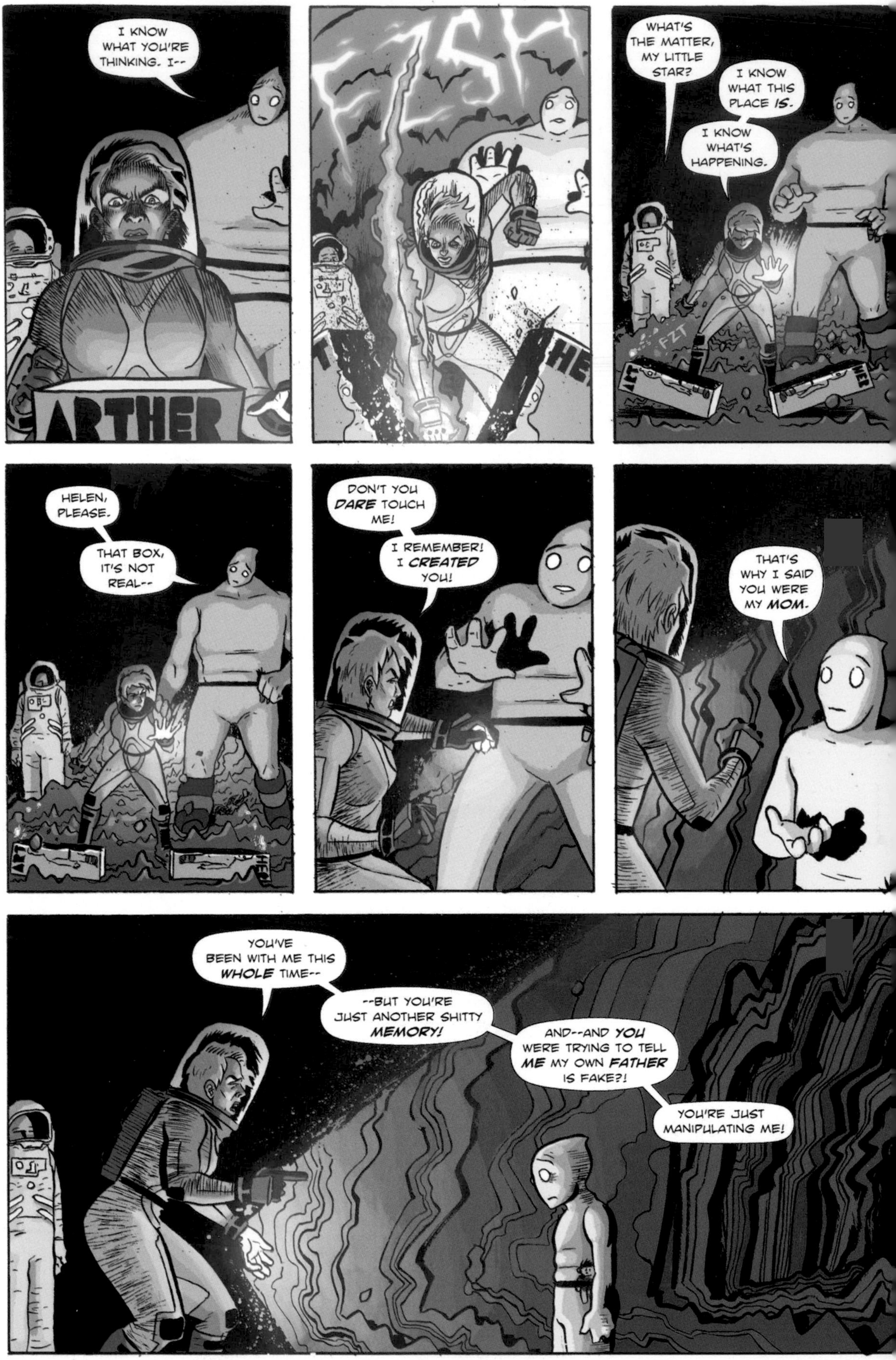
I KNOW WHAT YOU'RE THINKING. I--
ARTHER
FZSH
WHAT'S THE MATTER, MY LITTLE STAR?
I KNOW WHAT THIS PLACE *IS.*
I KNOW WHAT'S HAPPENING.
FZT
HELEN, PLEASE.
THAT BOX, IT'S NOT REAL--
DON'T YOU *DARE* TOUCH ME!
I REMEMBER! I *CREATED* YOU!
THAT'S WHY I SAID YOU WERE MY *MOM.*
YOU'VE BEEN WITH ME THIS *WHOLE* TIME--
--BUT YOU'RE JUST ANOTHER SHITTY *MEMORY!*
AND--AND *YOU* WERE TRYING TO TELL *ME* MY OWN *FATHER* IS FAKE?!
YOU'RE JUST MANIPULATING ME!

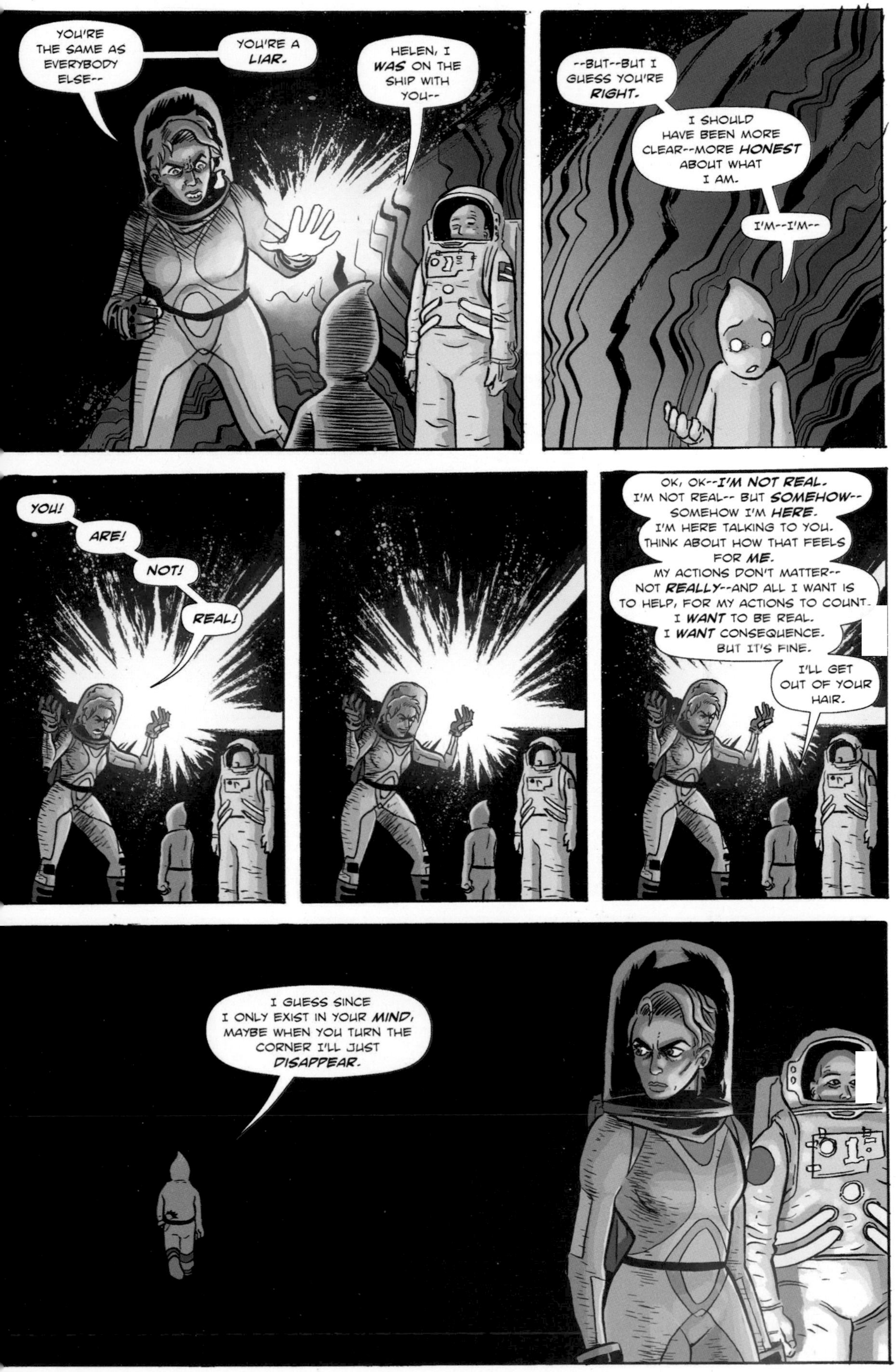
YOU'RE THE SAME AS EVERYBODY ELSE--
YOU'RE A LIAR.
HELEN, I WAS ON THE SHIP WITH YOU--
--BUT--BUT I GUESS YOU'RE RIGHT.
I SHOULD HAVE BEEN MORE CLEAR--MORE HONEST ABOUT WHAT I AM.
I'M--I'M--
YOU!
ARE!
NOT!
REAL!
OK, OK--I'M NOT REAL. I'M NOT REAL-- BUT SOMEHOW-- SOMEHOW I'M HERE. I'M HERE TALKING TO YOU. THINK ABOUT HOW THAT FEELS FOR ME. MY ACTIONS DON'T MATTER-- NOT REALLY--AND ALL I WANT IS TO HELP, FOR MY ACTIONS TO COUNT. I WANT TO BE REAL. I WANT CONSEQUENCE. BUT IT'S FINE.
I'LL GET OUT OF YOUR HAIR.
I GUESS SINCE I ONLY EXIST IN YOUR MIND, MAYBE WHEN YOU TURN THE CORNER I'LL JUST DISAPPEAR.

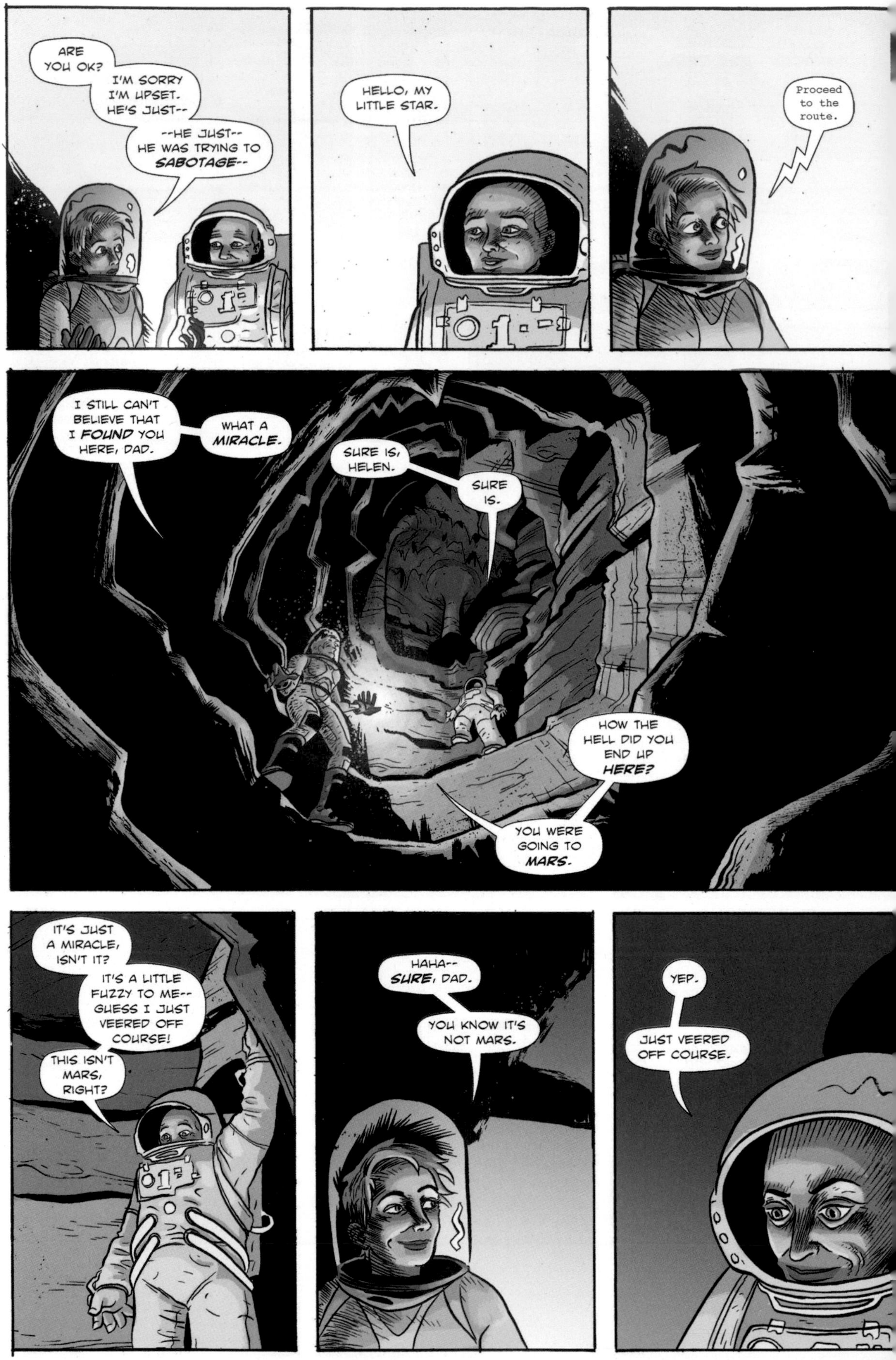
ARE YOU OK?
I'M SORRY I'M UPSET. HE'S JUST--
--HE JUST-- HE WAS TRYING TO SABOTAGE--
HELLO, MY LITTLE STAR.
Proceed to the route.
I STILL CAN'T BELIEVE THAT I FOUND YOU HERE, DAD.
WHAT A MIRACLE.
SURE IS, HELEN.
SURE IS.
HOW THE HELL DID YOU END UP HERE?
YOU WERE GOING TO MARS.
IT'S JUST A MIRACLE, ISN'T IT?
IT'S A LITTLE FUZZY TO ME-- GUESS I JUST VEERED OFF COURSE!
THIS ISN'T MARS, RIGHT?
HAHA-- SURE, DAD.
YOU KNOW IT'S NOT MARS.
YEP.
JUST VEERED OFF COURSE.

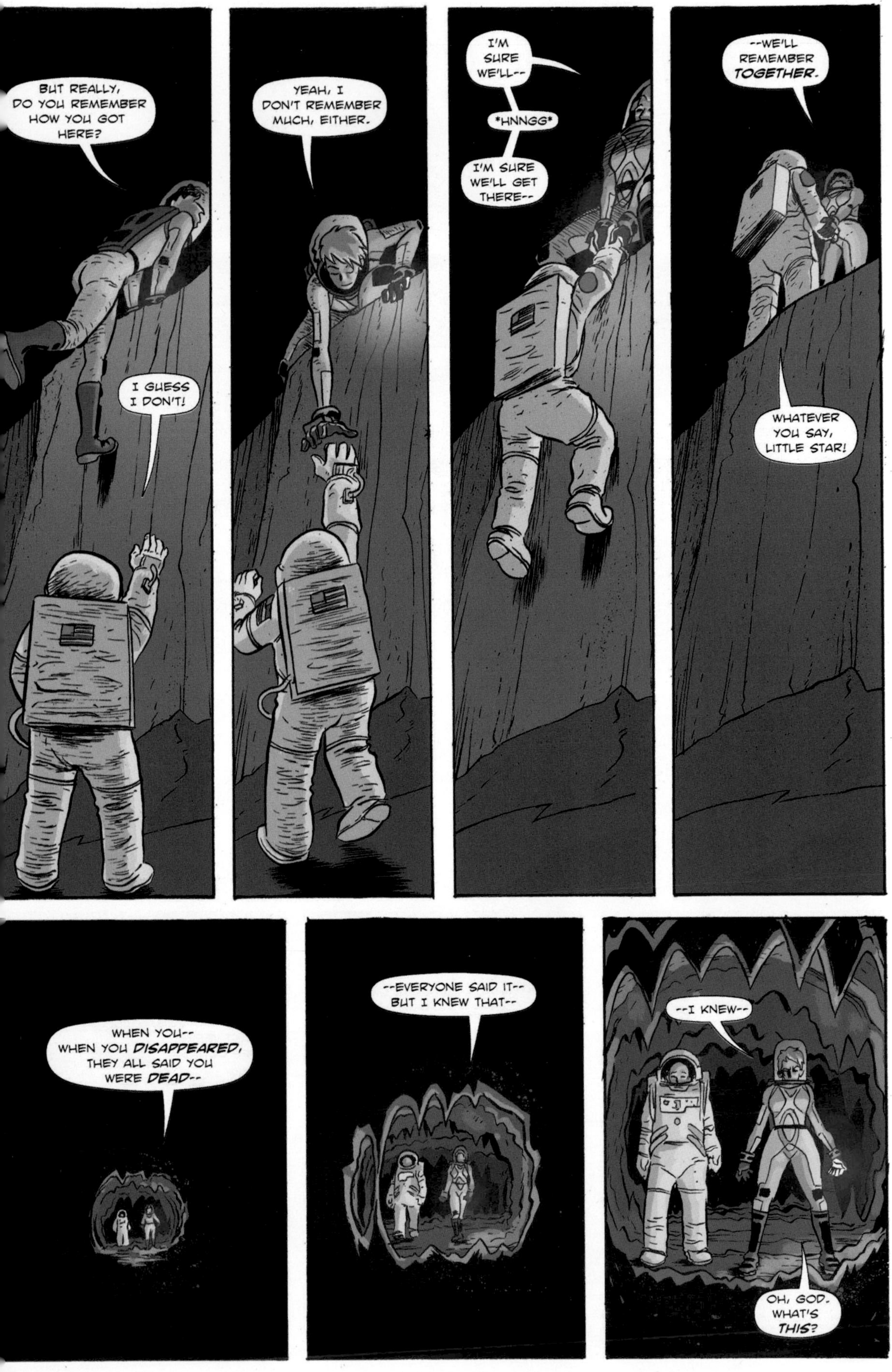
BUT REALLY, DO YOU REMEMBER HOW YOU GOT HERE?
I GUESS I DON'T!
YEAH, I DON'T REMEMBER MUCH, EITHER.
I'M SURE WE'LL--
HNNGG
I'M SURE WE'LL GET THERE--
--WE'LL REMEMBER TOGETHER.
WHATEVER YOU SAY, LITTLE STAR!
WHEN YOU-- WHEN YOU DISAPPEARED, THEY ALL SAID YOU WERE DEAD--
--EVERYONE SAID IT-- BUT I KNEW THAT--
--I KNEW--
OH, GOD. WHAT'S THIS?

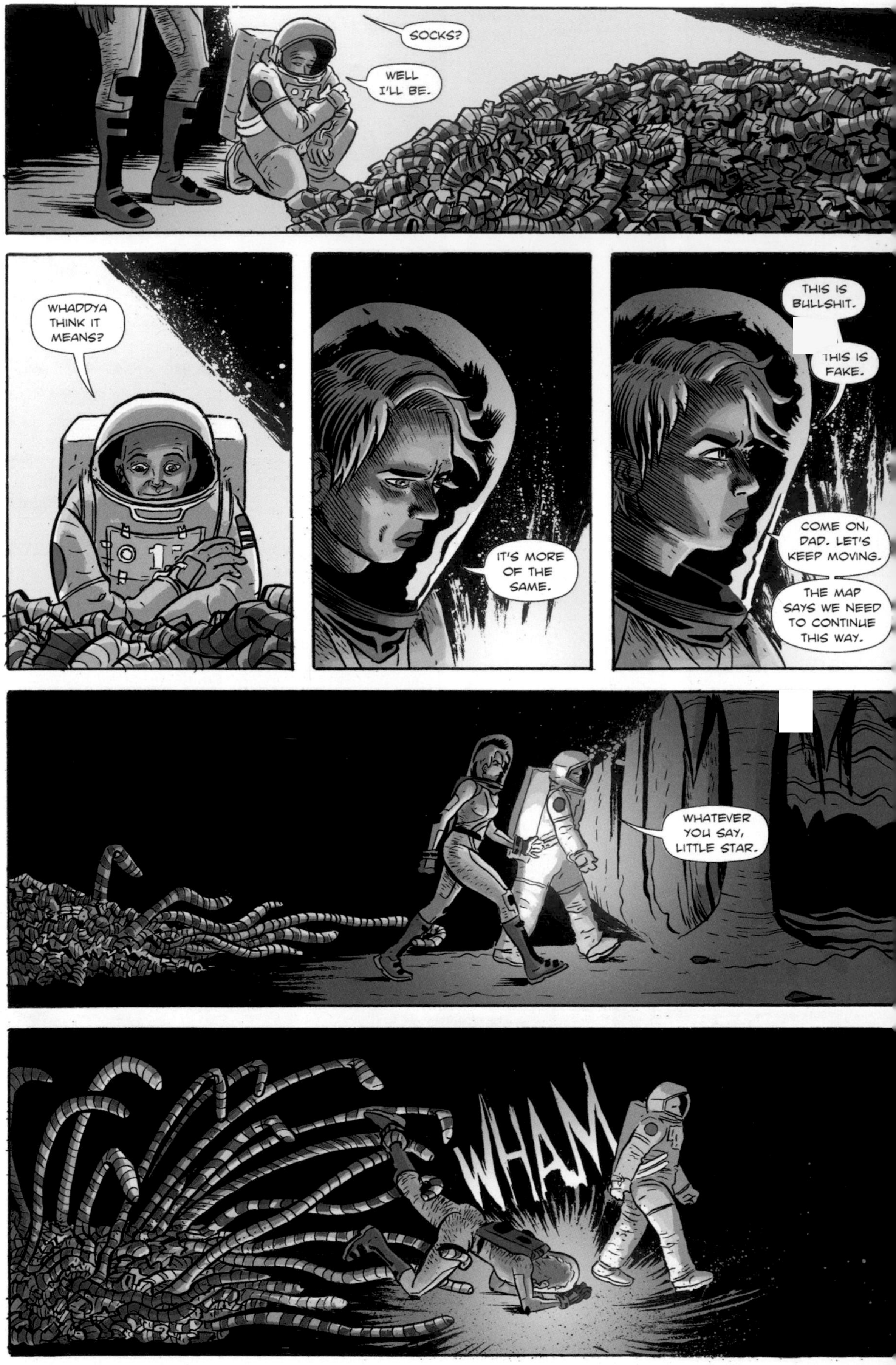
SOCKS?
WELL I'LL BE.
WHADDYA THINK IT MEANS?
IT'S MORE OF THE SAME.
THIS IS BULLSHIT.
THIS IS FAKE.
COME ON, DAD. LET'S KEEP MOVING.
THE MAP SAYS WE NEED TO CONTINUE THIS WAY.
WHATEVER YOU SAY, LITTLE STAR.
WHAM

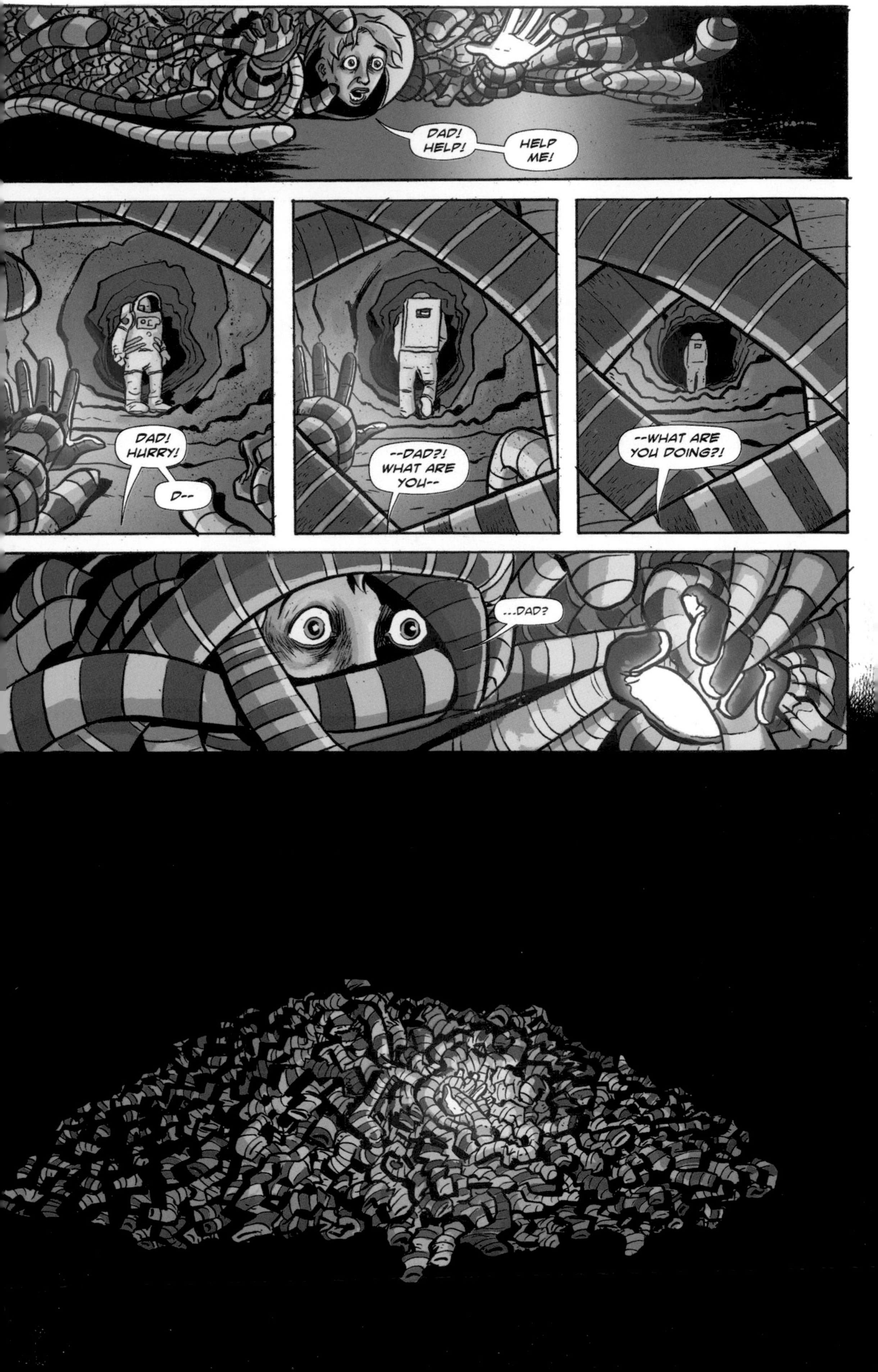
DAD! HELP!
HELP ME!
DAD! HURRY!
D--
--DAD?! WHAT ARE YOU--
--WHAT ARE YOU DOING?!
...DAD?

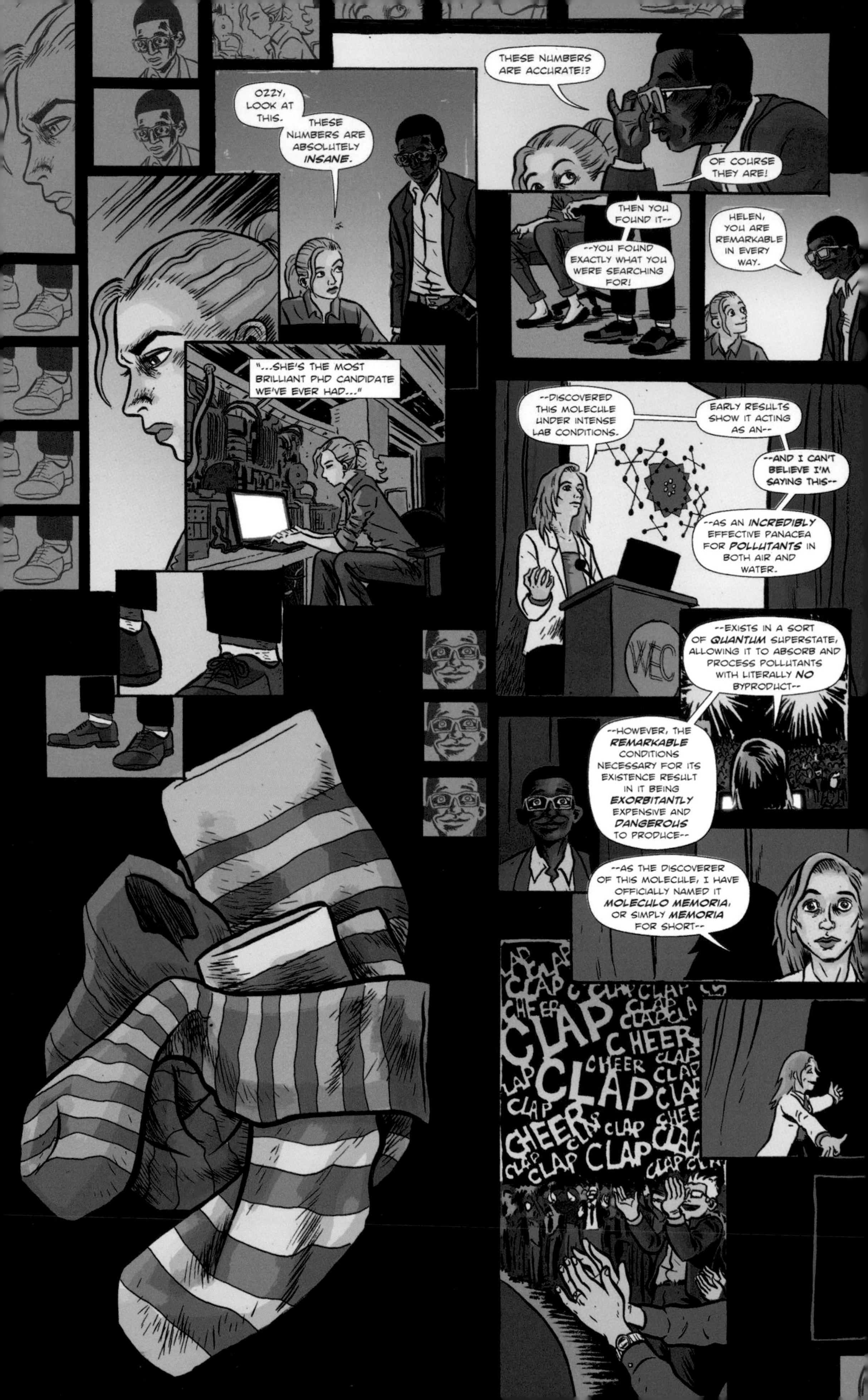
OZZY, LOOK AT THIS.
THESE NUMBERS ARE ABSOLUTELY INSANE.
THESE NUMBERS ARE ACCURATE!?
OF COURSE THEY ARE!
THEN YOU FOUND IT--
--YOU FOUND EXACTLY WHAT YOU WERE SEARCHING FOR!
HELEN, YOU ARE REMARKABLE IN EVERY WAY.
"...SHE'S THE MOST BRILLIANT PHD CANDIDATE WE'VE EVER HAD..."
--DISCOVERED THIS MOLECULE UNDER INTENSE LAB CONDITIONS.
EARLY RESULTS SHOW IT ACTING AS AN--
--AND I CAN'T BELIEVE I'M SAYING THIS--
--AS AN INCREDIBLY EFFECTIVE PANACEA FOR POLLUTANTS IN BOTH AIR AND WATER.
WEC
--EXISTS IN A SORT OF QUANTUM SUPERSTATE, ALLOWING IT TO ABSORB AND PROCESS POLLUTANTS WITH LITERALLY NO BYPRODUCT--
--HOWEVER, THE REMARKABLE CONDITIONS NECESSARY FOR ITS EXISTENCE RESULT IN IT BEING EXORBITANTLY EXPENSIVE AND DANGEROUS TO PRODUCE--
--AS THE DISCOVERER OF THIS MOLECULE, I HAVE OFFICIALLY NAMED IT MOLECULO MEMORIA, OR SIMPLY MEMORIA FOR SHORT--
CLAP CLAP CHEER CLAP CLAP CHEER CLAP CHEER CLAP CLAP CHEER CLAP CLAP CLAP

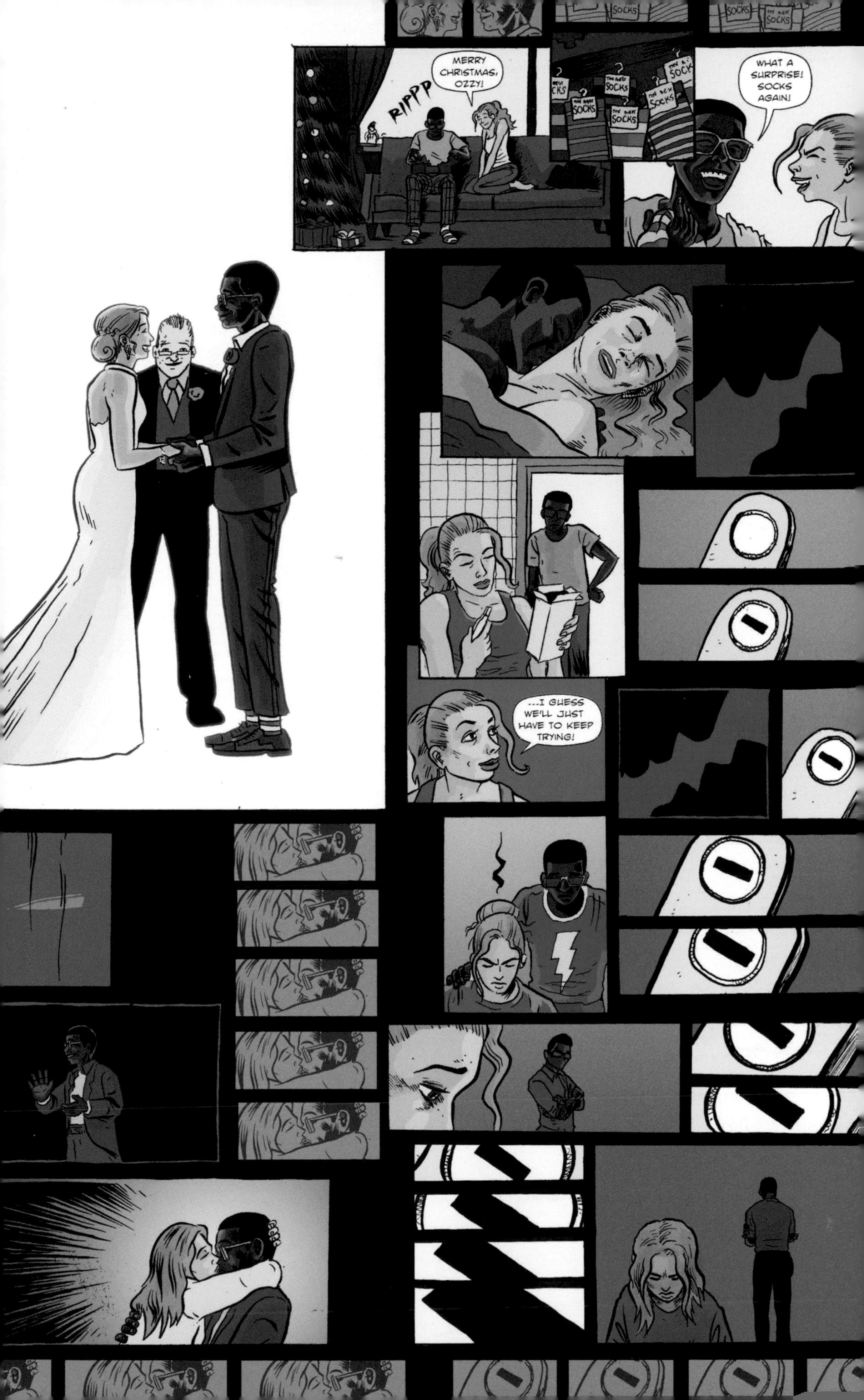
RIPPP
MERRY CHRISTMAS, OZZY!
WHAT A SURPRISE! SOCKS AGAIN!
...I GUESS WE'LL JUST HAVE TO KEEP TRYING!

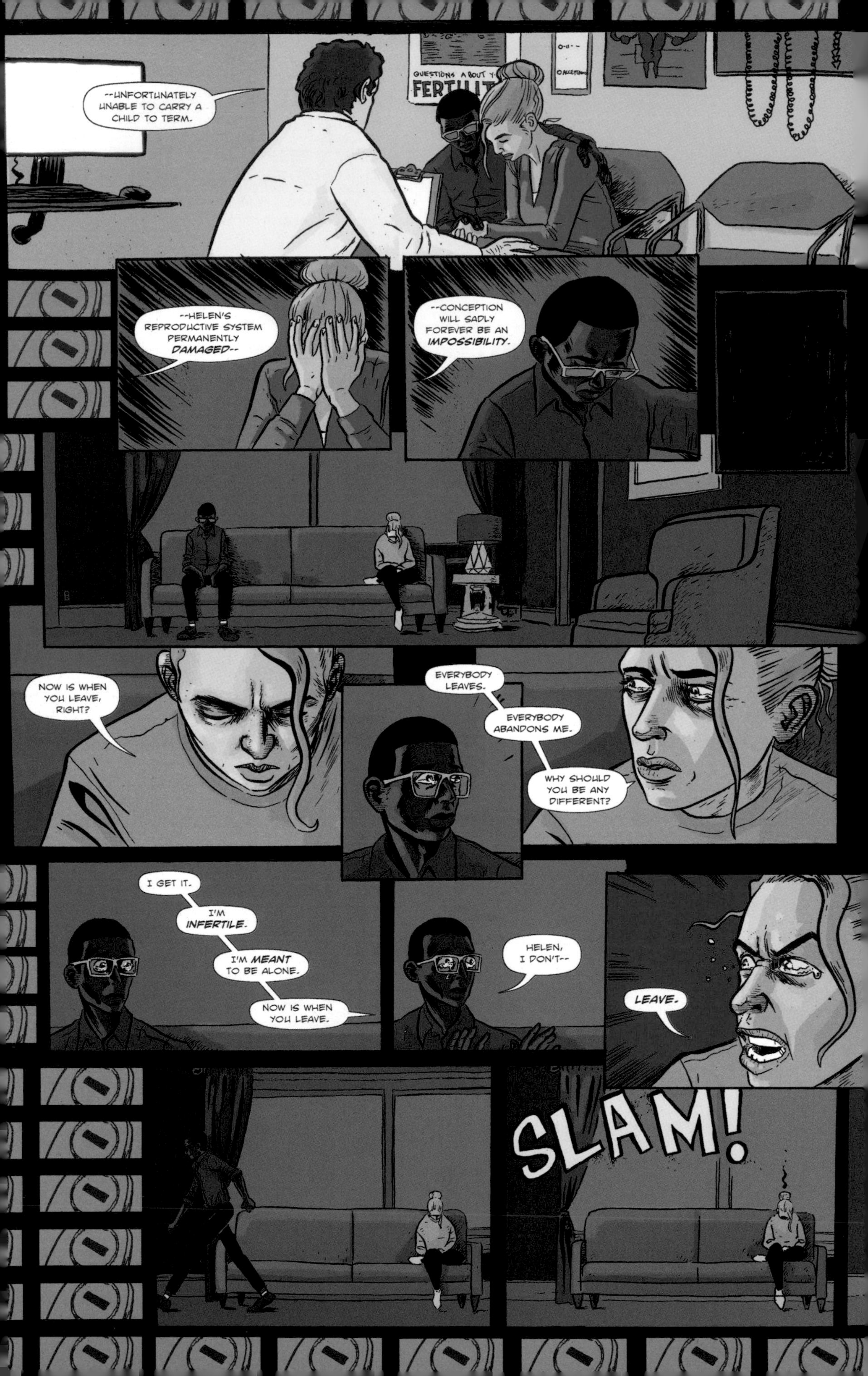

--UNFORTUNATELY UNABLE TO CARRY A CHILD TO TERM.
QUESTIONS ABOUT Y... FERTILIT...
--HELEN'S REPRODUCTIVE SYSTEM PERMANENTLY DAMAGED--
--CONCEPTION WILL SADLY FOREVER BE AN IMPOSSIBILITY.
NOW IS WHEN YOU LEAVE, RIGHT?
EVERYBODY LEAVES.
EVERYBODY ABANDONS ME.
WHY SHOULD YOU BE ANY DIFFERENT?
I GET IT.
I'M INFERTILE.
I'M MEANT TO BE ALONE.
NOW IS WHEN YOU LEAVE.
HELEN, I DON'T--
LEAVE.
SLAM!

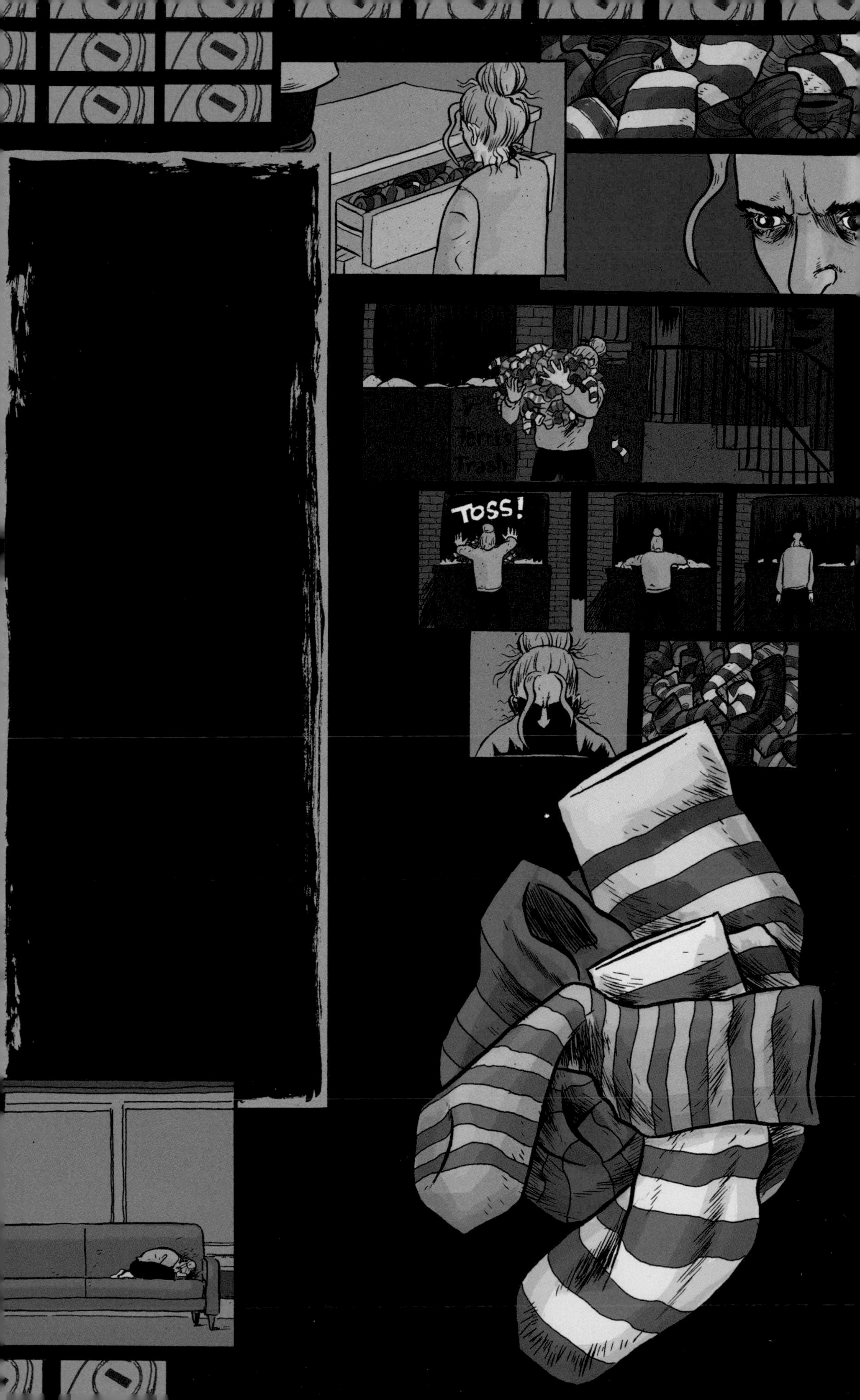

TOSS!

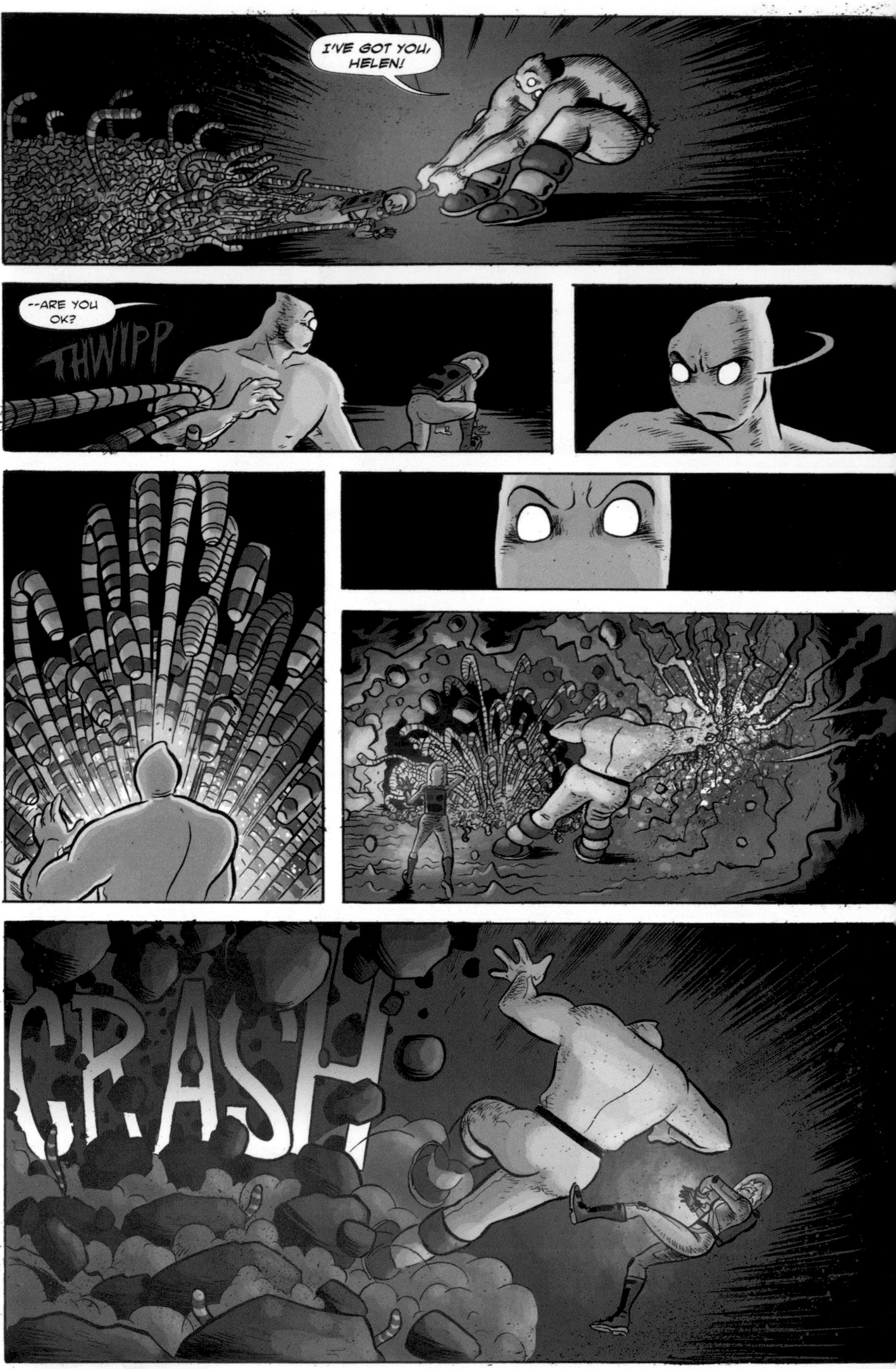
I'VE GOT YOU, HELEN!
--ARE YOU OK?
THWIPP
CRASH

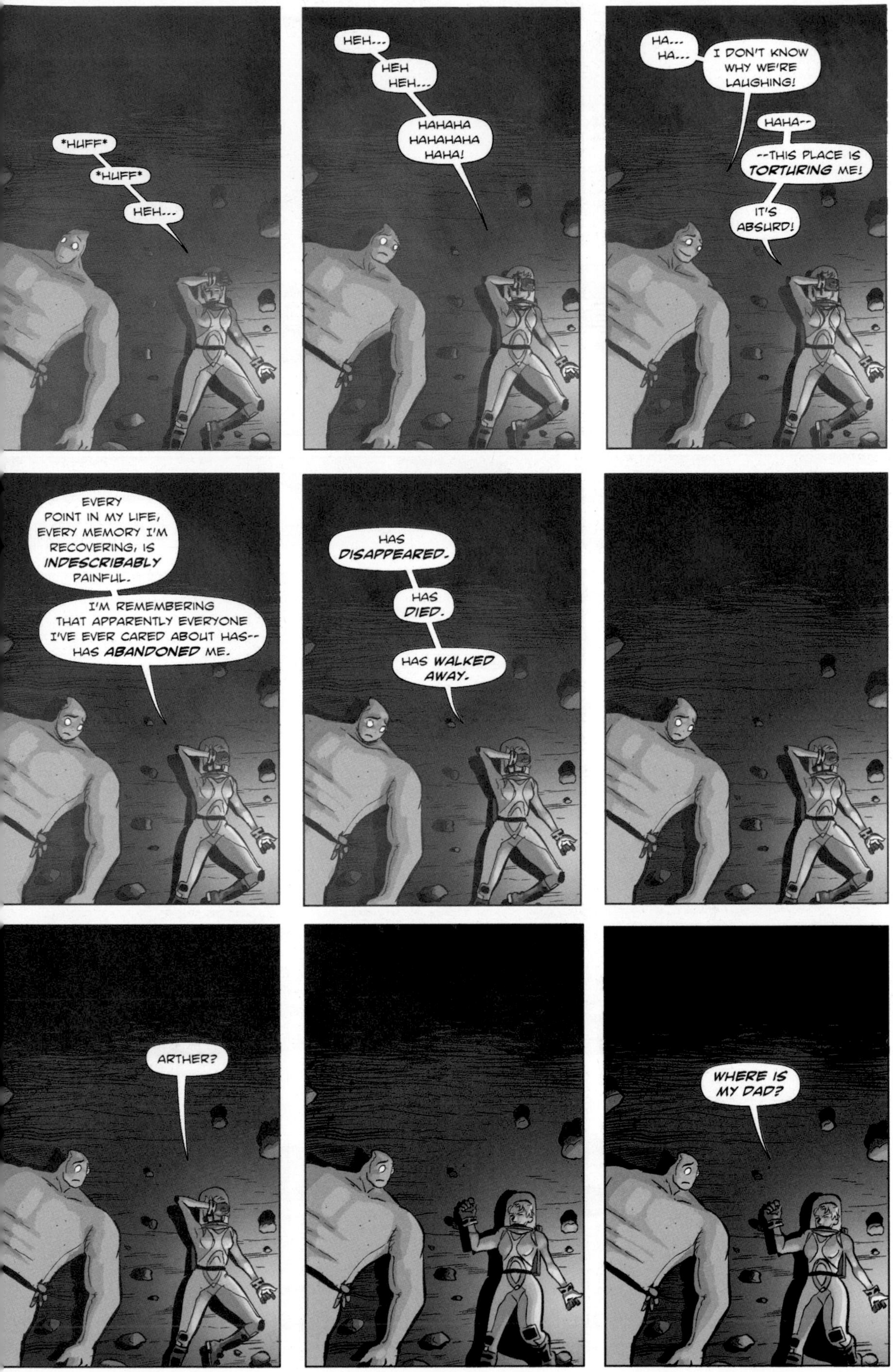
HUFF
HUFF
HEH...
HEH...
HEH HEH...
HAHAHA HAHAHAHA HAHA!
HA... HA...
I DON'T KNOW WHY WE'RE LAUGHING!
HAHA--
--THIS PLACE IS TORTURING ME!
IT'S ABSURD!
EVERY POINT IN MY LIFE, EVERY MEMORY I'M RECOVERING, IS INDESCRIBABLY PAINFUL.
I'M REMEMBERING THAT APPARENTLY EVERYONE I'VE EVER CARED ABOUT HAS-- HAS ABANDONED ME.
HAS DISAPPEARED.
HAS DIED.
HAS WALKED AWAY.
ARTHER?
WHERE IS MY DAD?

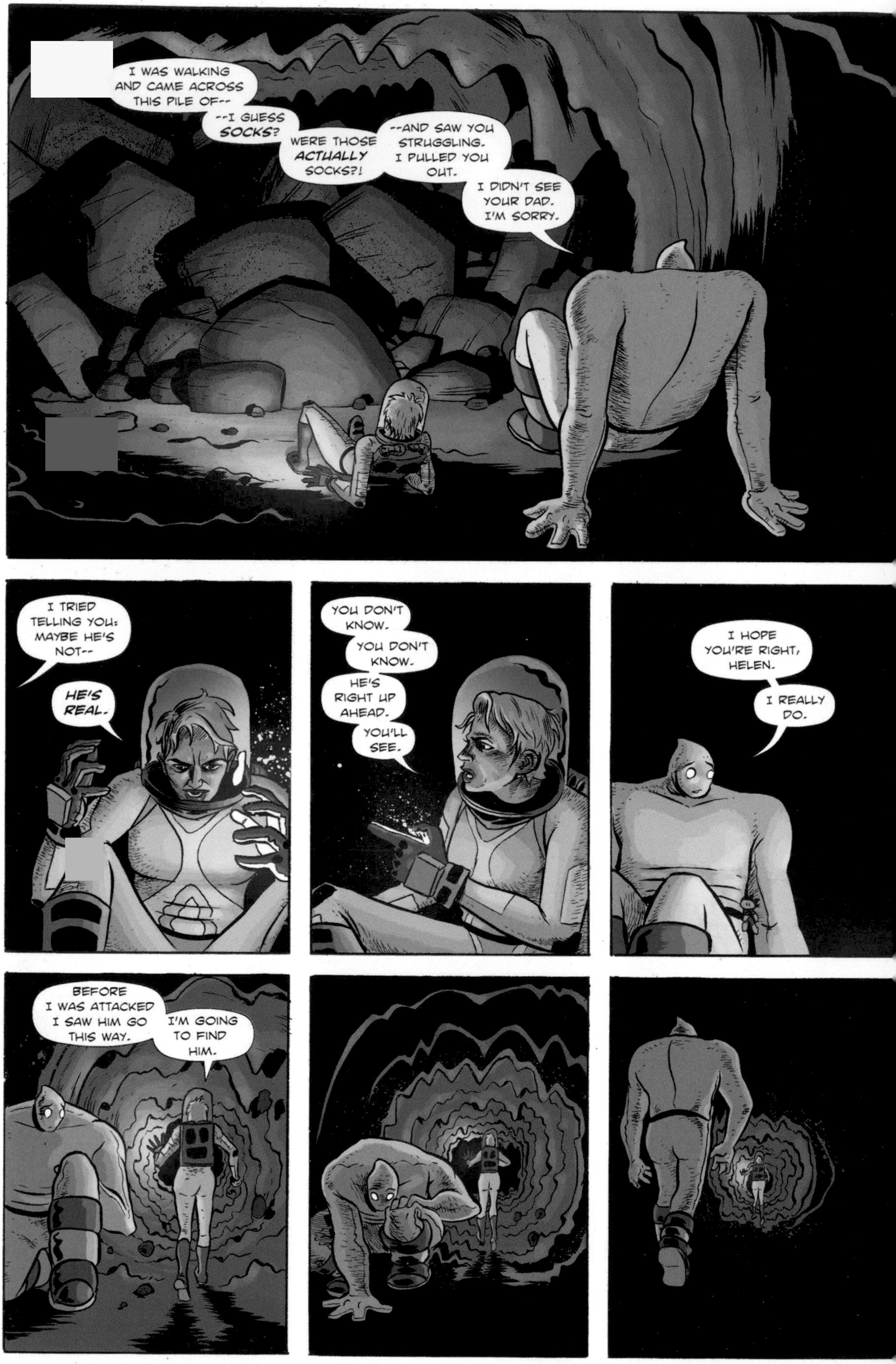
I WAS WALKING AND CAME ACROSS THIS PILE OF--
--I GUESS SOCKS?
WERE THOSE ACTUALLY SOCKS?!
--AND SAW YOU STRUGGLING. I PULLED YOU OUT.
I DIDN'T SEE YOUR DAD. I'M SORRY.
I TRIED TELLING YOU: MAYBE HE'S NOT--
HE'S REAL.
YOU DON'T KNOW.
YOU DON'T KNOW.
HE'S RIGHT UP AHEAD.
YOU'LL SEE.
I HOPE YOU'RE RIGHT, HELEN.
I REALLY DO.
BEFORE I WAS ATTACKED I SAW HIM GO THIS WAY.
I'M GOING TO FIND HIM.

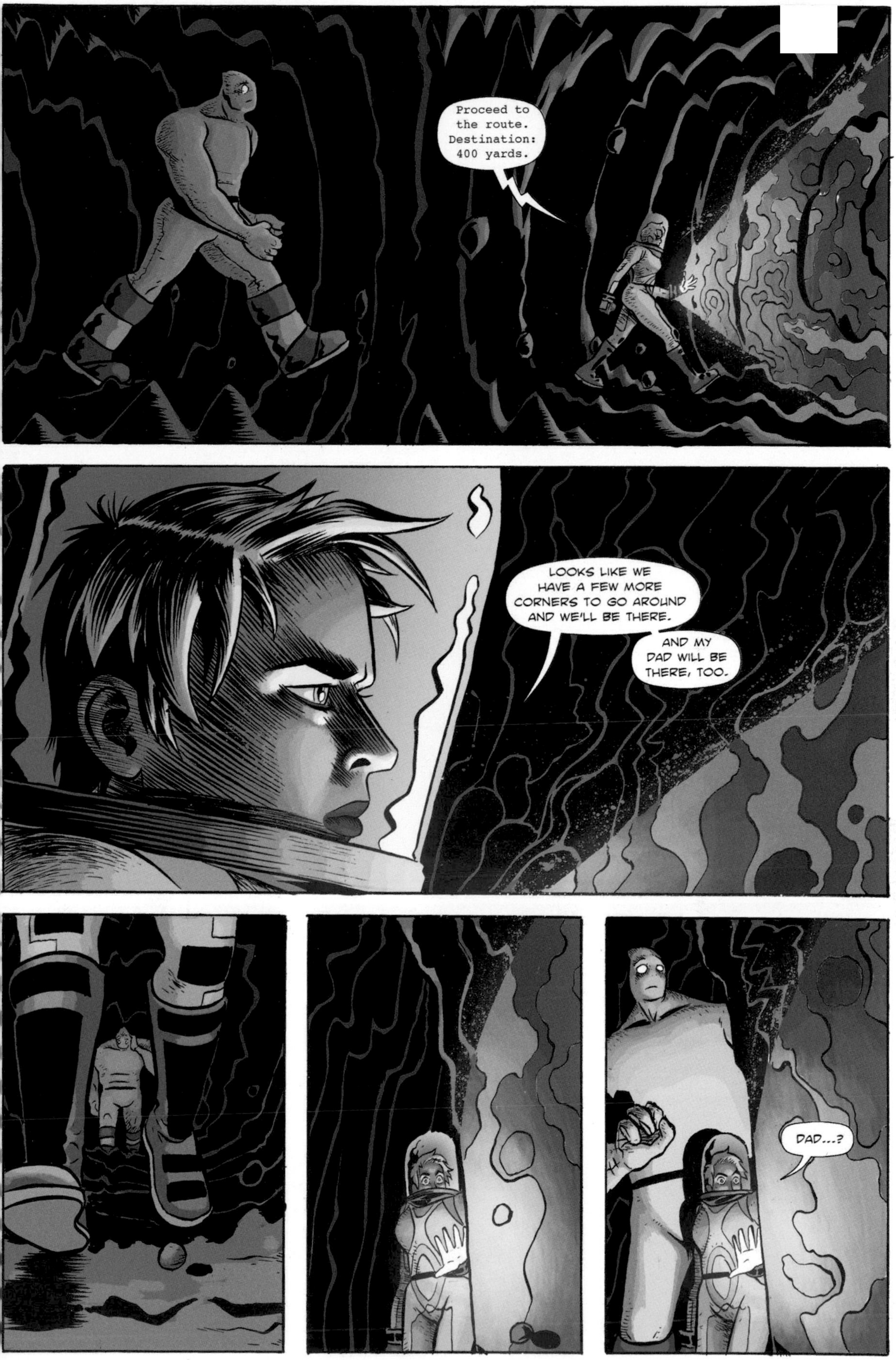
Proceed to the route. Destination: 400 yards.
LOOKS LIKE WE HAVE A FEW MORE CORNERS TO GO AROUND AND WE'LL BE THERE.
AND MY DAD WILL BE THERE, TOO.
DAD...?

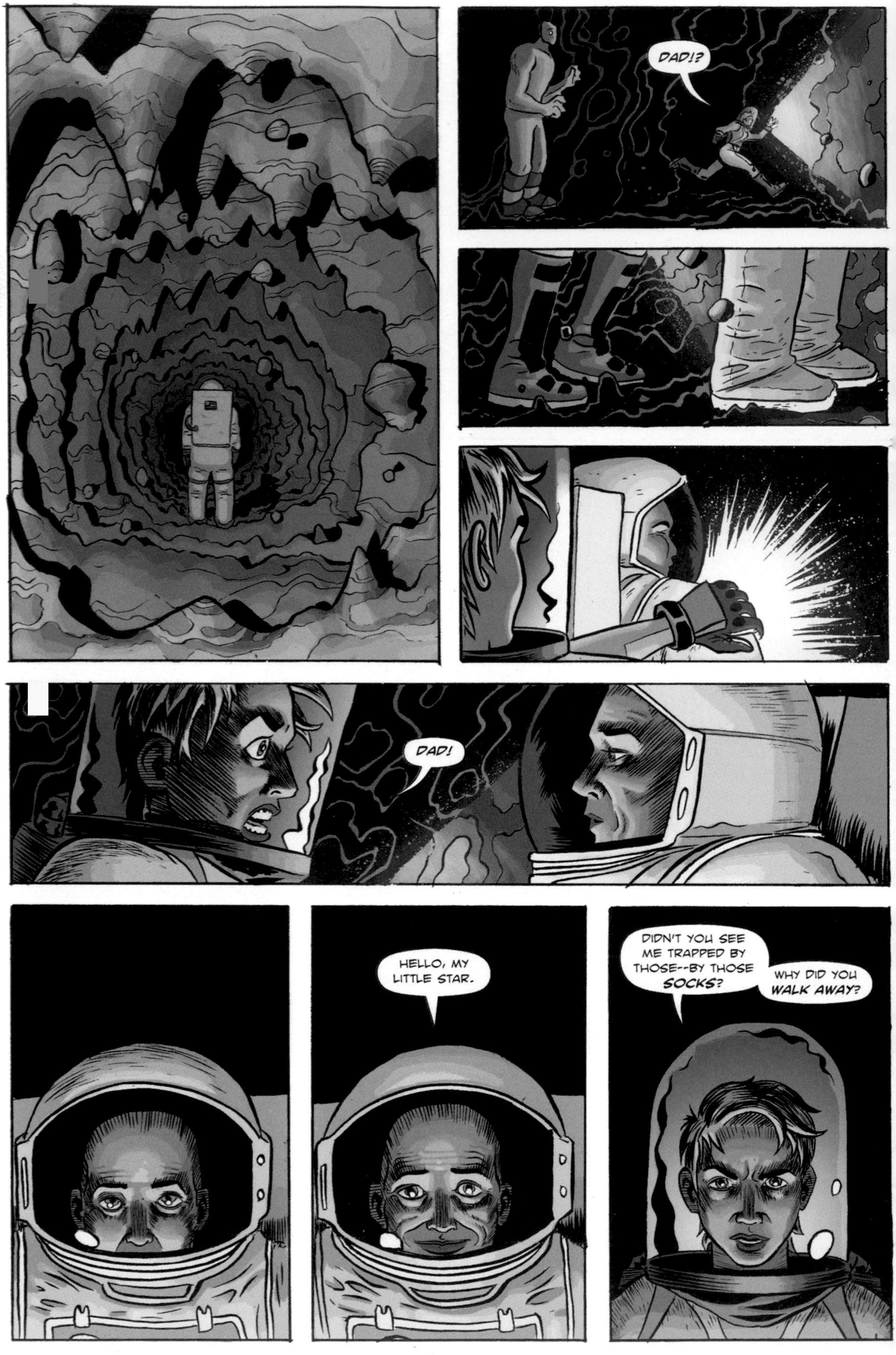
DAD!?
DAD!
HELLO, MY LITTLE STAR.
DIDN'T YOU SEE ME TRAPPED BY THOSE--BY THOSE SOCKS?
WHY DID YOU WALK AWAY?

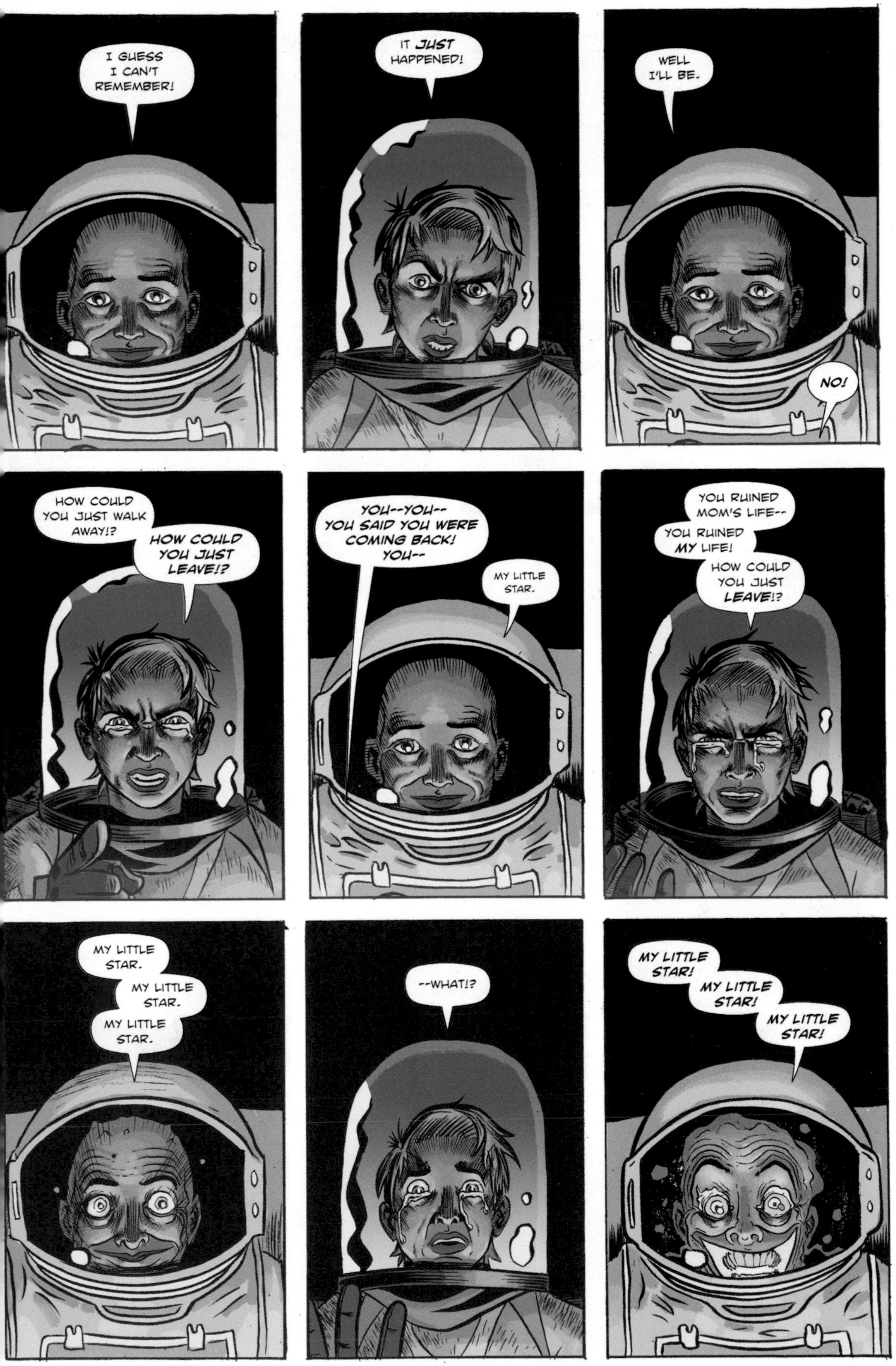
I GUESS I CAN'T REMEMBER!
IT JUST HAPPENED!
WELL I'LL BE.
NO!
HOW COULD YOU JUST WALK AWAY!?
HOW COULD YOU JUST LEAVE!?
YOU--YOU-- YOU SAID YOU WERE COMING BACK! YOU--
MY LITTLE STAR.
YOU RUINED MOM'S LIFE--
YOU RUINED MY LIFE!
HOW COULD YOU JUST LEAVE!?
MY LITTLE STAR.
MY LITTLE STAR.
MY LITTLE STAR.
--WHAT!?
MY LITTLE STAR!
MY LITTLE STAR!
MY LITTLE STAR!

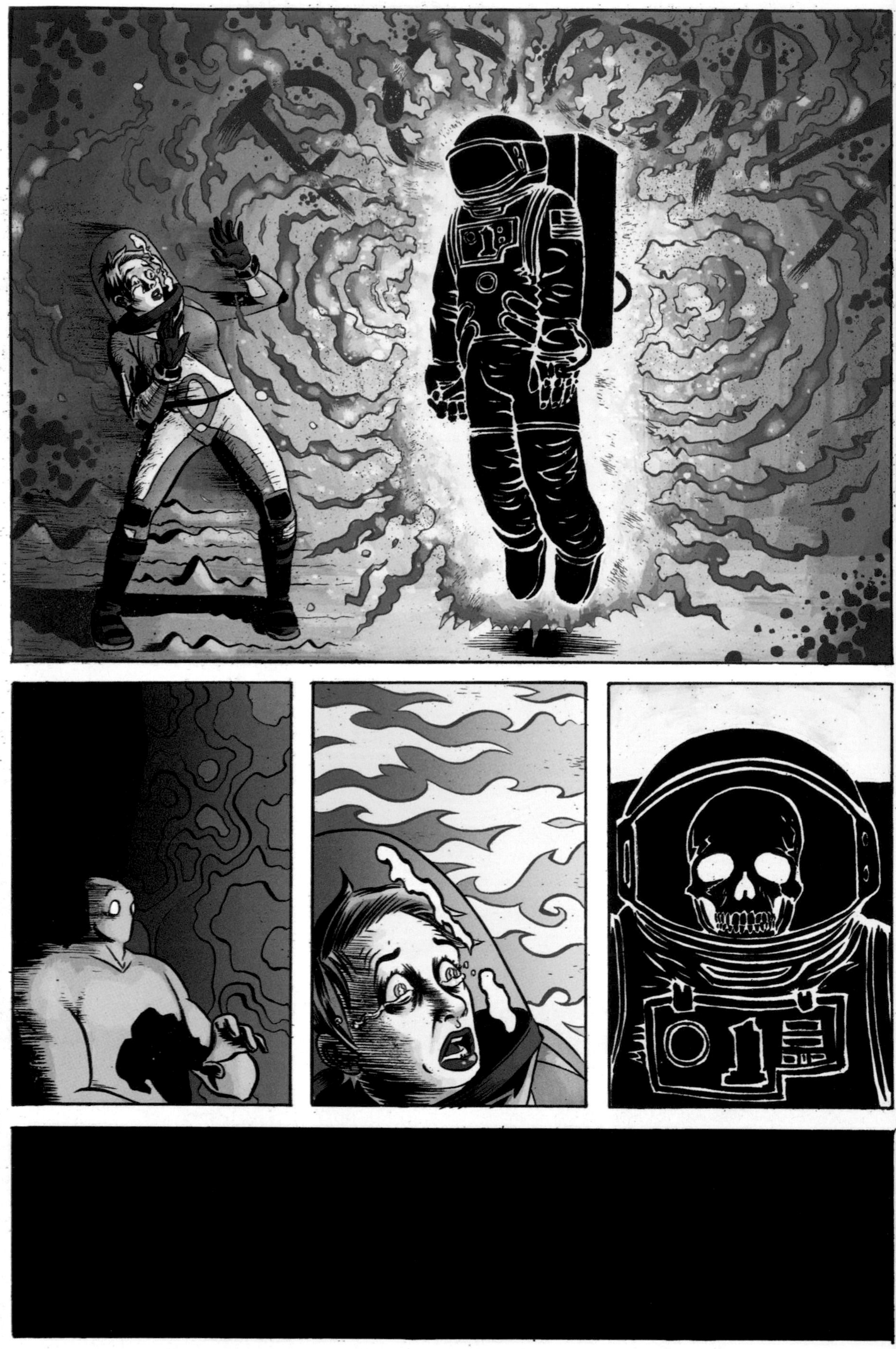

CHAPTER 3

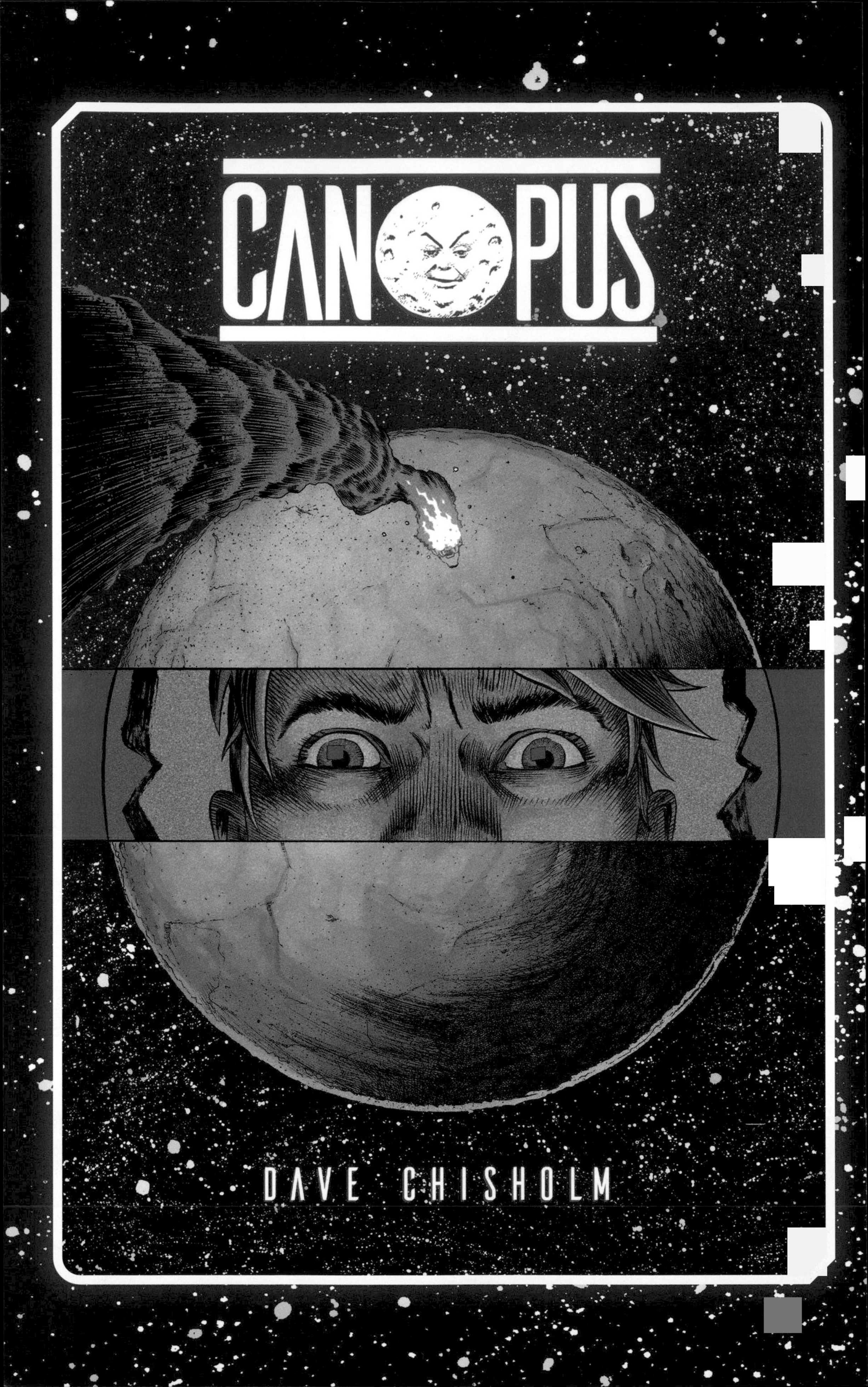
CANOPUS
DAVE CHISHOLM

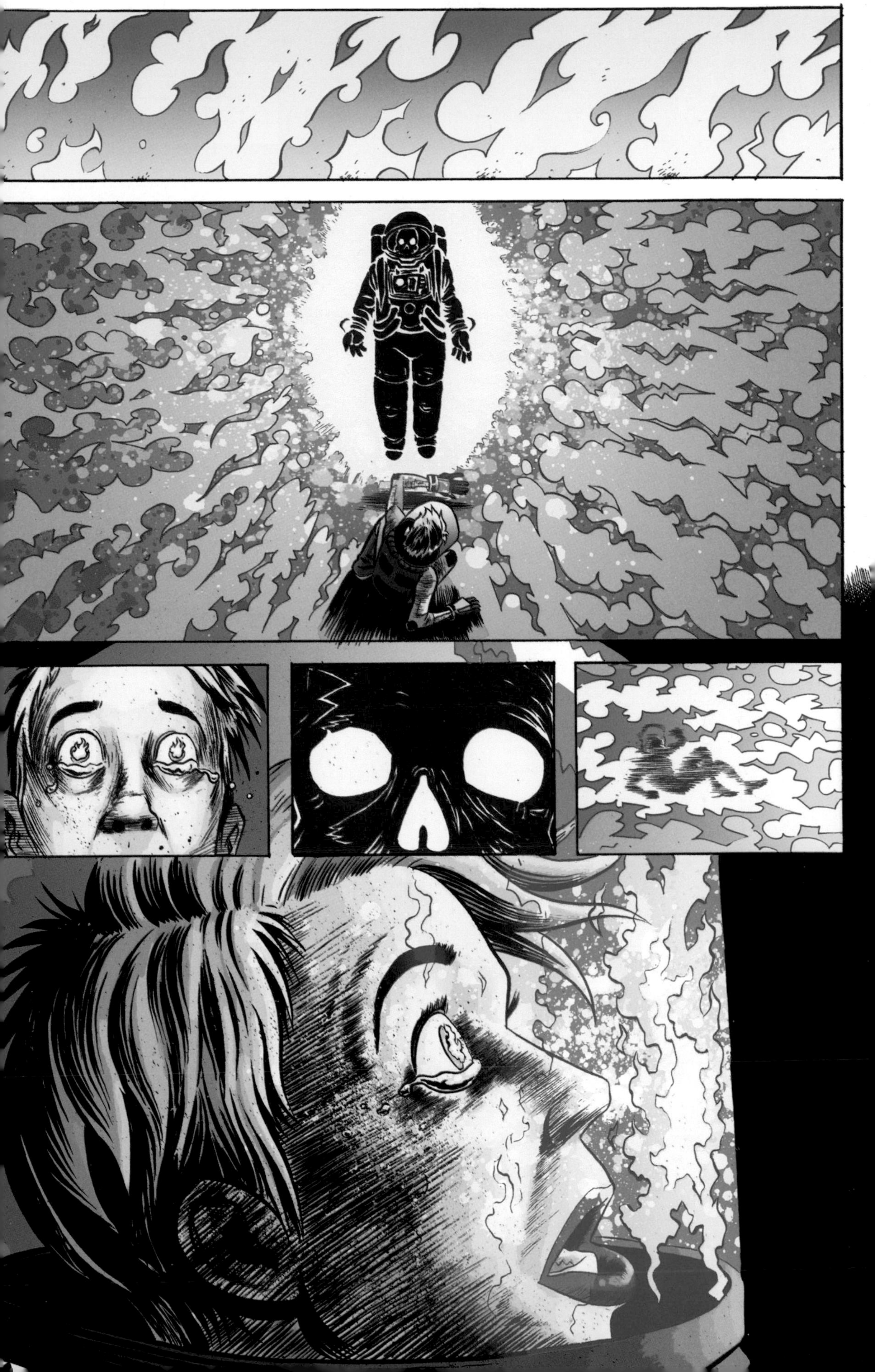

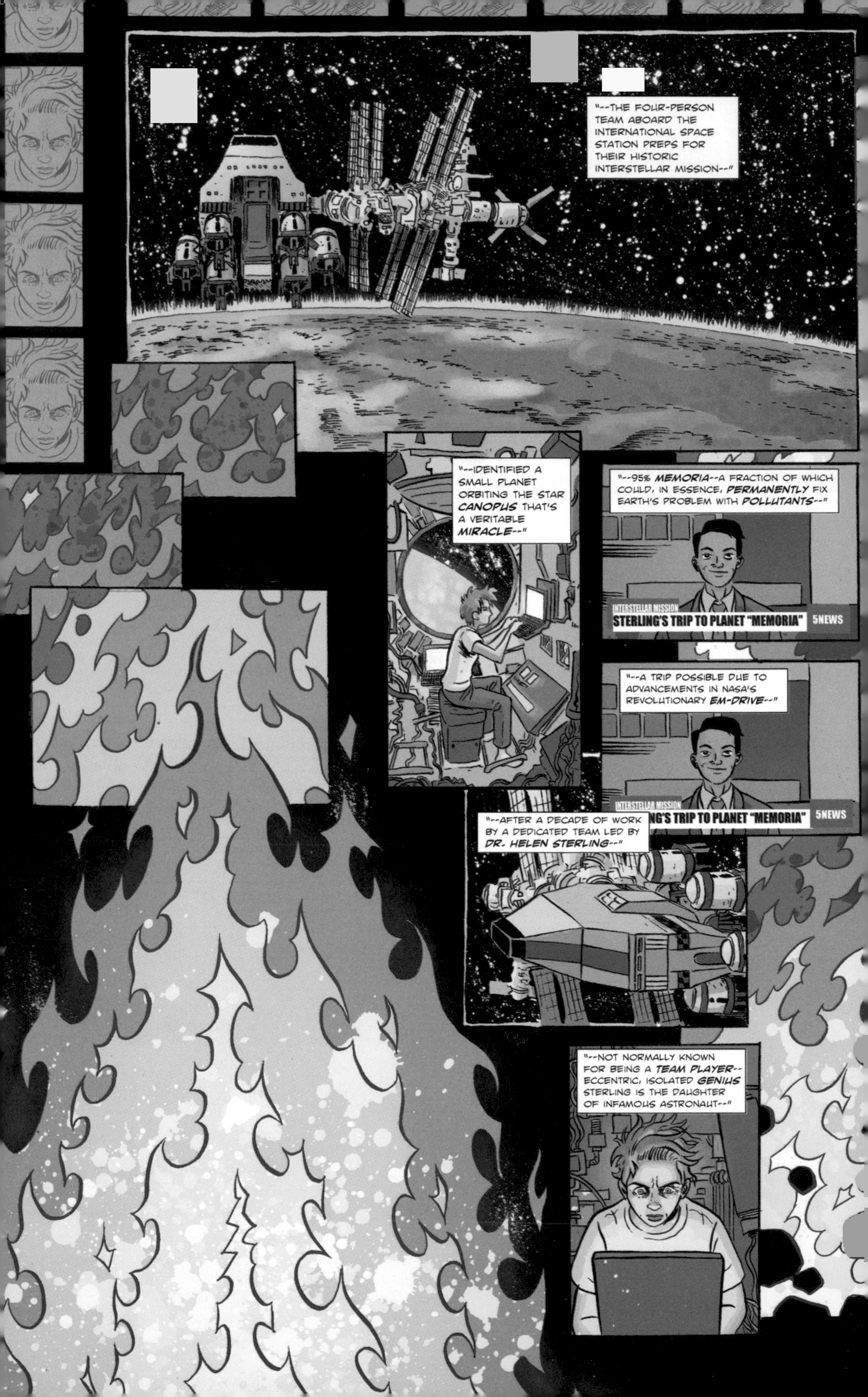
"--THE FOUR-PERSON TEAM ABOARD THE INTERNATIONAL SPACE STATION PREPS FOR THEIR HISTORIC INTERSTELLAR MISSION--"
"--IDENTIFIED A SMALL PLANET ORBITING THE STAR CANOPUS THAT'S A VERITABLE MIRACLE--"
"--95% MEMORIA--A FRACTION OF WHICH COULD, IN ESSENCE, PERMANENTLY FIX EARTH'S PROBLEM WITH POLLUTANTS--"
INTERSTELLAR MISSION
STERLING'S TRIP TO PLANET "MEMORIA"
5NEWS
"--A TRIP POSSIBLE DUE TO ADVANCEMENTS IN NASA'S REVOLUTIONARY EM-DRIVE--"
INTERSTELLAR MISSION
NG'S TRIP TO PLANET "MEMORIA"
5NEWS
"--AFTER A DECADE OF WORK BY A DEDICATED TEAM LED BY DR. HELEN STERLING--"
"--NOT NORMALLY KNOWN FOR BEING A TEAM PLAYER--ECCENTRIC, ISOLATED GENIUS STERLING IS THE DAUGHTER OF INFAMOUS ASTRONAUT--"

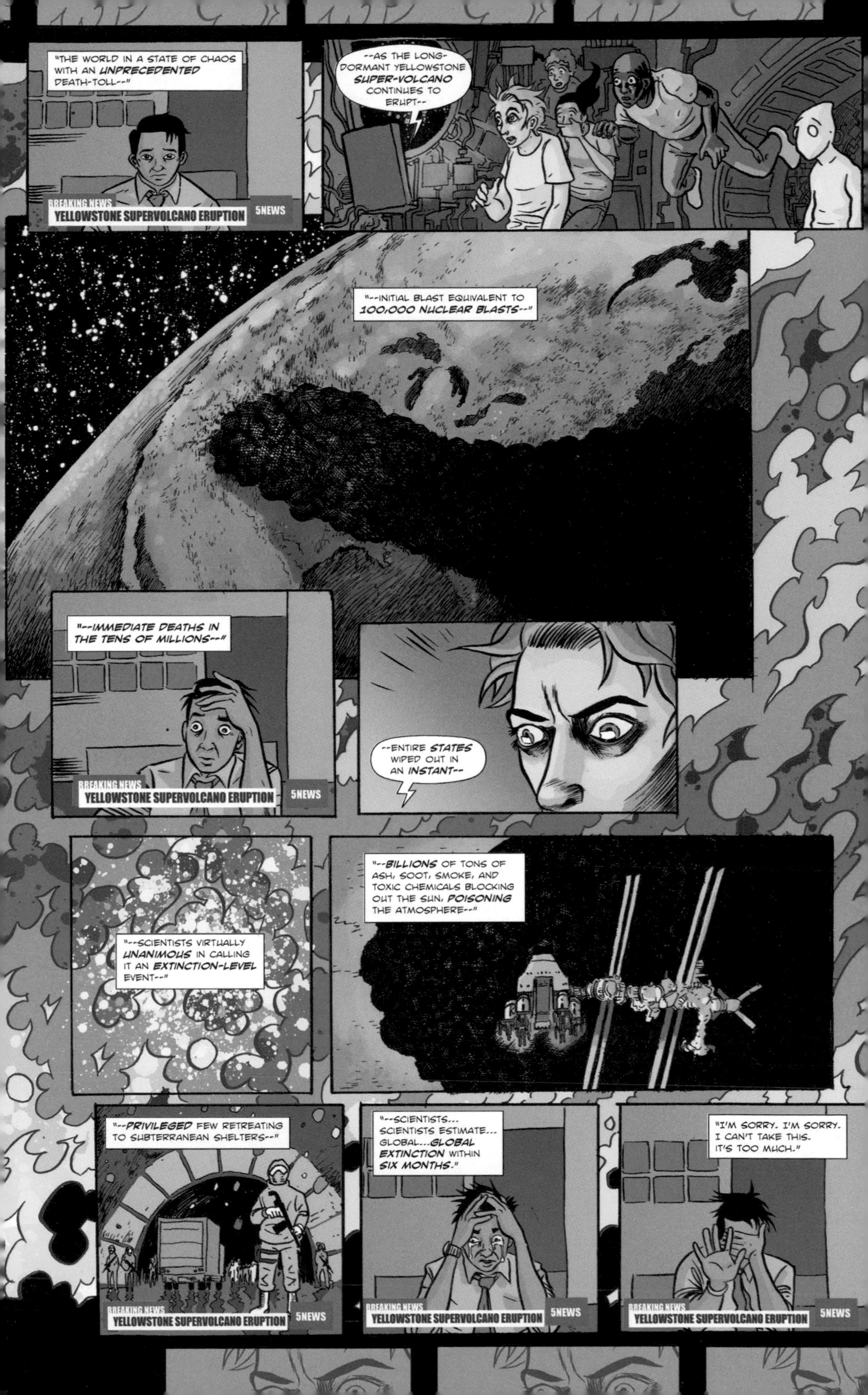
"THE WORLD IN A STATE OF CHAOS WITH AN UNPRECEDENTED DEATH-TOLL--"
BREAKING NEWS
YELLOWSTONE SUPERVOLCANO ERUPTION
5NEWS
--AS THE LONG-DORMANT YELLOWSTONE SUPER-VOLCANO CONTINUES TO ERUPT--
"--INITIAL BLAST EQUIVALENT TO 100,000 NUCLEAR BLASTS--"
"--IMMEDIATE DEATHS IN THE TENS OF MILLIONS--"
BREAKING NEWS
YELLOWSTONE SUPERVOLCANO ERUPTION
5NEWS
--ENTIRE STATES WIPED OUT IN AN INSTANT--
"--SCIENTISTS VIRTUALLY UNANIMOUS IN CALLING IT AN EXTINCTION-LEVEL EVENT--"
"--BILLIONS OF TONS OF ASH, SOOT, SMOKE, AND TOXIC CHEMICALS BLOCKING OUT THE SUN, POISONING THE ATMOSPHERE--"
"--PRIVILEGED FEW RETREATING TO SUBTERRANEAN SHELTERS--"
BREAKING NEWS
YELLOWSTONE SUPERVOLCANO ERUPTION
5NEWS
"--SCIENTISTS... SCIENTISTS ESTIMATE... GLOBAL...GLOBAL EXTINCTION WITHIN SIX MONTHS."
BREAKING NEWS
YELLOWSTONE SUPERVOLCANO ERUPTION
5NEWS
"I'M SORRY. I'M SORRY. I CAN'T TAKE THIS. IT'S TOO MUCH."
BREAKING NEWS
YELLOWSTONE SUPERVOLCANO ERUPTION
5NEWS

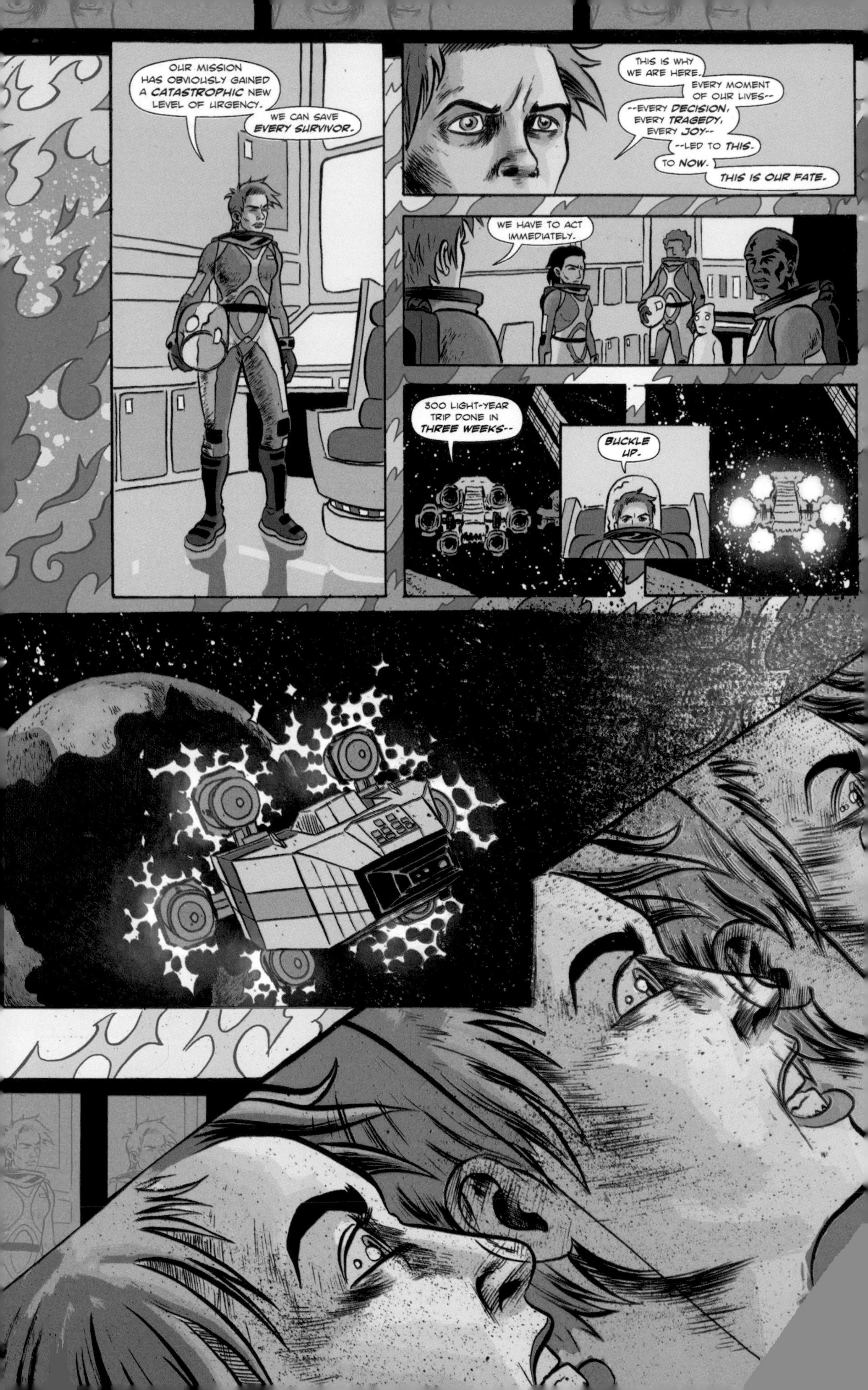

OUR MISSION HAS OBVIOUSLY GAINED A CATASTROPHIC NEW LEVEL OF URGENCY.
WE CAN SAVE EVERY SURVIVOR.
THIS IS WHY WE ARE HERE.
EVERY MOMENT OF OUR LIVES--
--EVERY DECISION, EVERY TRAGEDY, EVERY JOY--
--LED TO THIS.
TO NOW.
THIS IS OUR FATE.
WE HAVE TO ACT IMMEDIATELY.
300 LIGHT-YEAR TRIP DONE IN THREE WEEKS--
BUCKLE UP.

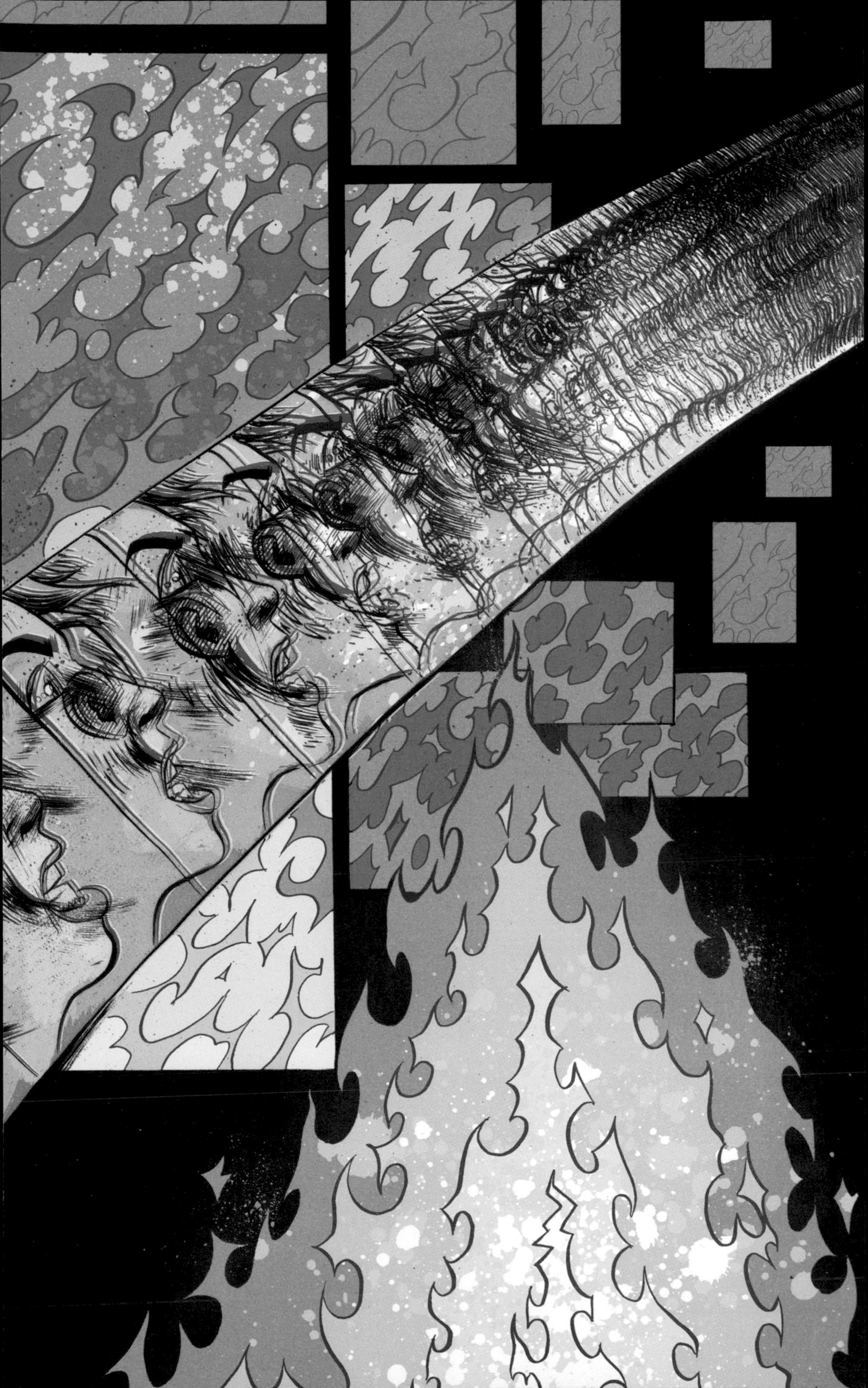

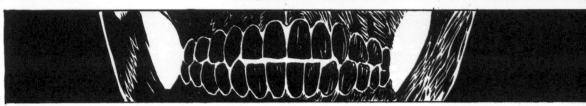

OH NO.
OH, NO NO NO NO NO.

HELEN! YOU-- YOU'RE--

YOU ARE THE STRONGEST PERSON I'VE EVER MET! YOU'RE GONNA BE FINE!

I'M STRONG-- --I'M STRONG-- --I'M STRONG-- --I'M STRONG-- --I'M STRONG-- --I'M--

--STRONG.

THAT WORKED...?!

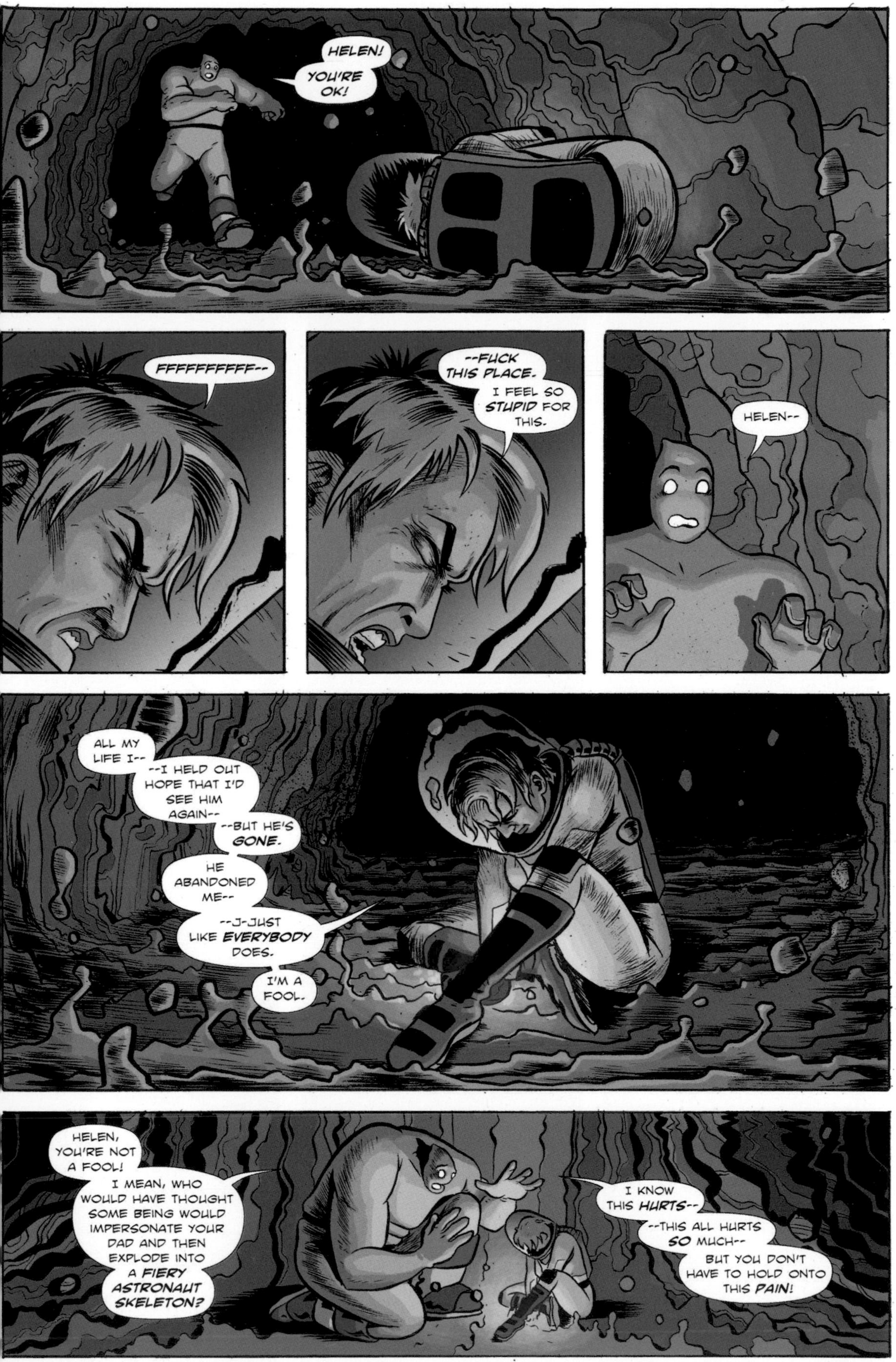
HELEN! YOU'RE OK!
FFFFFFFFFF--
--FUCK THIS PLACE.
I FEEL SO STUPID FOR THIS.
HELEN--
ALL MY LIFE I--
--I HELD OUT HOPE THAT I'D SEE HIM AGAIN--
--BUT HE'S GONE.
HE ABANDONED ME--
--J-JUST LIKE EVERYBODY DOES.
I'M A FOOL.
HELEN, YOU'RE NOT A FOOL!
I MEAN, WHO WOULD HAVE THOUGHT SOME BEING WOULD IMPERSONATE YOUR DAD AND THEN EXPLODE INTO A FIERY ASTRONAUT SKELETON?
I KNOW THIS HURTS--
--THIS ALL HURTS SO MUCH--
BUT YOU DON'T HAVE TO HOLD ONTO THIS PAIN!

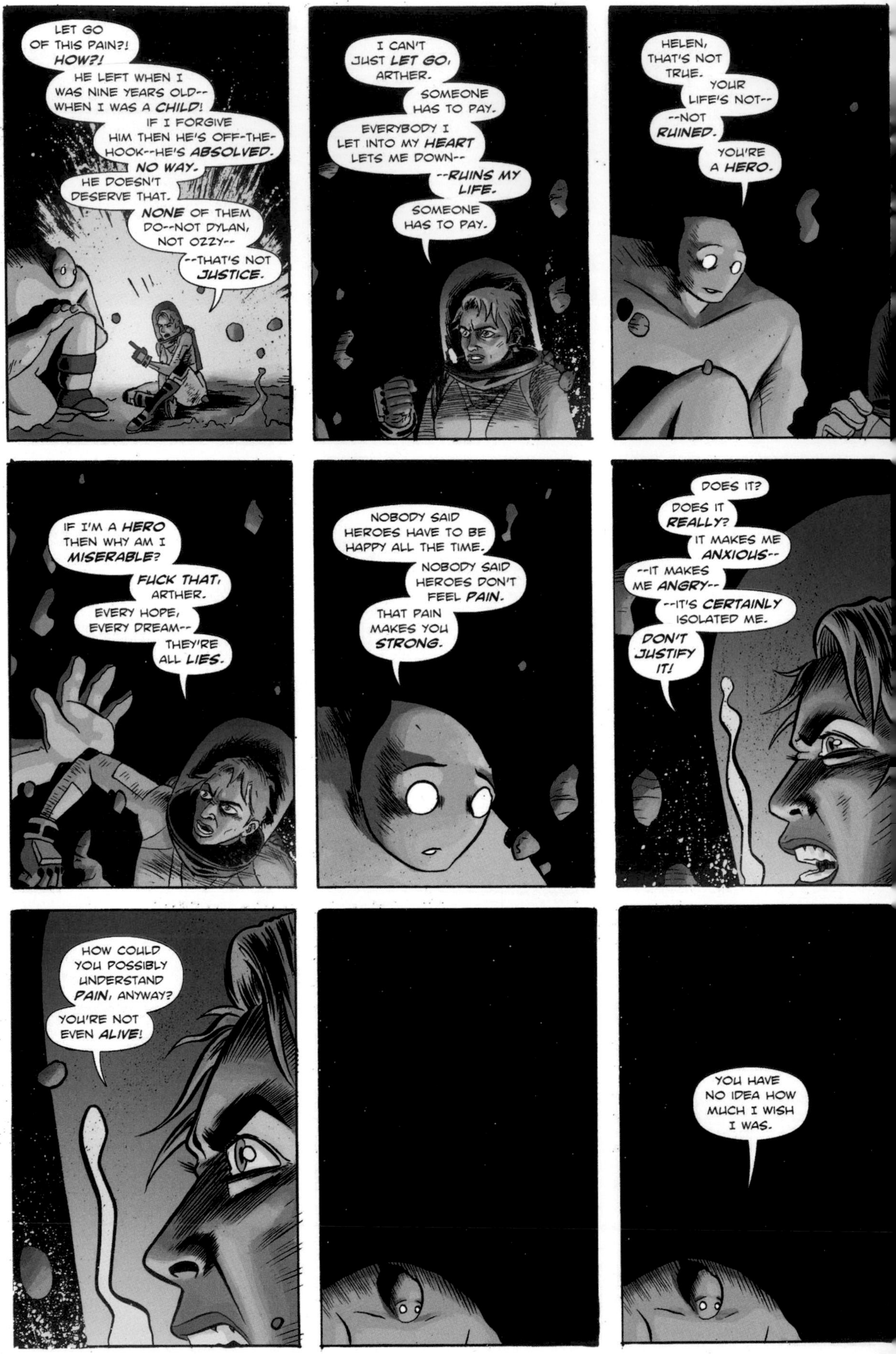

LET GO OF THIS PAIN?! HOW?!
HE LEFT WHEN I WAS NINE YEARS OLD-- WHEN I WAS A CHILD!
IF I FORGIVE HIM THEN HE'S OFF-THE-HOOK--HE'S ABSOLVED. NO WAY.
HE DOESN'T DESERVE THAT.
NONE OF THEM DO--NOT DYLAN, NOT OZZY--
--THAT'S NOT JUSTICE.
I CAN'T JUST LET GO, ARTHER.
SOMEONE HAS TO PAY.
EVERYBODY I LET INTO MY HEART LETS ME DOWN--
--RUINS MY LIFE.
SOMEONE HAS TO PAY.
HELEN, THAT'S NOT TRUE.
YOUR LIFE'S NOT--
--NOT RUINED.
YOU'RE A HERO.
IF I'M A HERO THEN WHY AM I MISERABLE?
FUCK THAT, ARTHER.
EVERY HOPE, EVERY DREAM--
THEY'RE ALL LIES.
NOBODY SAID HEROES HAVE TO BE HAPPY ALL THE TIME.
NOBODY SAID HEROES DON'T FEEL PAIN.
THAT PAIN MAKES YOU STRONG.
DOES IT?
DOES IT REALLY?
IT MAKES ME ANXIOUS--
--IT MAKES ME ANGRY--
--IT'S CERTAINLY ISOLATED ME.
DON'T JUSTIFY IT!
HOW COULD YOU POSSIBLY UNDERSTAND PAIN, ANYWAY?
YOU'RE NOT EVEN ALIVE!
YOU HAVE NO IDEA HOW MUCH I WISH I WAS.

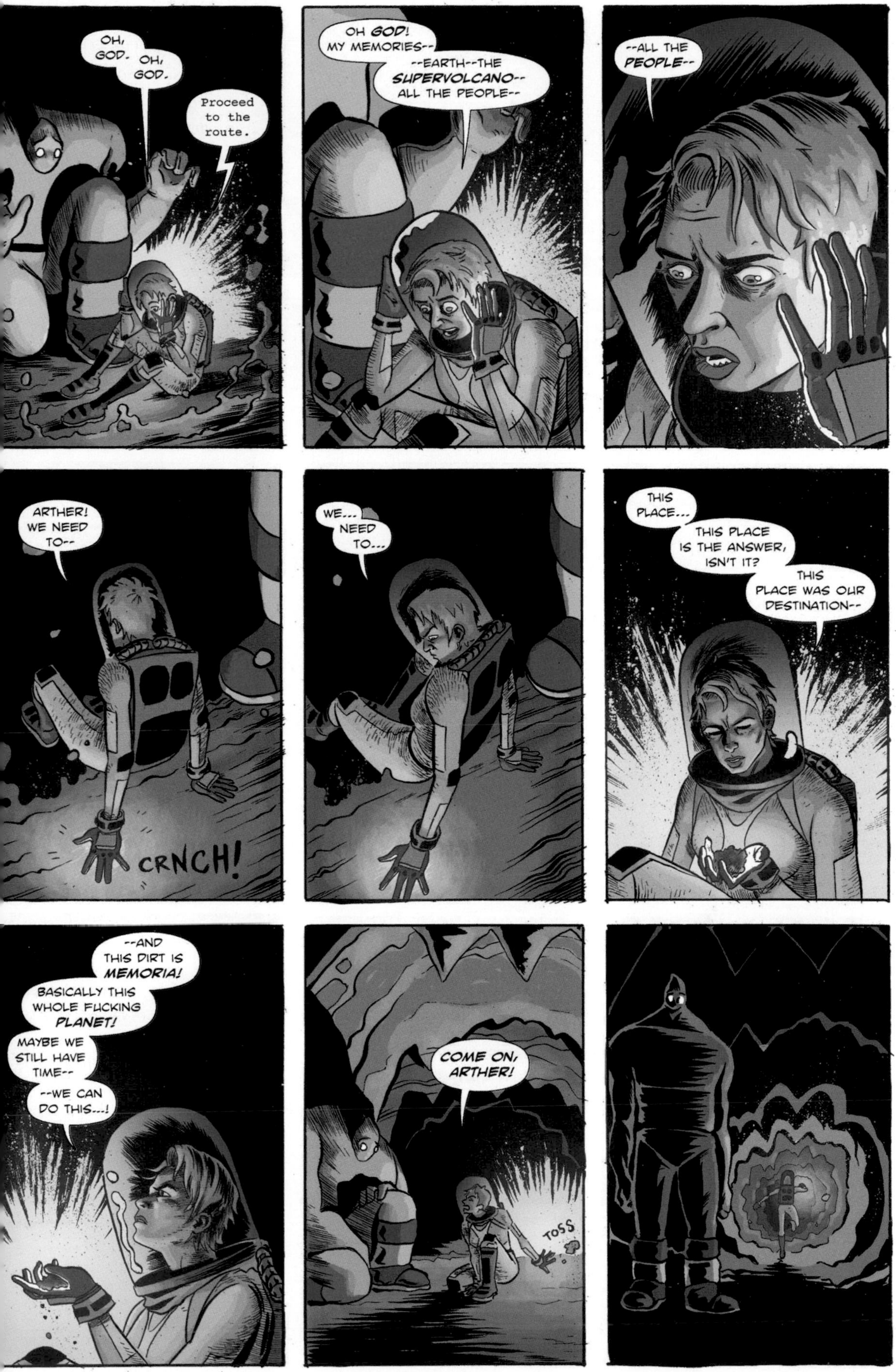
OH, GOD.
OH, GOD.
Proceed to the route.
OH GOD! MY MEMORIES--
--EARTH--THE SUPERVOLCANO-- ALL THE PEOPLE--
--ALL THE PEOPLE--
ARTHER! WE NEED TO--
CRNCH!
WE... NEED TO...
THIS PLACE...
THIS PLACE IS THE ANSWER, ISN'T IT?
THIS PLACE WAS OUR DESTINATION--
--AND THIS DIRT IS MEMORIA!
BASICALLY THIS WHOLE FUCKING PLANET!
MAYBE WE STILL HAVE TIME--
--WE CAN DO THIS...!
COME ON, ARTHER!
TOSS

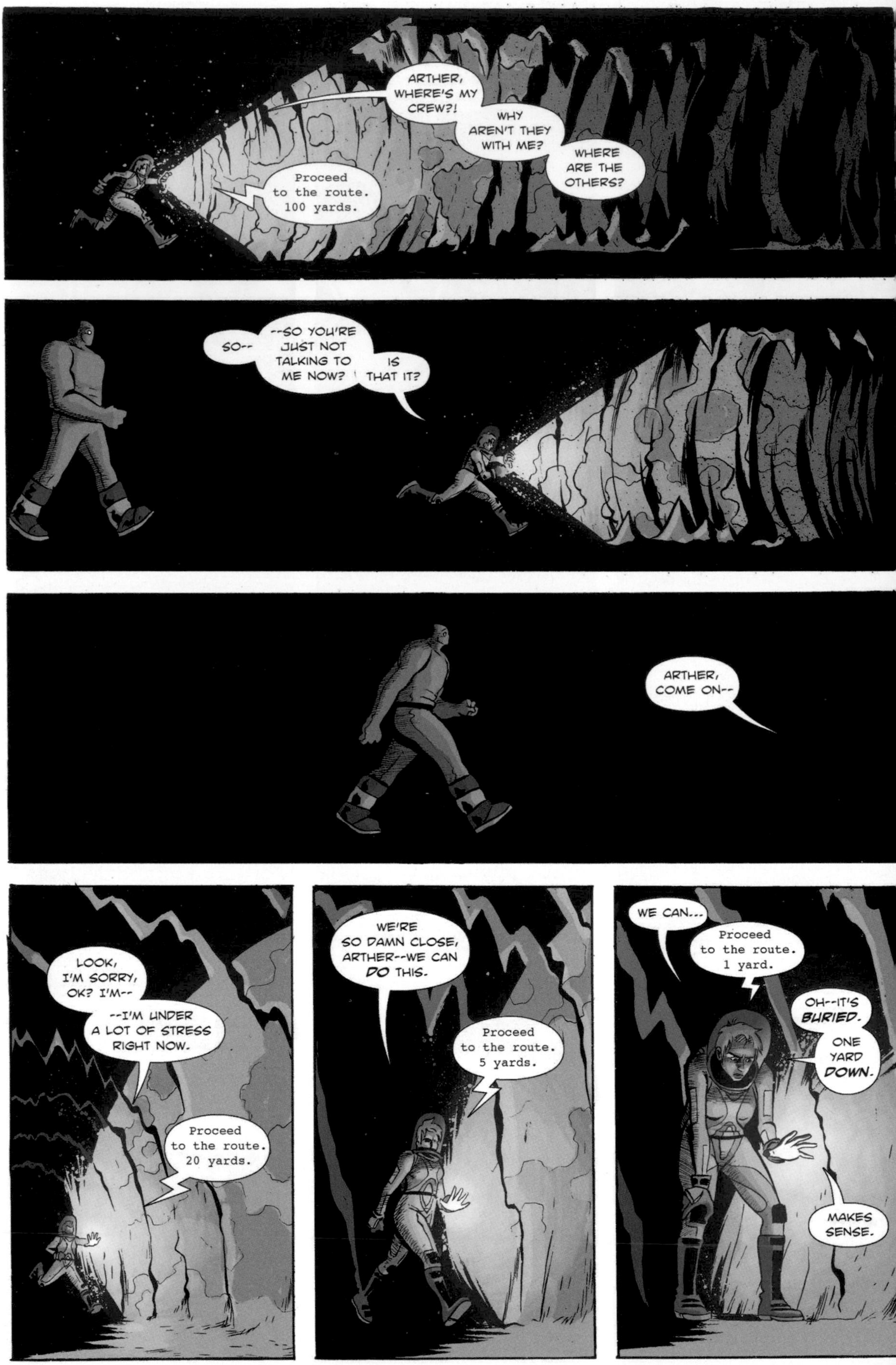
ARTHER, WHERE'S MY CREW?!
WHY AREN'T THEY WITH ME?
WHERE ARE THE OTHERS?
Proceed to the route. 100 yards.
SO--
--SO YOU'RE JUST NOT TALKING TO ME NOW?
IS THAT IT?
ARTHER, COME ON--
LOOK, I'M SORRY, OK? I'M--
--I'M UNDER A LOT OF STRESS RIGHT NOW.
Proceed to the route. 20 yards.
WE'RE SO DAMN CLOSE, ARTHER--WE CAN DO THIS.
Proceed to the route. 5 yards.
WE CAN...
Proceed to the route. 1 yard.
OH--IT'S BURIED.
ONE YARD DOWN.
MAKES SENSE.

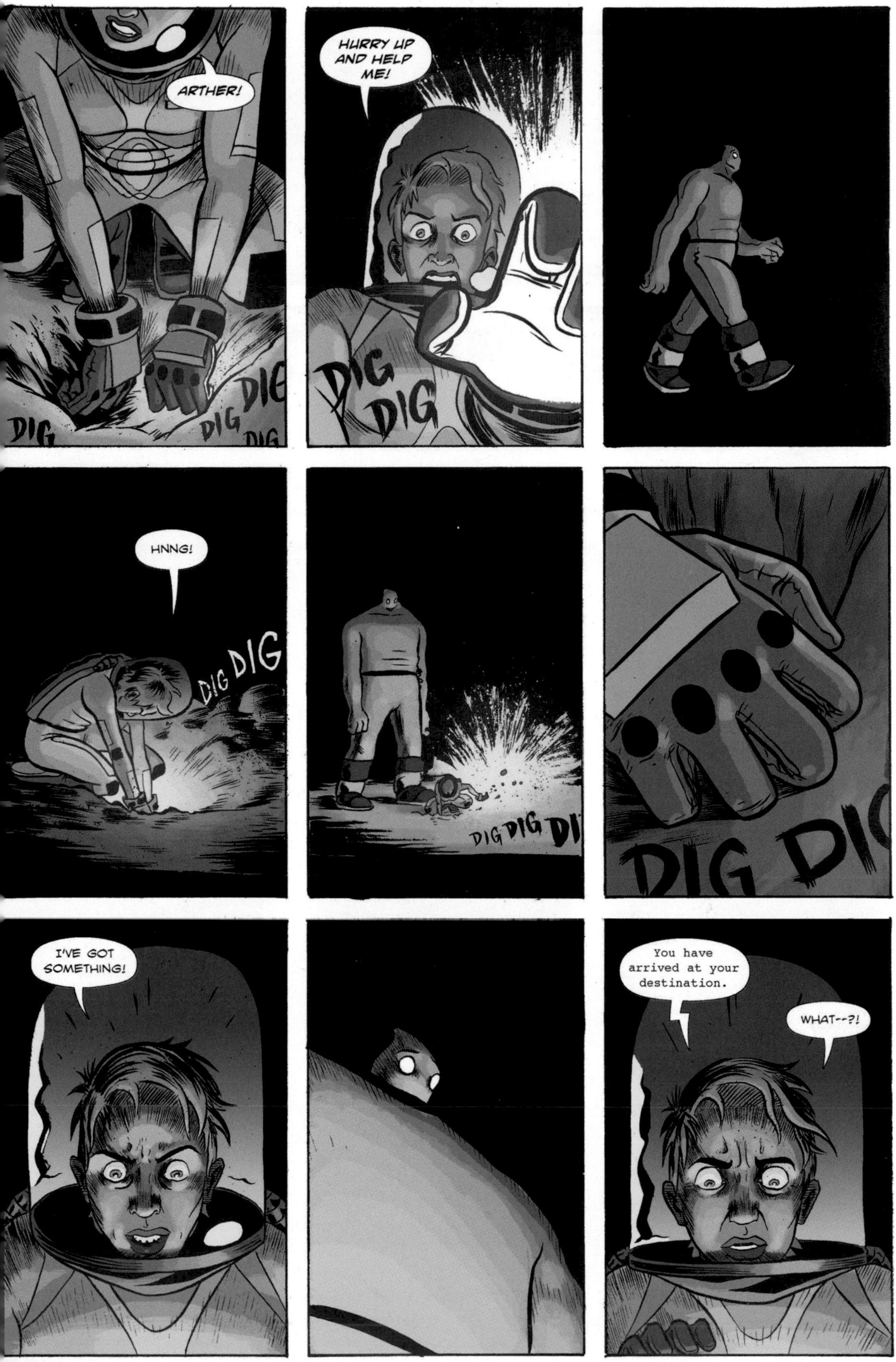
ARTHER!
DIG
DIG
DIG
DIG
HURRY UP AND HELP ME!
DIG
DIG
HNNG!
DIG DIG
DIG DIG
DIG DIG
I'VE GOT SOMETHING!
You have arrived at your destination.
WHAT--?!

IT'S ONE OF MY *CREWMEMBERS*, ARTHER!

HELP ME!

DIG DIG DIG

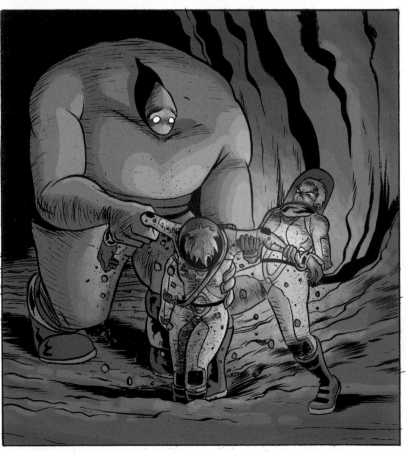

WAIT-- IS THAT--

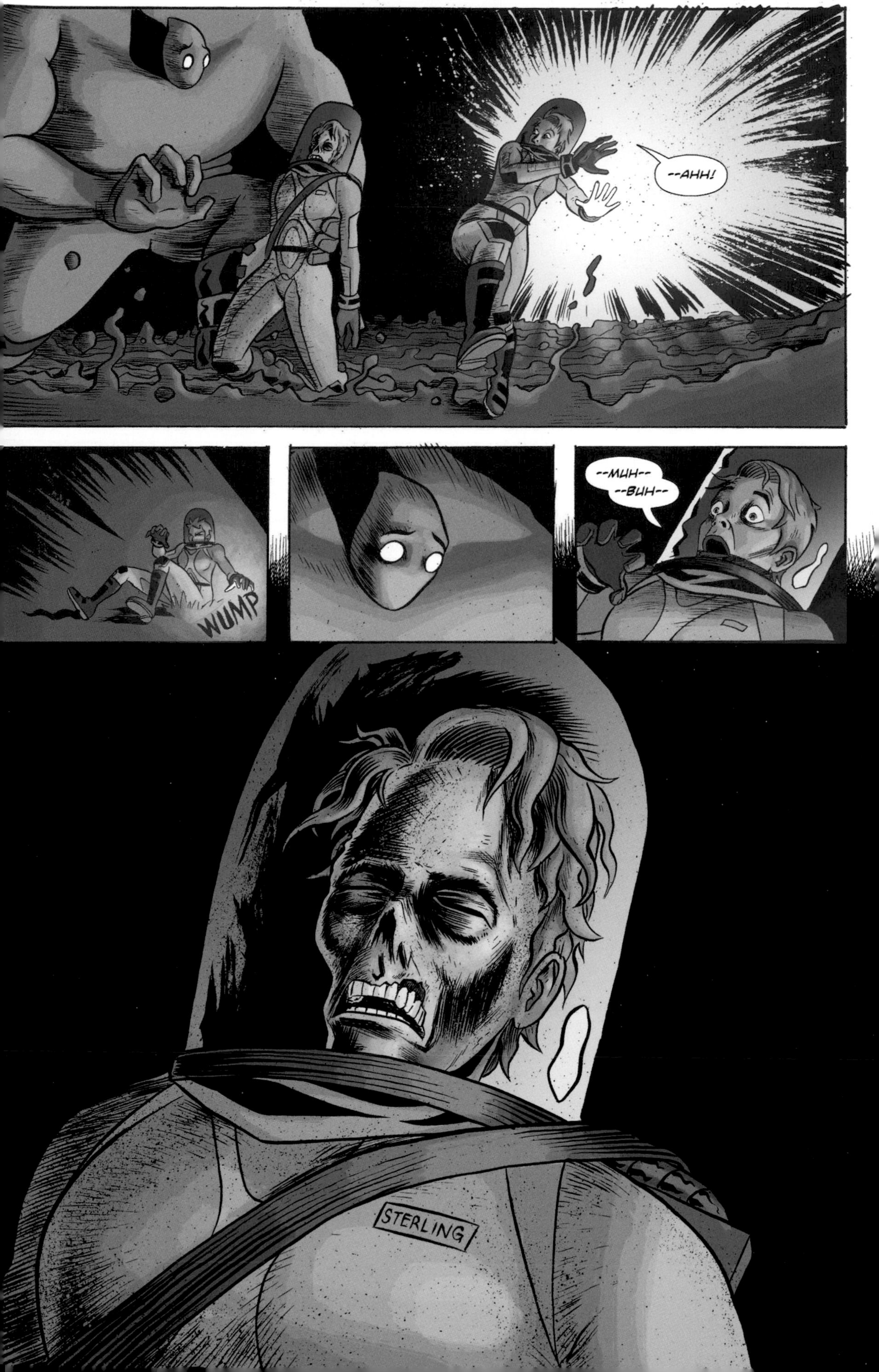
--AHH!
WUMP
--MUH--
--BUH--
STERLING

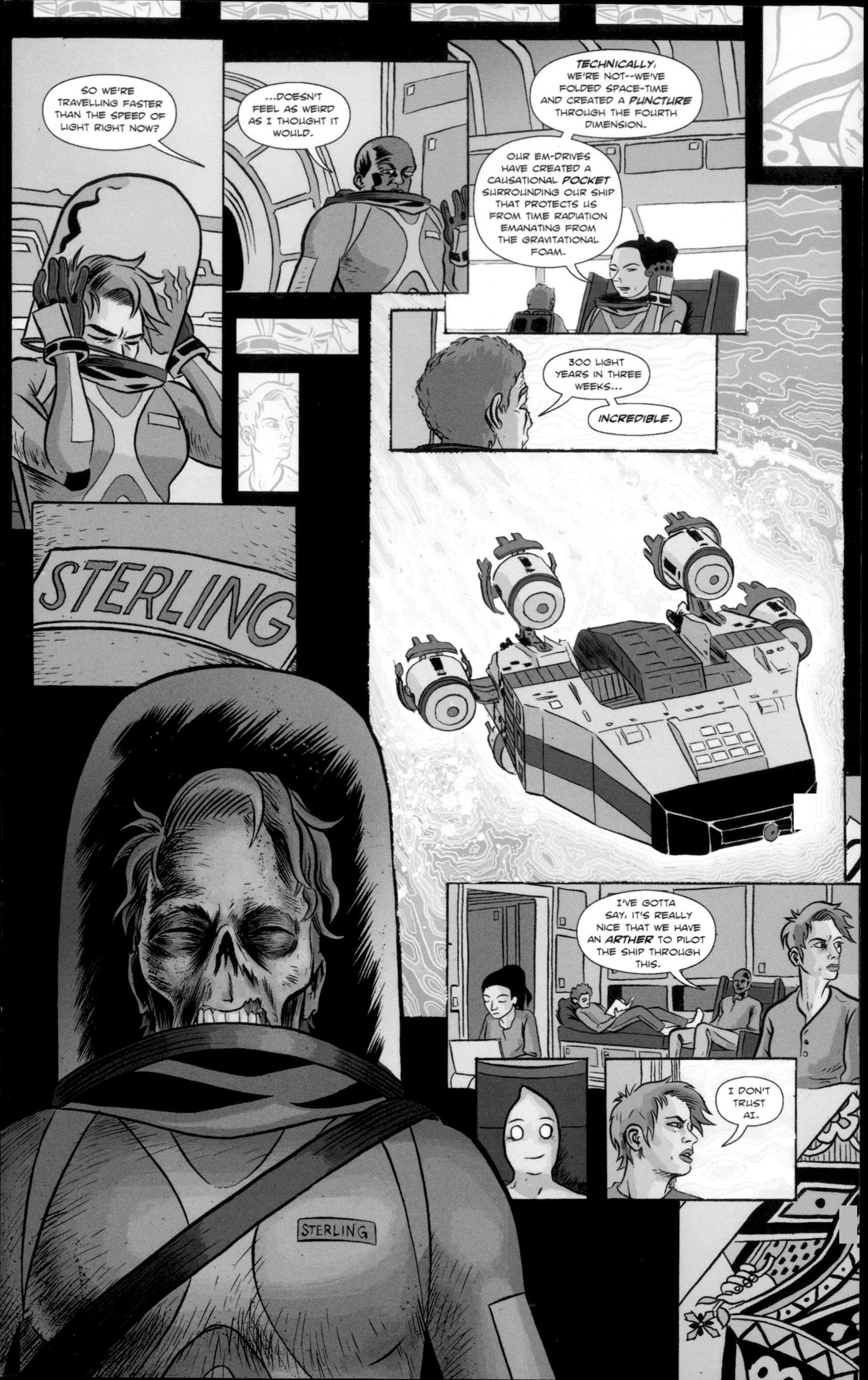
SO WE'RE TRAVELLING FASTER THAN THE SPEED OF LIGHT RIGHT NOW?
...DOESN'T FEEL AS WEIRD AS I THOUGHT IT WOULD.
TECHNICALLY, WE'RE NOT--WE'VE FOLDED SPACE-TIME AND CREATED A PUNCTURE THROUGH THE FOURTH DIMENSION.
OUR EM-DRIVES HAVE CREATED A CAUSATIONAL POCKET SURROUNDING OUR SHIP THAT PROTECTS US FROM TIME RADIATION EMANATING FROM THE GRAVITATIONAL FOAM.
300 LIGHT YEARS IN THREE WEEKS...
INCREDIBLE.
STERLING
STERLING
I'VE GOTTA SAY, IT'S REALLY NICE THAT WE HAVE AN ARTHER TO PILOT THE SHIP THROUGH THIS.
I DON'T TRUST AI.

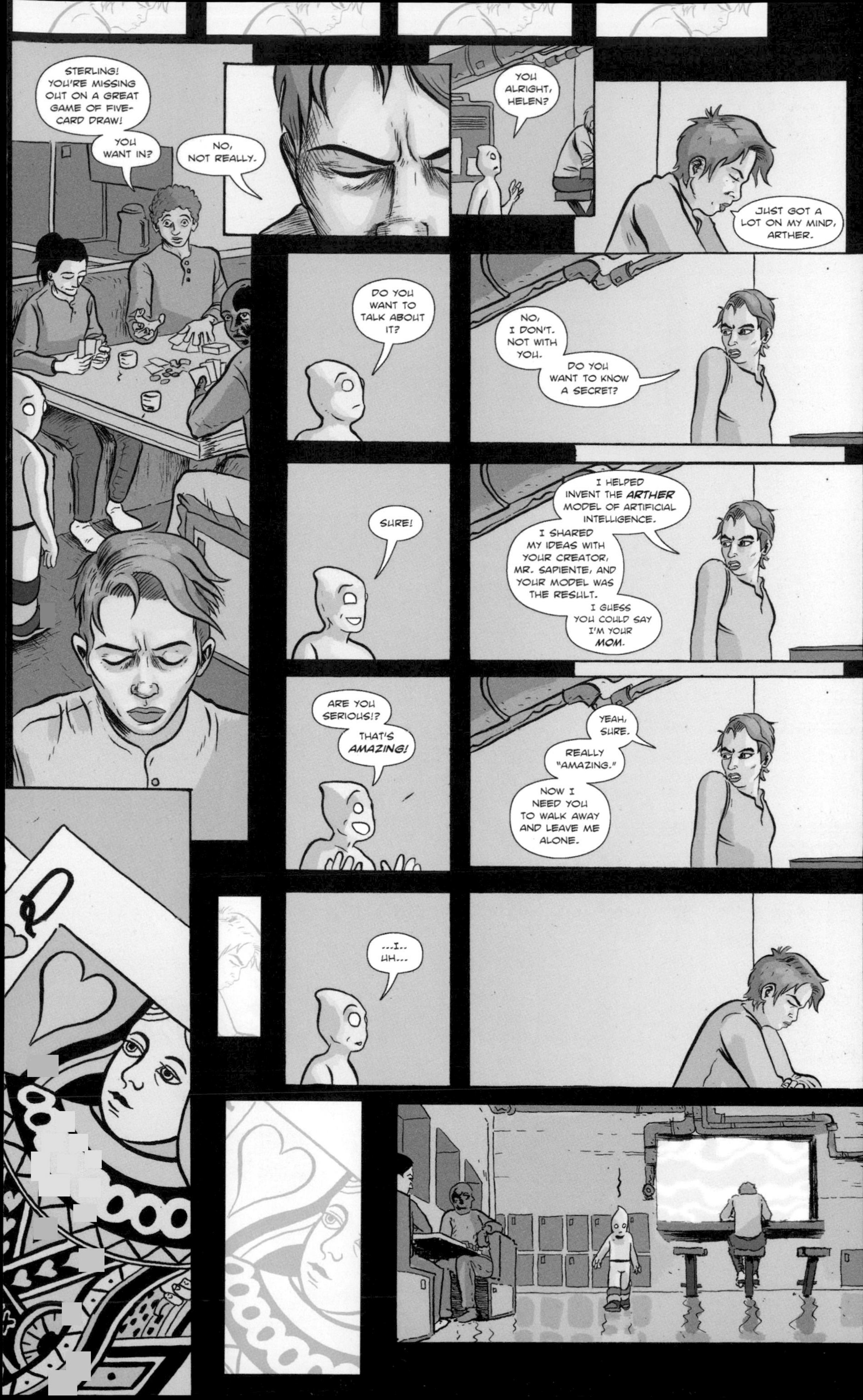
STERLING! YOU'RE MISSING OUT ON A GREAT GAME OF FIVE-CARD DRAW!
YOU WANT IN?
NO, NOT REALLY.
YOU ALRIGHT, HELEN?
JUST GOT A LOT ON MY MIND, ARTHER.
DO YOU WANT TO TALK ABOUT IT?
NO, I DON'T. NOT WITH YOU.
DO YOU WANT TO KNOW A SECRET?
SURE!
I HELPED INVENT THE ARTHER MODEL OF ARTIFICIAL INTELLIGENCE.
I SHARED MY IDEAS WITH YOUR CREATOR, MR. SAPIENTE, AND YOUR MODEL WAS THE RESULT.
I GUESS YOU COULD SAY I'M YOUR MOM.
ARE YOU SERIOUS!?
THAT'S AMAZING!
YEAH, SURE.
REALLY "AMAZING."
NOW I NEED YOU TO WALK AWAY AND LEAVE ME ALONE.
...I... UH...

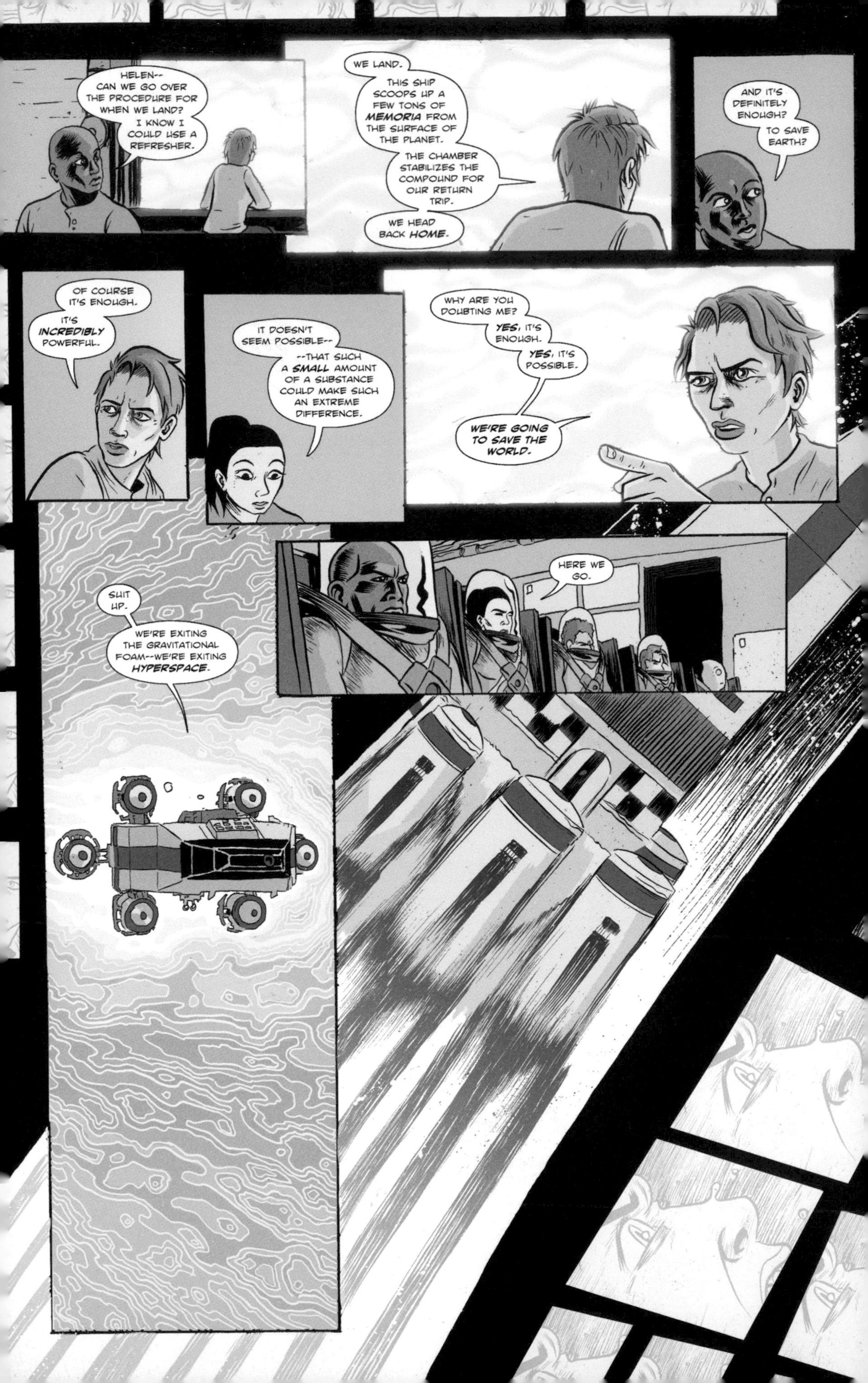
HELEN--
CAN WE GO OVER THE PROCEDURE FOR WHEN WE LAND?
I KNOW I COULD USE A REFRESHER.
WE LAND.
THIS SHIP SCOOPS UP A FEW TONS OF MEMORIA FROM THE SURFACE OF THE PLANET.
THE CHAMBER STABILIZES THE COMPOUND FOR OUR RETURN TRIP.
WE HEAD BACK HOME.
AND IT'S DEFINITELY ENOUGH?
TO SAVE EARTH?
OF COURSE IT'S ENOUGH.
IT'S INCREDIBLY POWERFUL.
IT DOESN'T SEEM POSSIBLE--
--THAT SUCH A SMALL AMOUNT OF A SUBSTANCE COULD MAKE SUCH AN EXTREME DIFFERENCE.
WHY ARE YOU DOUBTING ME?
YES, IT'S ENOUGH.
YES, IT'S POSSIBLE.
WE'RE GOING TO SAVE THE WORLD.
SUIT UP.
WE'RE EXITING THE GRAVITATIONAL FOAM--WE'RE EXITING HYPERSPACE.
HERE WE GO.

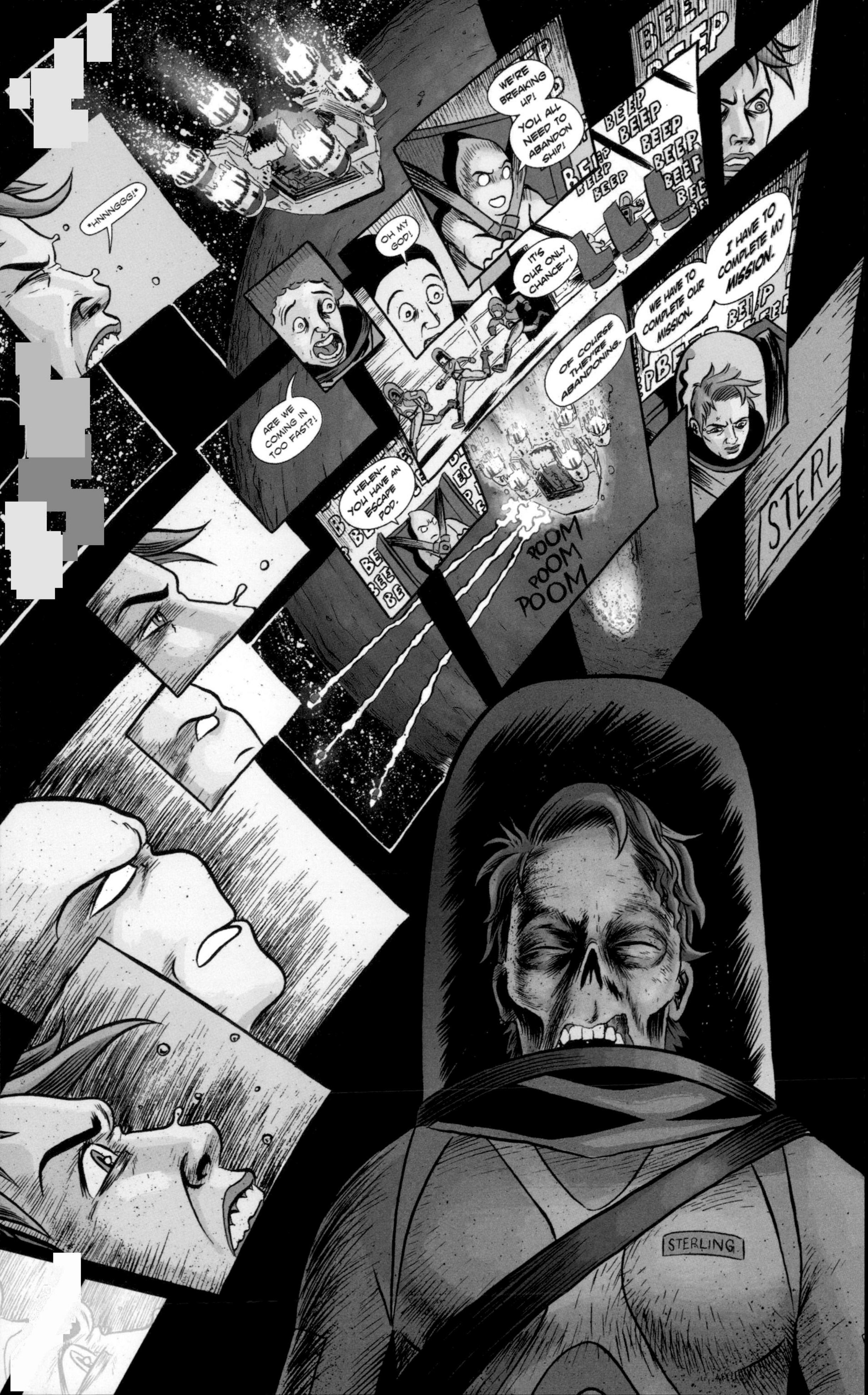
HNNNGGG!
WE'RE BREAKING UP! YOU ALL NEED TO ABANDON SHIP!
BEEP BEEP BEEP BEEP
OH MY GOD!
IT'S OUR ONLY CHANCE--!
ARE WE COMING IN TOO FAST?!
HELEN-- YOU HAVE AN ESCAPE POD.
OF COURSE THEY'RE ABANDONING.
WE HAVE TO COMPLETE OUR MISSION.
I HAVE TO COMPLETE MY MISSION.
POOM POOM POOM
STERL
STERLING

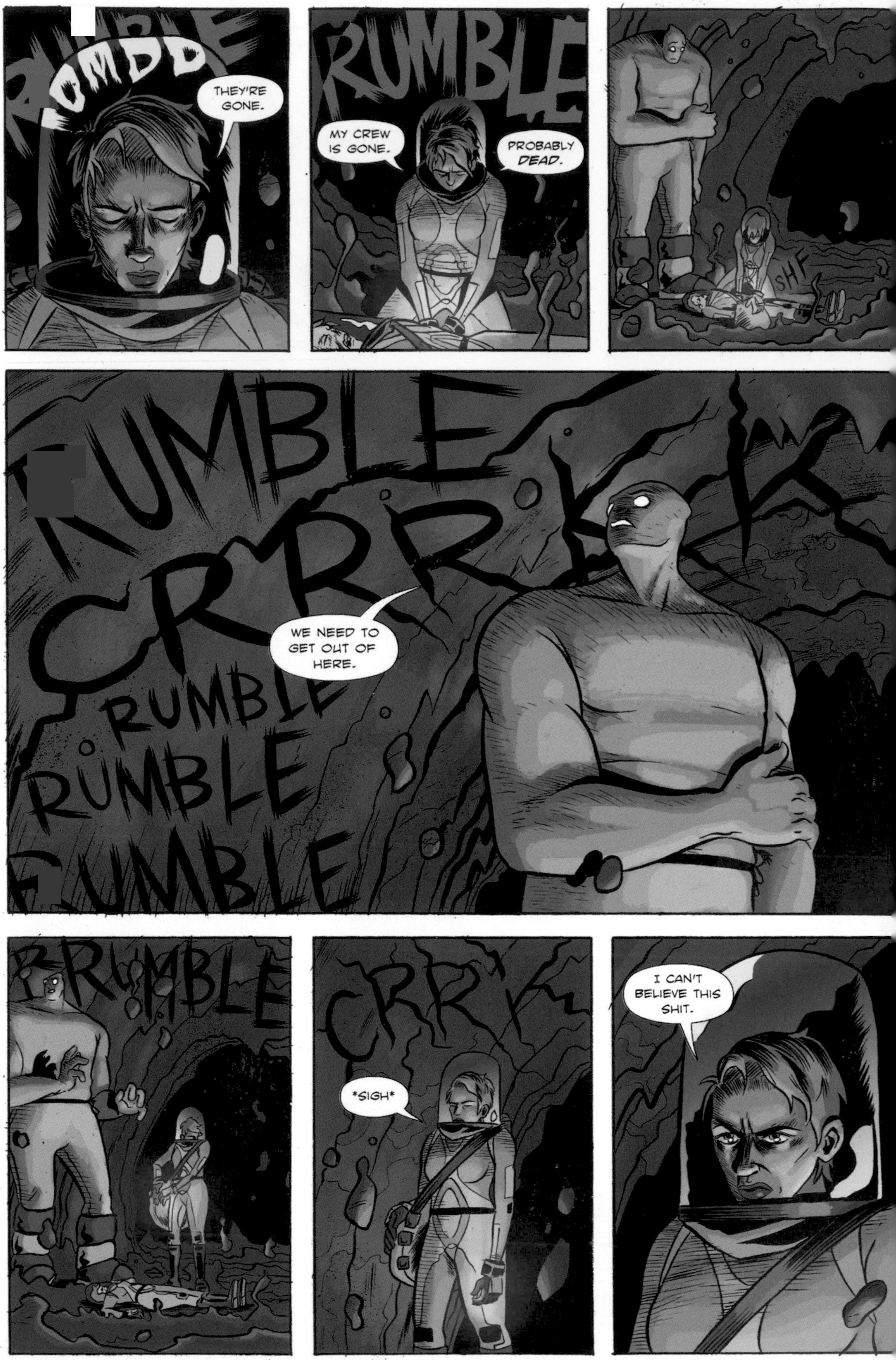
THEY'RE GONE.
RUMBLE
MY CREW IS GONE.
PROBABLY *DEAD*.
SHF
CRRRK
WE NEED TO GET OUT OF HERE.
RUMBLE
RUMBLE
RUMBLE
CRRK
SIGH
I CAN'T BELIEVE THIS SHIT.

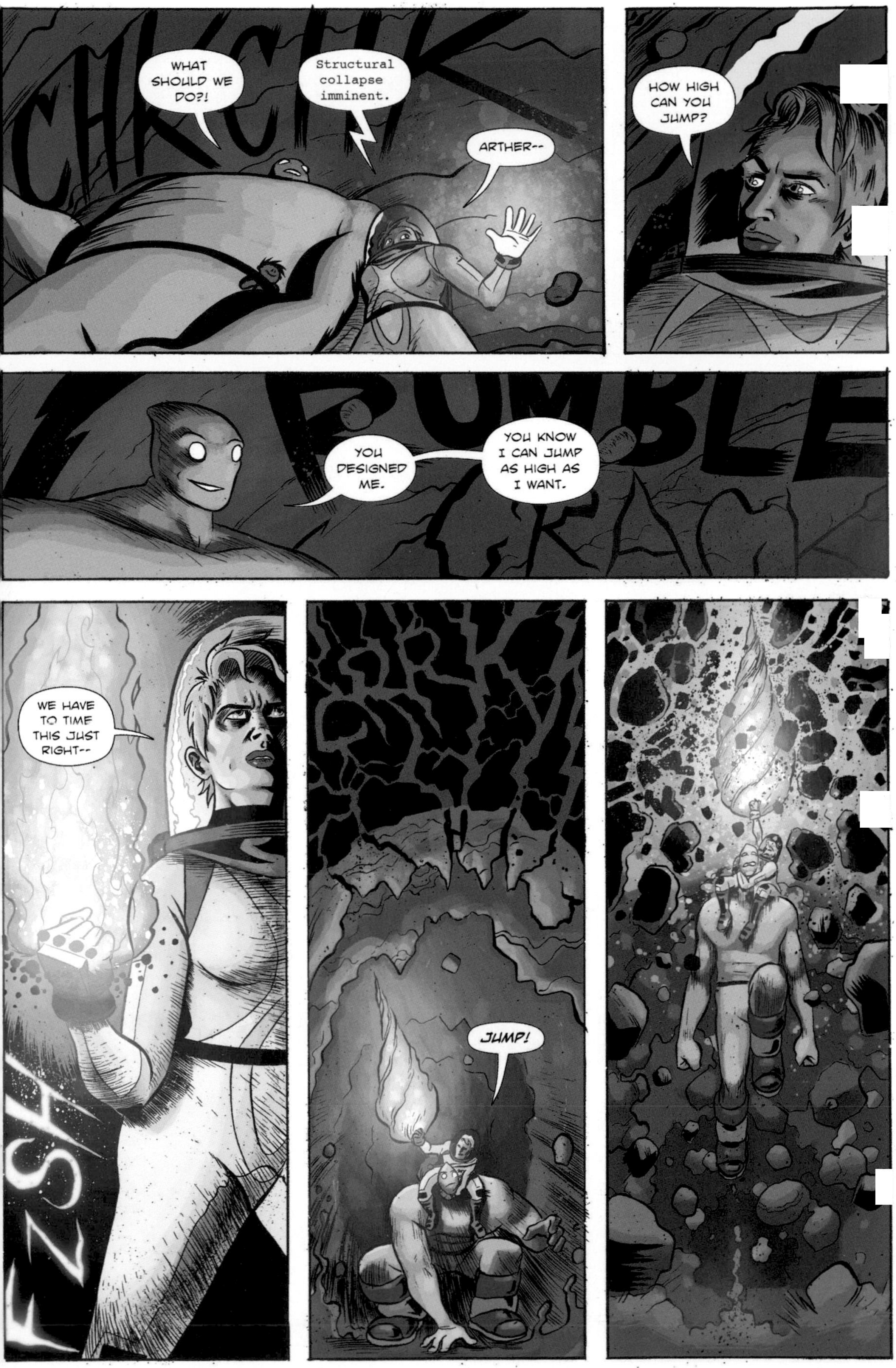
WHAT SHOULD WE DO?!
Structural collapse imminent.
ARTHER--
HOW HIGH CAN YOU JUMP?
YOU KNOW I CAN JUMP AS HIGH AS I WANT.
YOU DESIGNED ME.
WE HAVE TO TIME THIS JUST RIGHT--
JUMP!

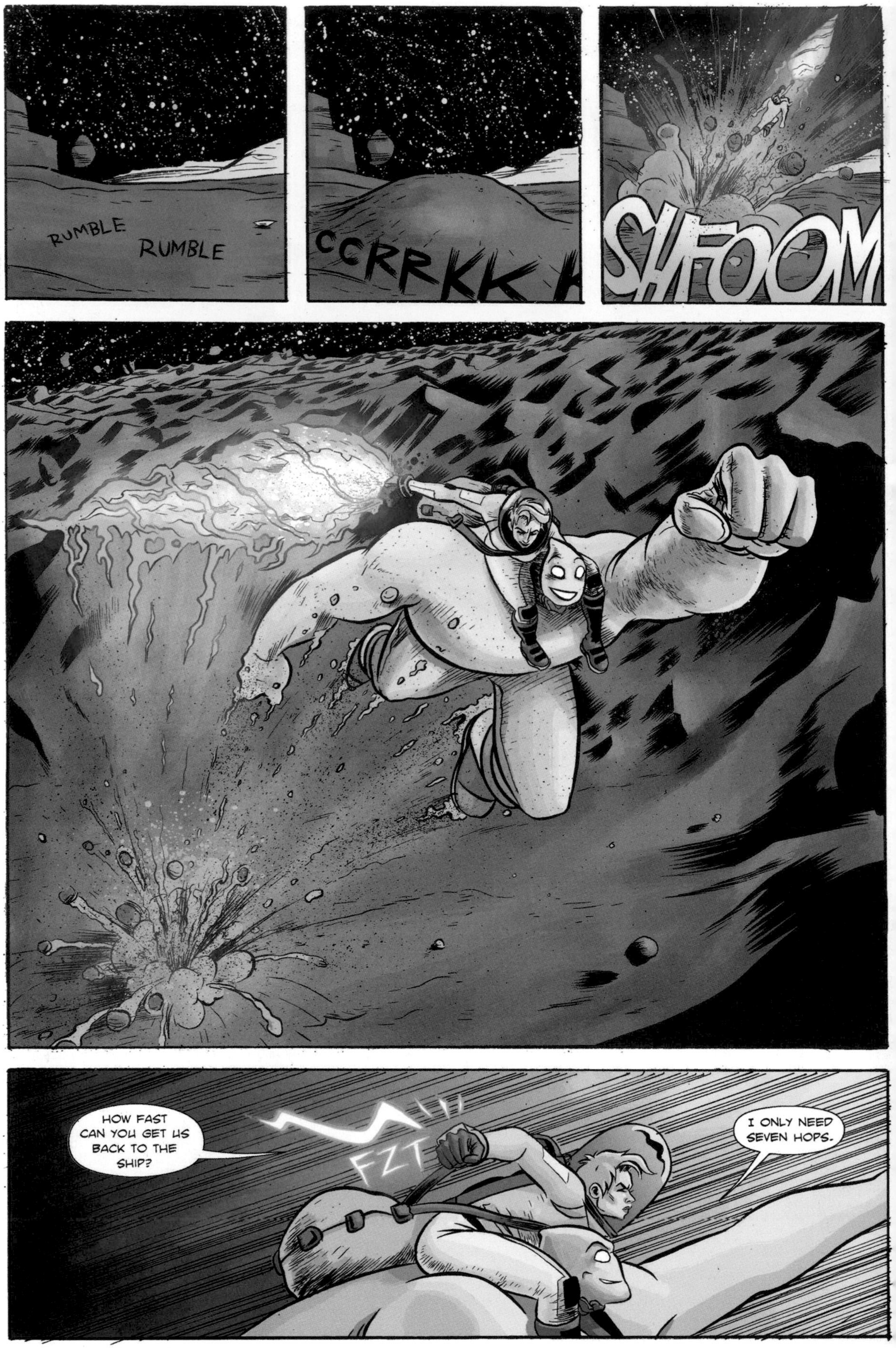
RUMBLE
RUMBLE
CCRRKKK
SHFOOM
HOW FAST CAN YOU GET US BACK TO THE SHIP?
FZT
I ONLY NEED SEVEN HOPS.

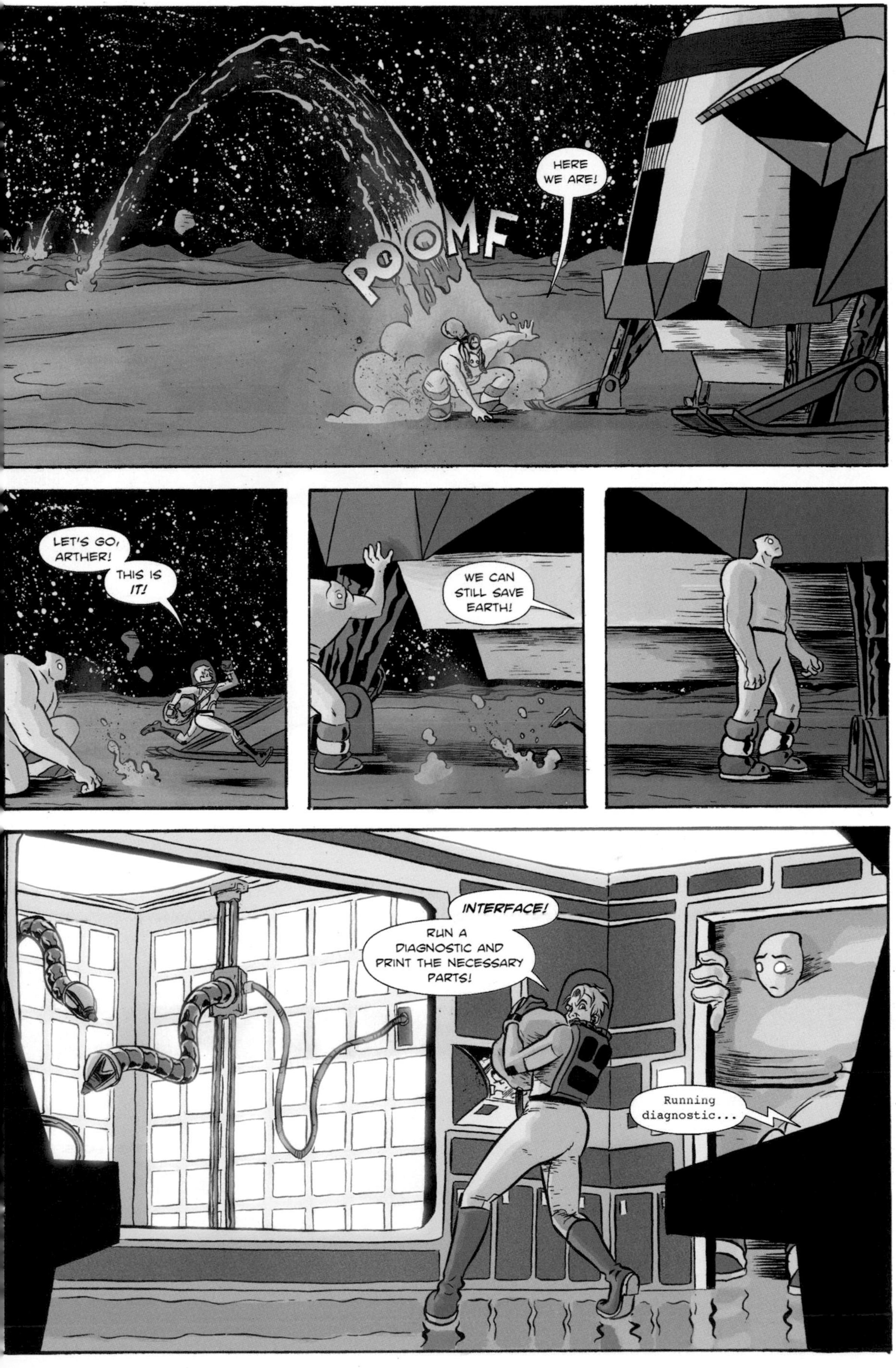
HERE WE ARE!
POOMF
LET'S GO, ARTHER!
THIS IS *IT!*
WE CAN STILL SAVE EARTH!
INTERFACE!
RUN A DIAGNOSTIC AND PRINT THE NECESSARY PARTS!
Running diagnostic...

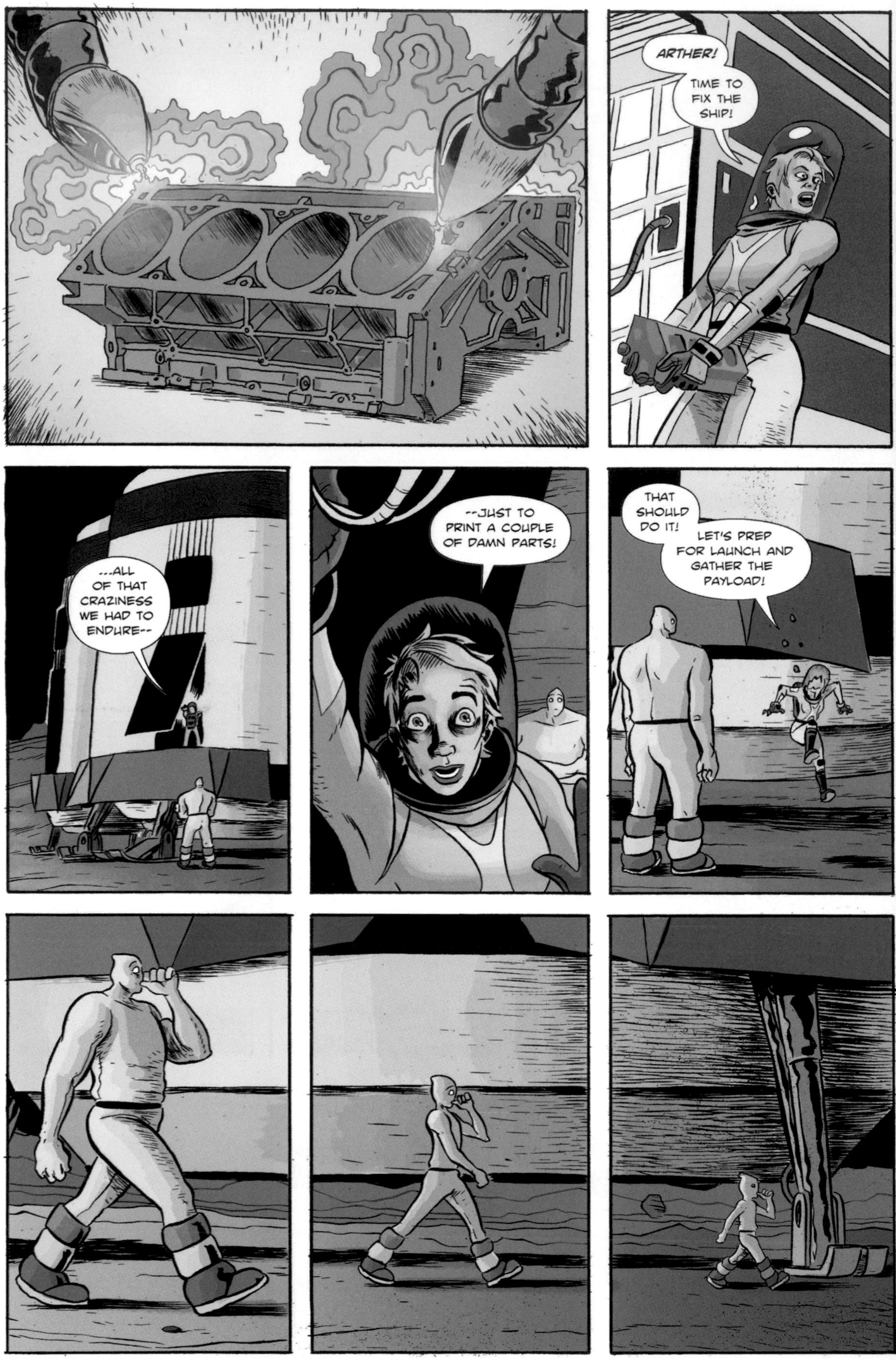
ARTHER!
TIME TO FIX THE SHIP!
---ALL OF THAT CRAZINESS WE HAD TO ENDURE--
--JUST TO PRINT A COUPLE OF DAMN PARTS!
THAT SHOULD DO IT!
LET'S PREP FOR LAUNCH AND GATHER THE PAYLOAD!

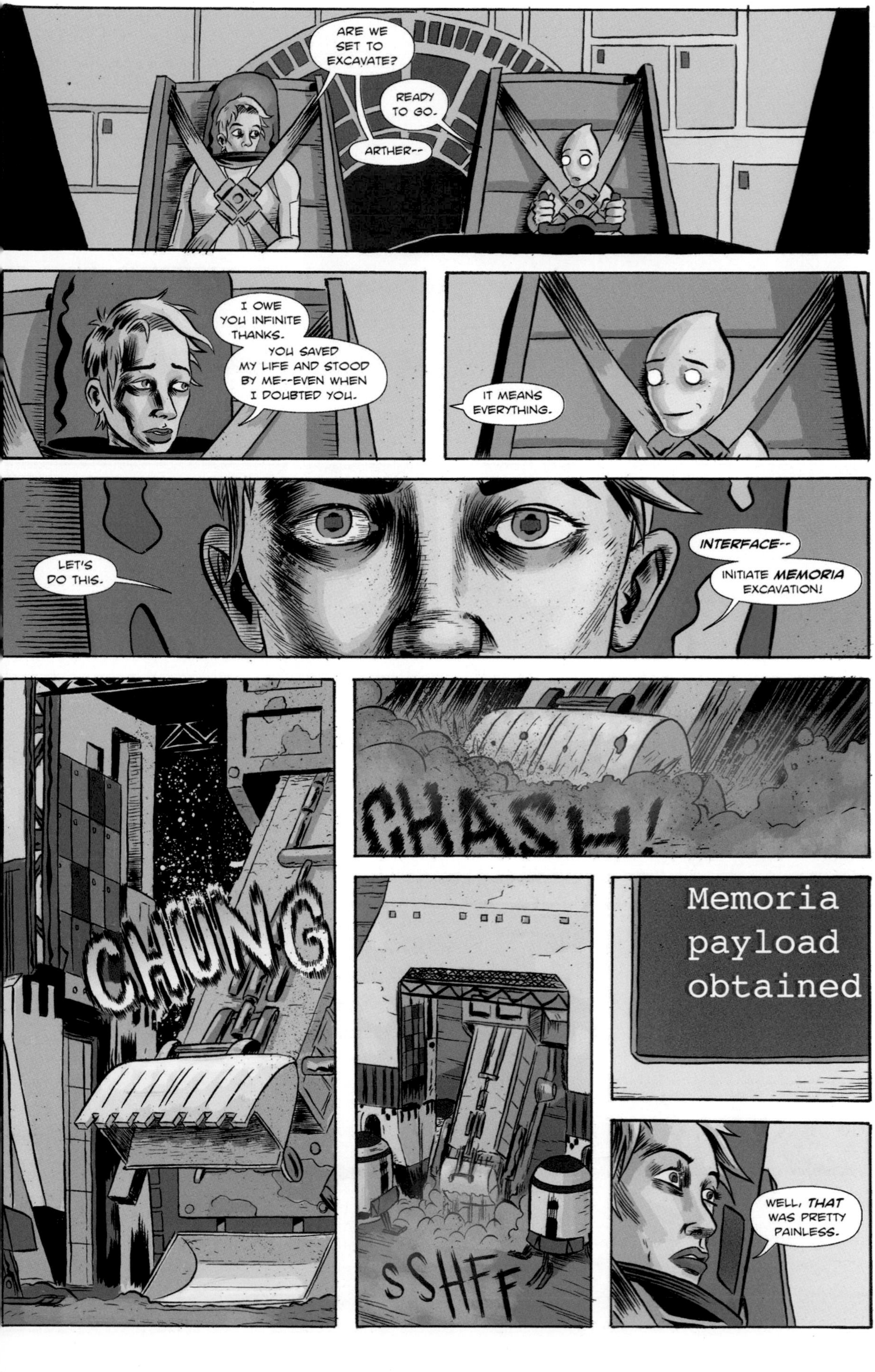
ARE WE SET TO EXCAVATE?
READY TO GO.
ARTHER--
I OWE YOU INFINITE THANKS.
YOU SAVED MY LIFE AND STOOD BY ME--EVEN WHEN I DOUBTED YOU.
IT MEANS EVERYTHING.
LET'S DO THIS.
INTERFACE--
INITIATE MEMORIA EXCAVATION!
CHUNG
CRASH!
SSHFF
Memoria payload obtained
WELL, THAT WAS PRETTY PAINLESS.

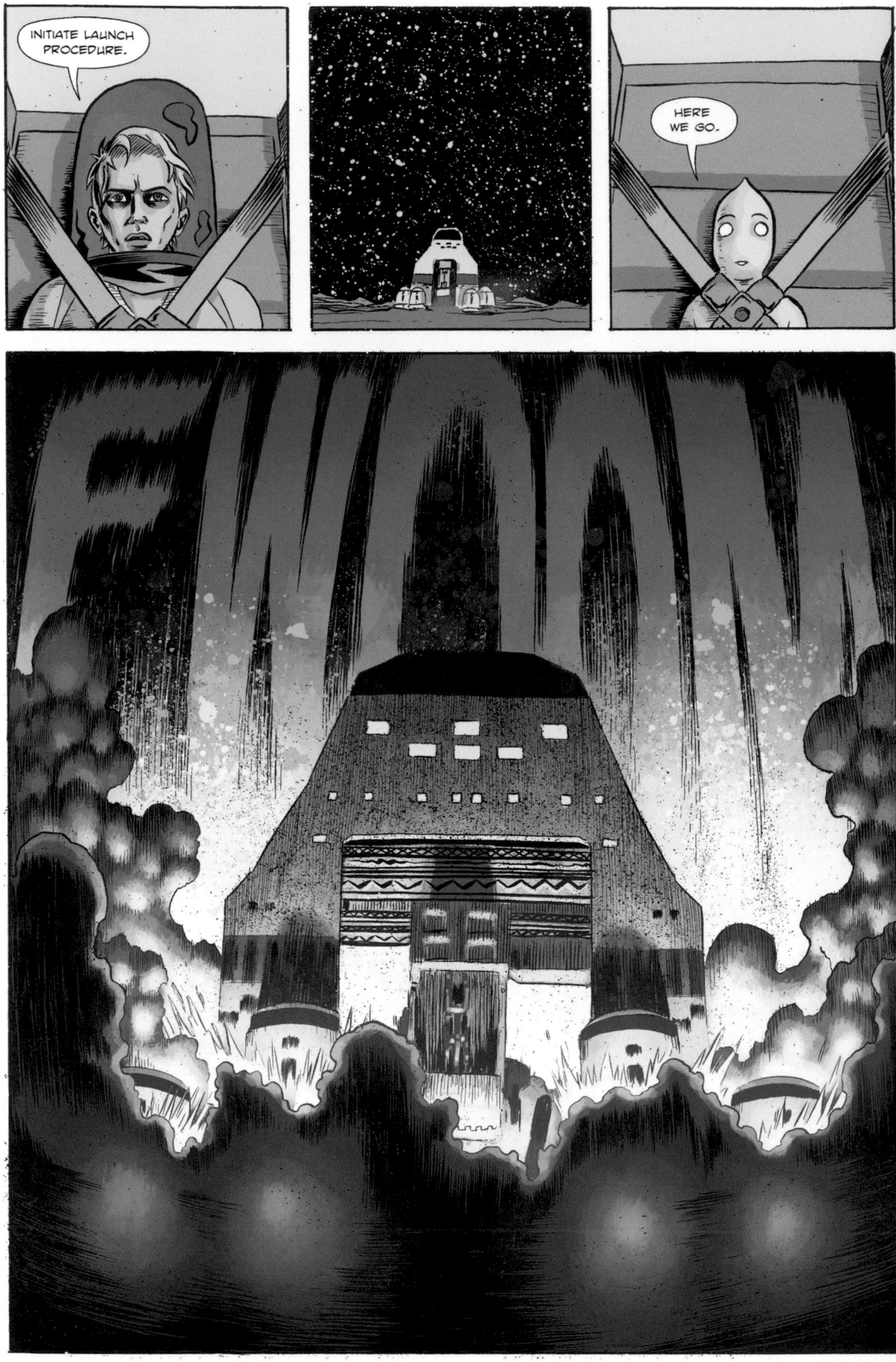
INITIATE LAUNCH PROCEDURE.
HERE WE GO.

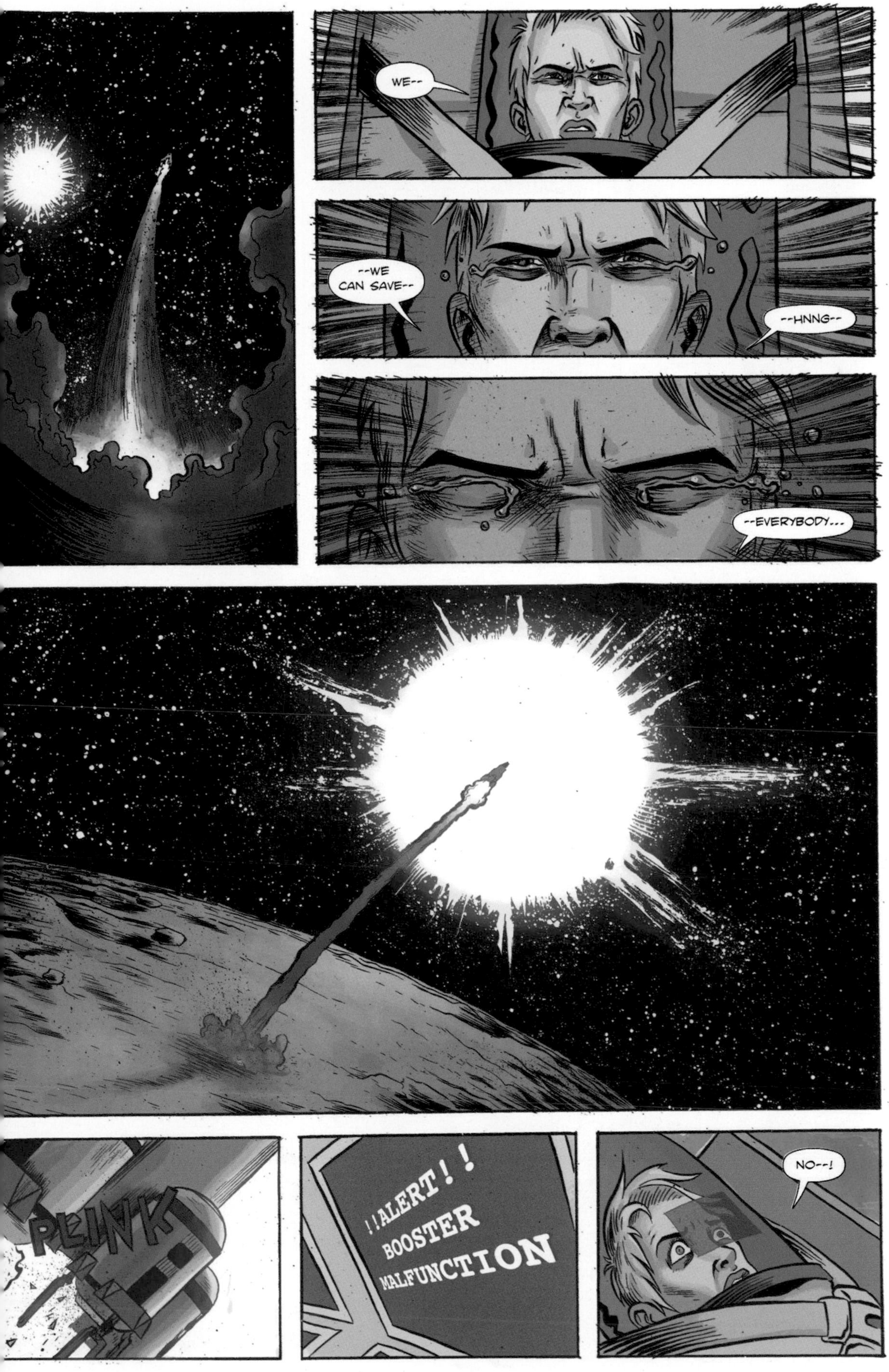
WE--
--WE CAN SAVE--
--HNNG--
--EVERYBODY...
PLINK
!!ALERT!! BOOSTER MALFUNCTION
NO--!

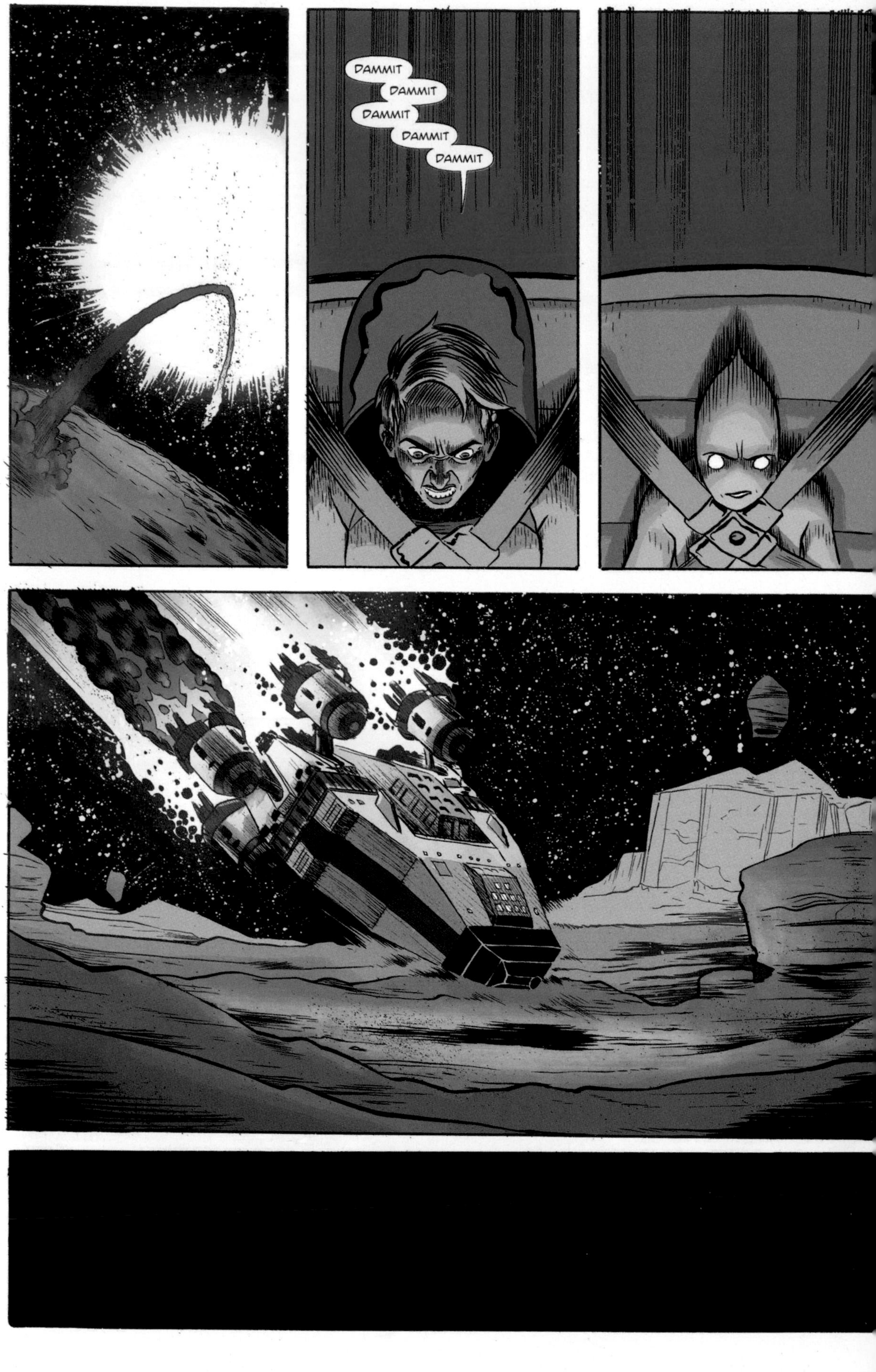
DAMMIT
DAMMIT
DAMMIT
DAMMIT
DAMMIT

CHAPTER 4

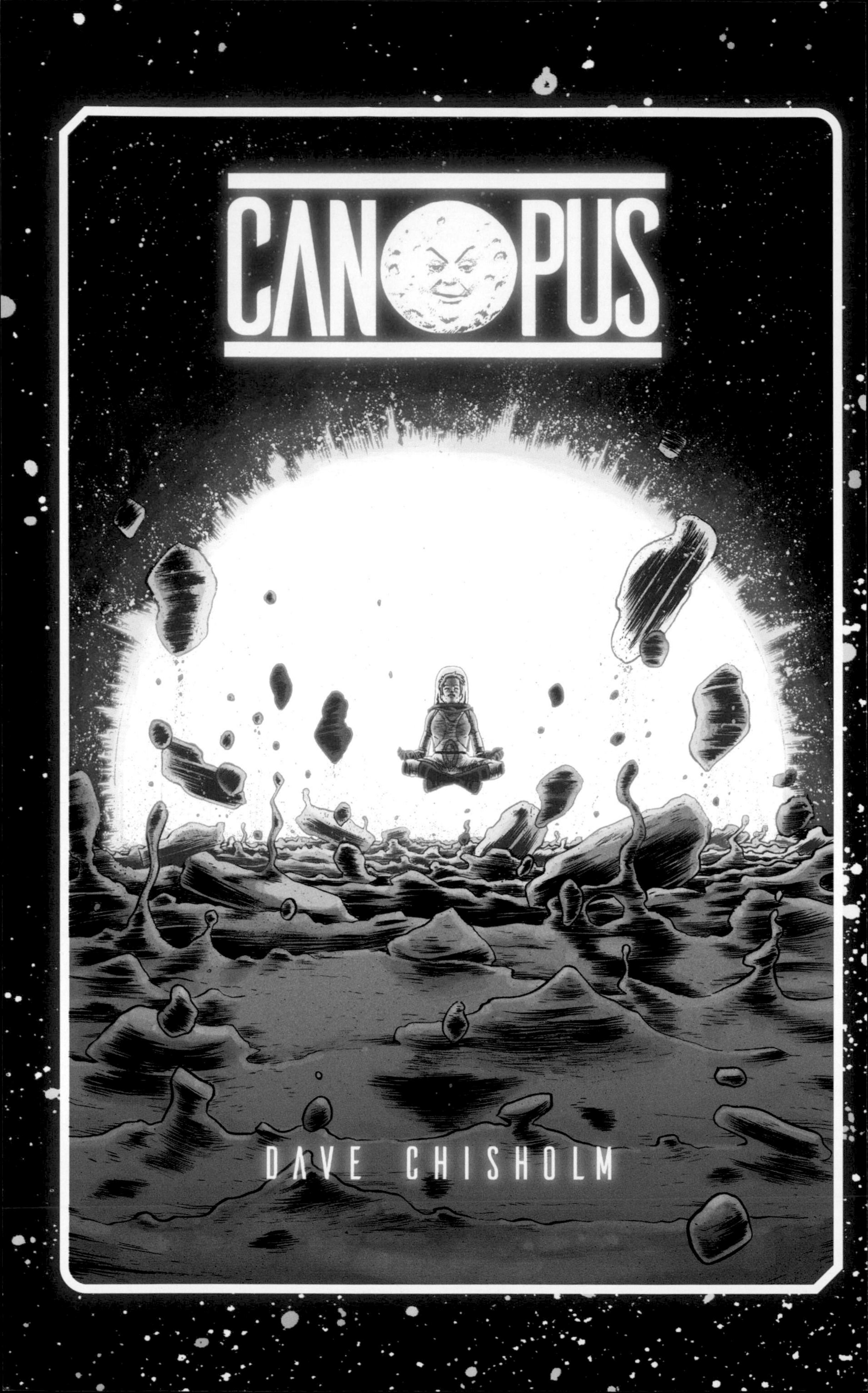
CANOPUS
DAVE CHISHOLM

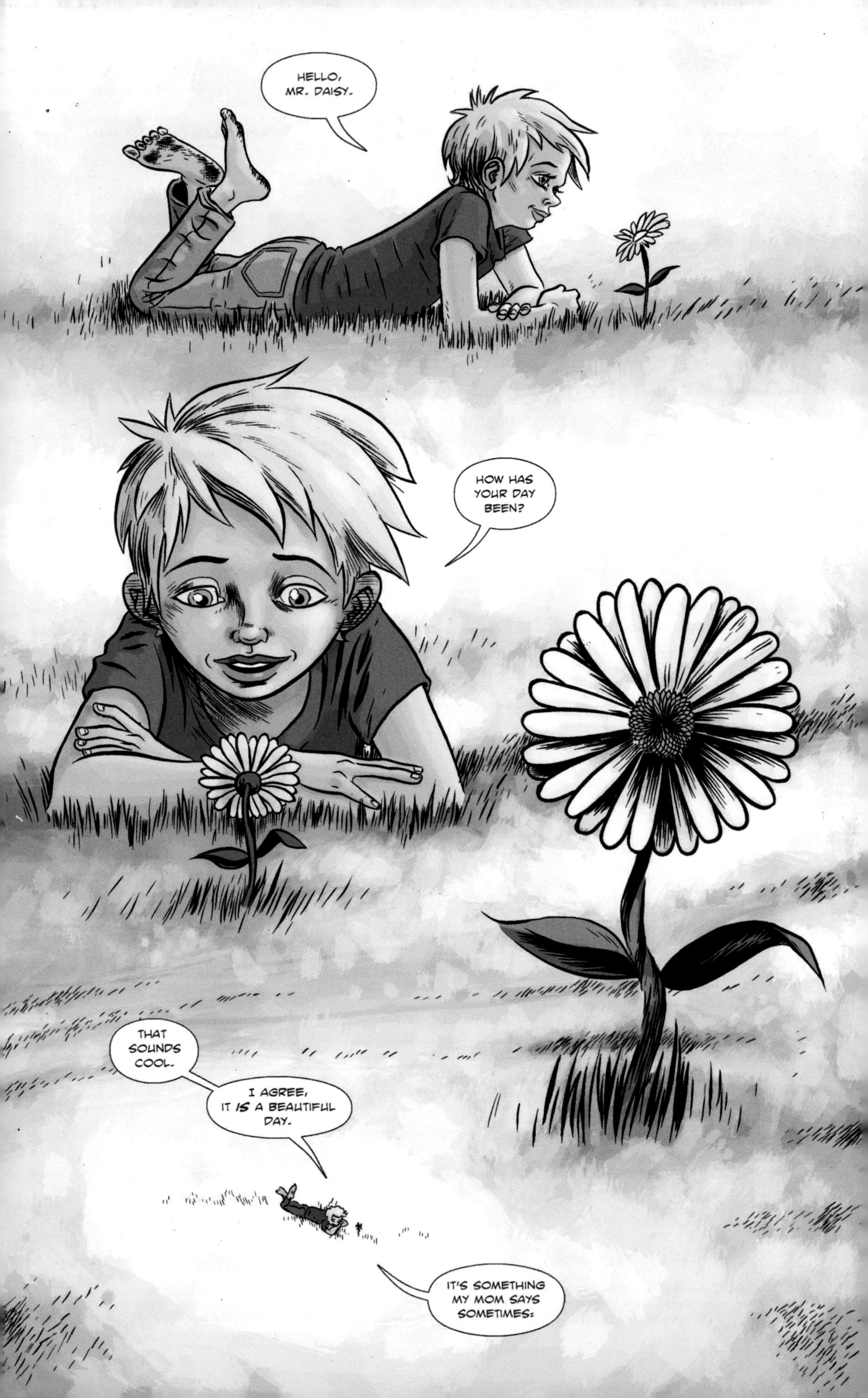
HELLO, MR. DAISY.
HOW HAS YOUR DAY BEEN?
THAT SOUNDS COOL.
I AGREE, IT *IS* A BEAUTIFUL DAY.
IT'S SOMETHING MY MOM SAYS SOMETIMES.

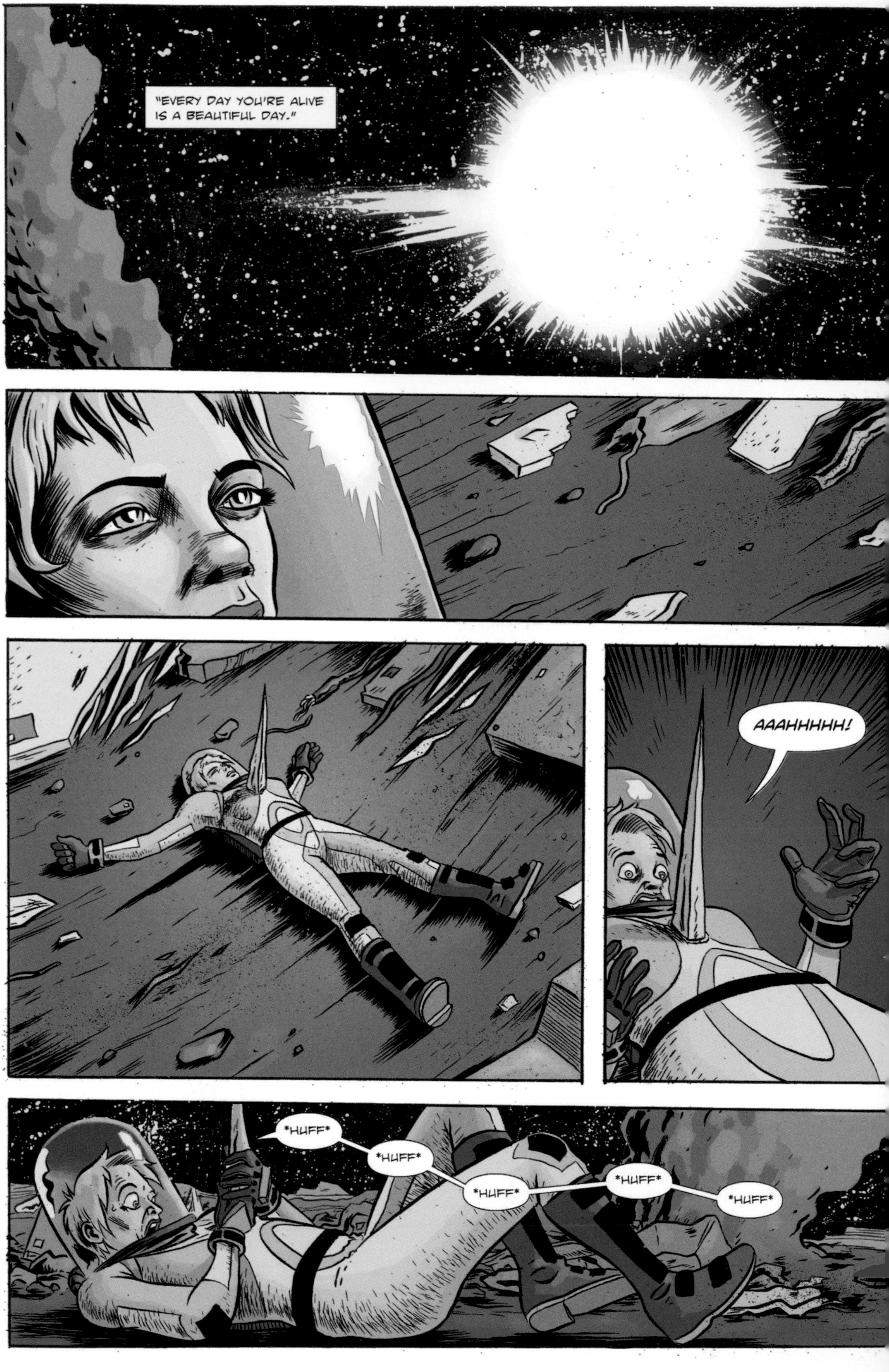
"EVERY DAY YOU'RE ALIVE IS A BEAUTIFUL DAY."
AAAHHHHH!
HUFF
HUFF
HUFF
HUFF
HUFF

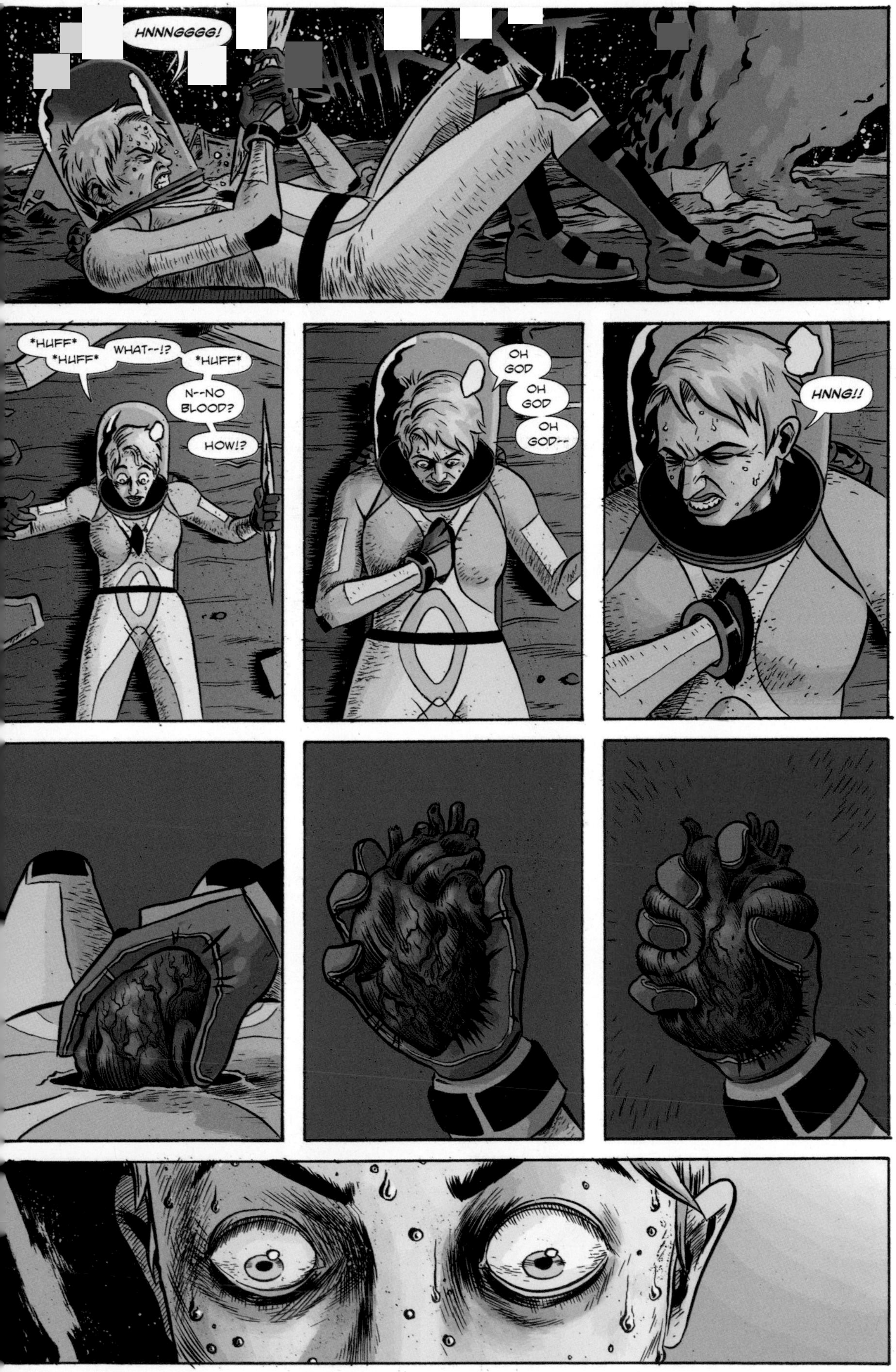

HNNNGGGG!
HUFF
HUFF
WHAT--!?
HUFF
N--NO BLOOD?
HOW!?
OH GOD
OH GOD
OH GOD--
HNNG!!

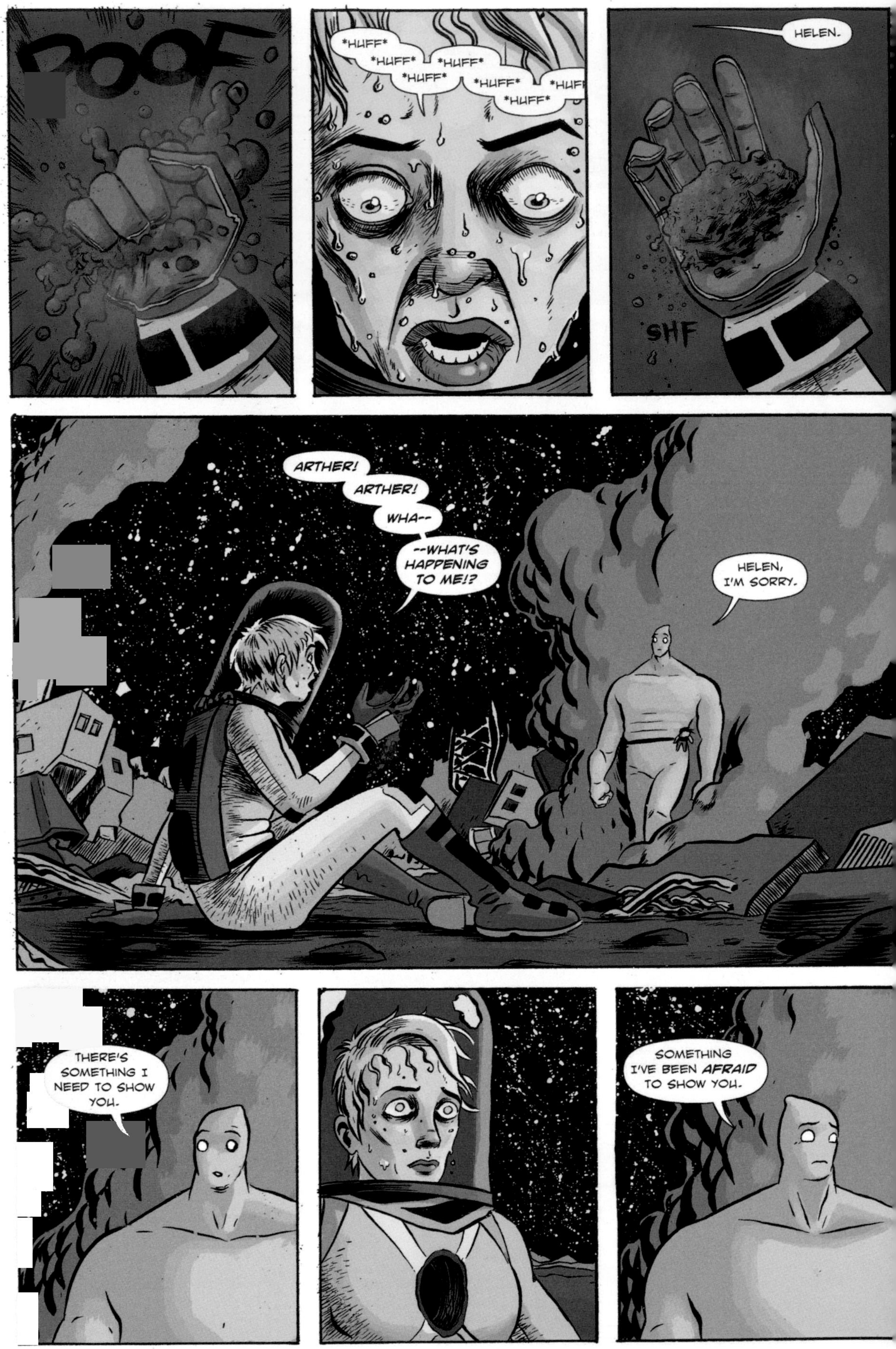
POOF
HUFF
HUFF
HUFF
HUFF
HUFF
HUFF
HELEN.
SHF
ARTHER!
ARTHER!
WHA--
--WHAT'S HAPPENING TO ME!?
HELEN, I'M SORRY.
THERE'S SOMETHING I NEED TO SHOW YOU.
SOMETHING I'VE BEEN AFRAID TO SHOW YOU.

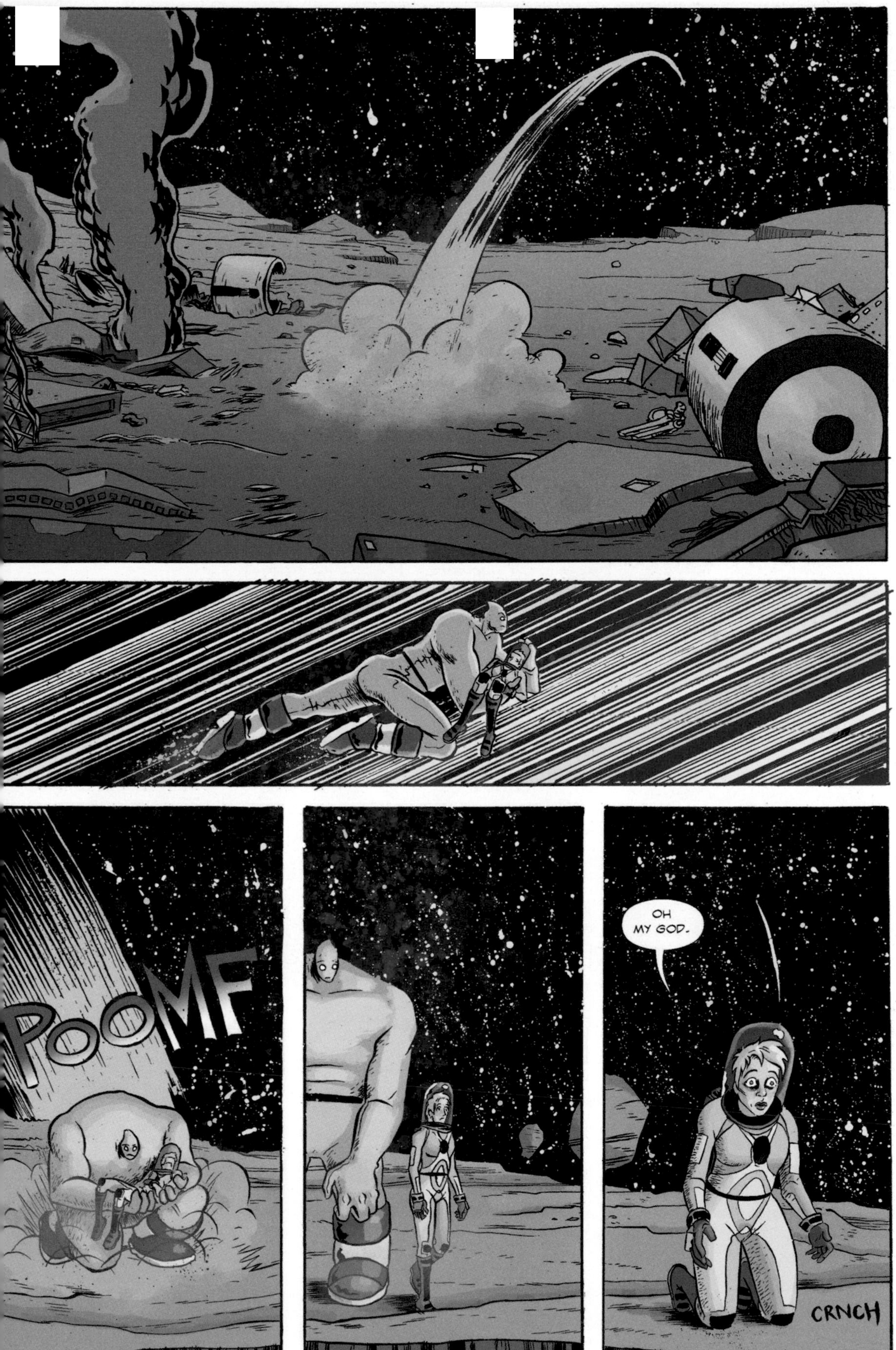
POOMF
OH MY GOD.
CRNCH

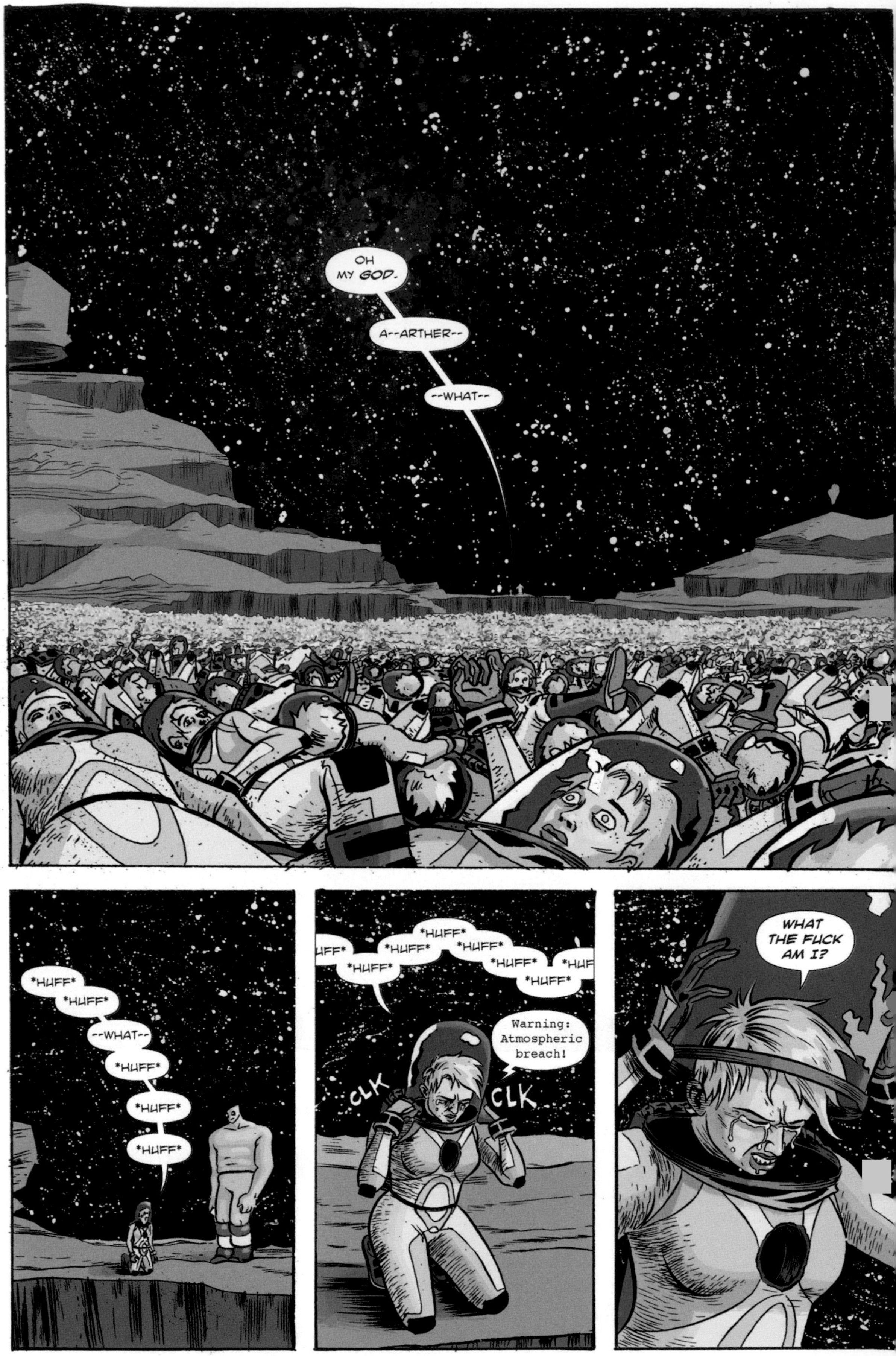

OH MY GOD.
A--ARTHER--
--WHAT--
HUFF
HUFF
--WHAT--
HUFF
HUFF
HUFF
HUFF
HUFF
HUFF
HUFF
HUFF
HUFF
CLK
Warning: Atmospheric breach!
CLK
WHAT THE FUCK AM I?

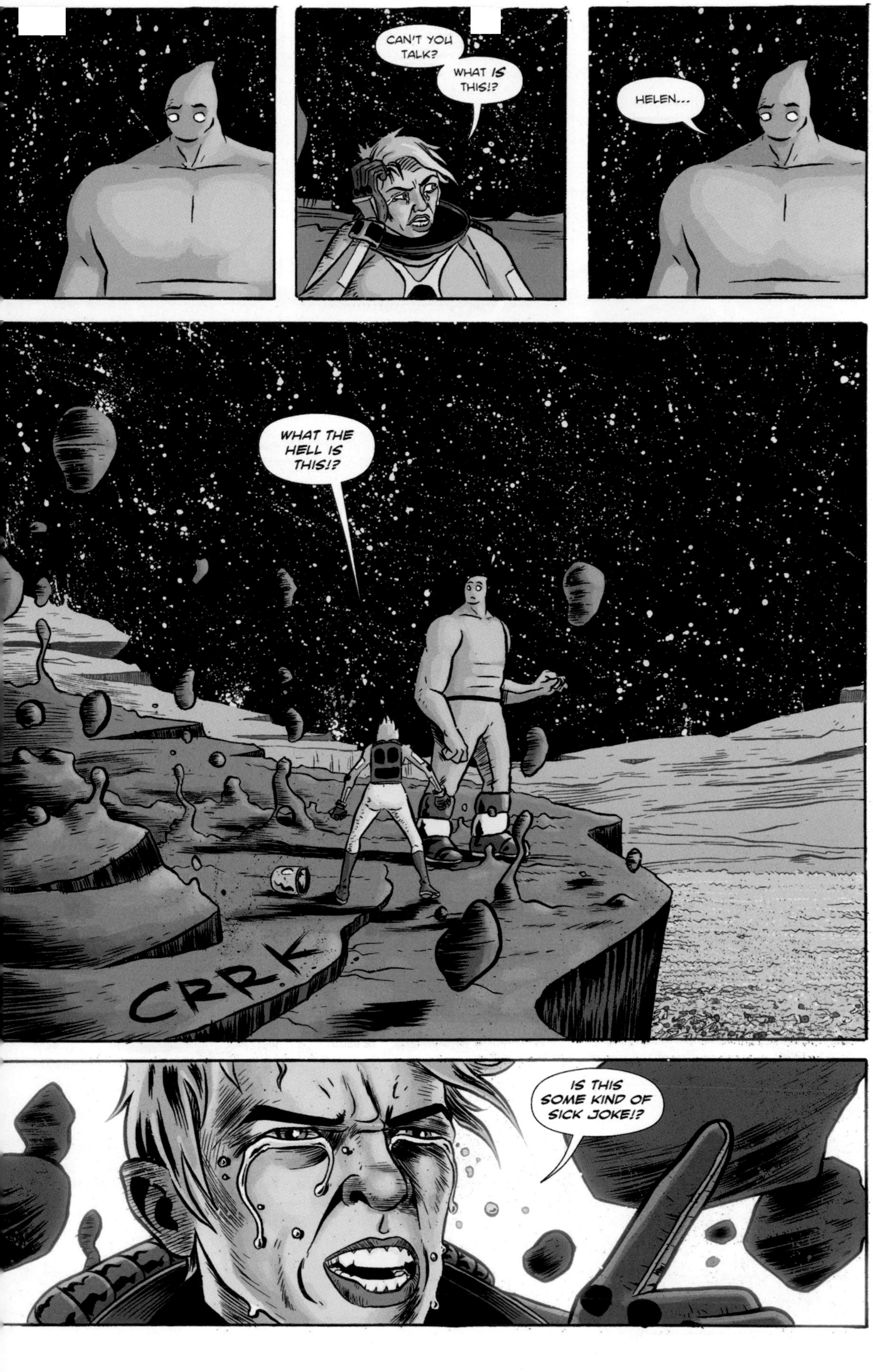
CAN'T YOU TALK?
WHAT IS THIS!?
HELEN...
WHAT THE HELL IS THIS!?
CRRK
IS THIS SOME KIND OF SICK JOKE!?

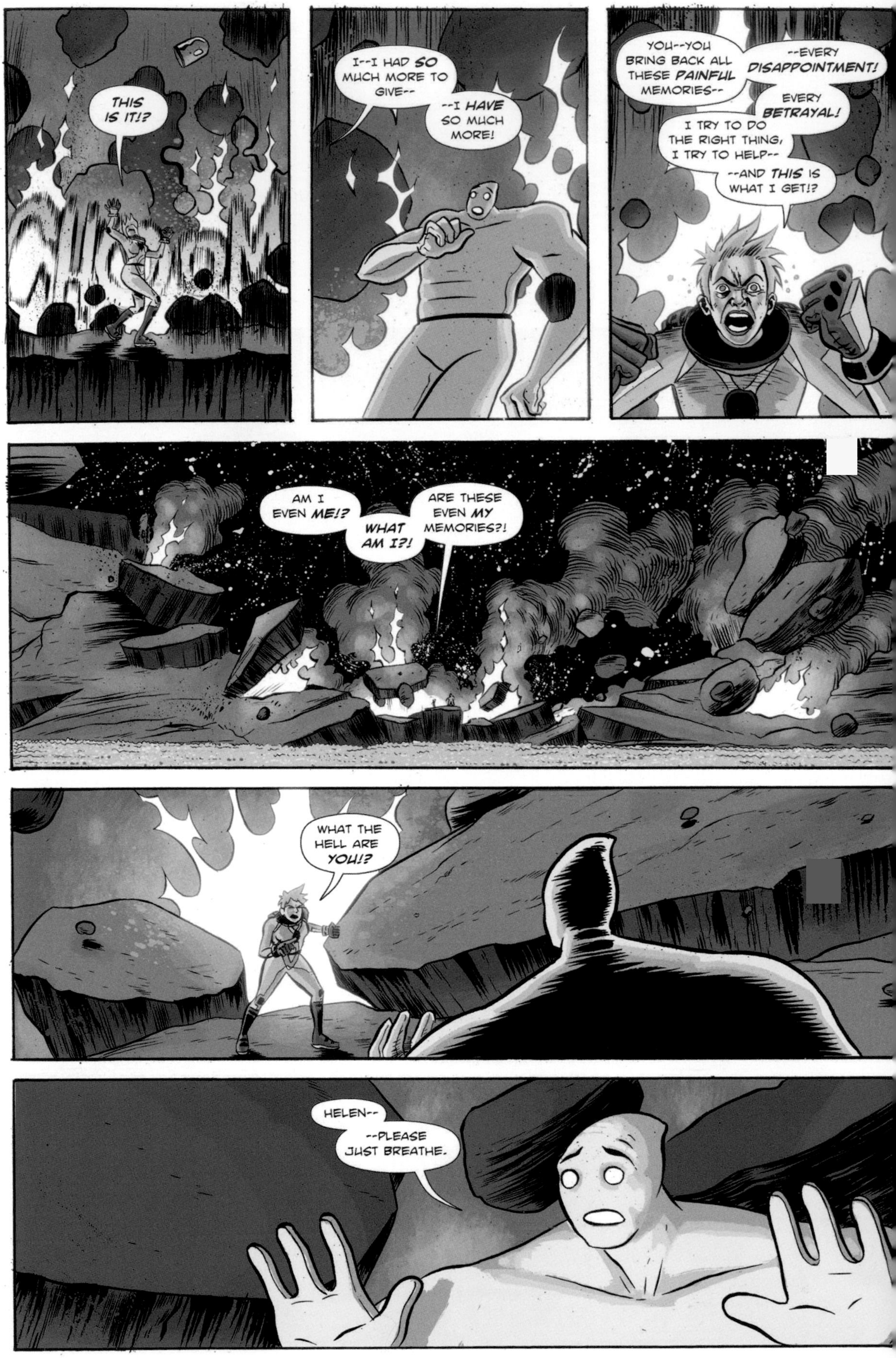
THIS IS IT!?
I--I HAD SO MUCH MORE TO GIVE--
--I HAVE SO MUCH MORE!
YOU--YOU BRING BACK ALL THESE PAINFUL MEMORIES--
--EVERY DISAPPOINTMENT!
EVERY BETRAYAL!
I TRY TO DO THE RIGHT THING, I TRY TO HELP--
--AND THIS IS WHAT I GET!?
AM I EVEN ME!?
WHAT AM I?!
ARE THESE EVEN MY MEMORIES?!
WHAT THE HELL ARE YOU!?
HELEN--
--PLEASE JUST BREATHE.

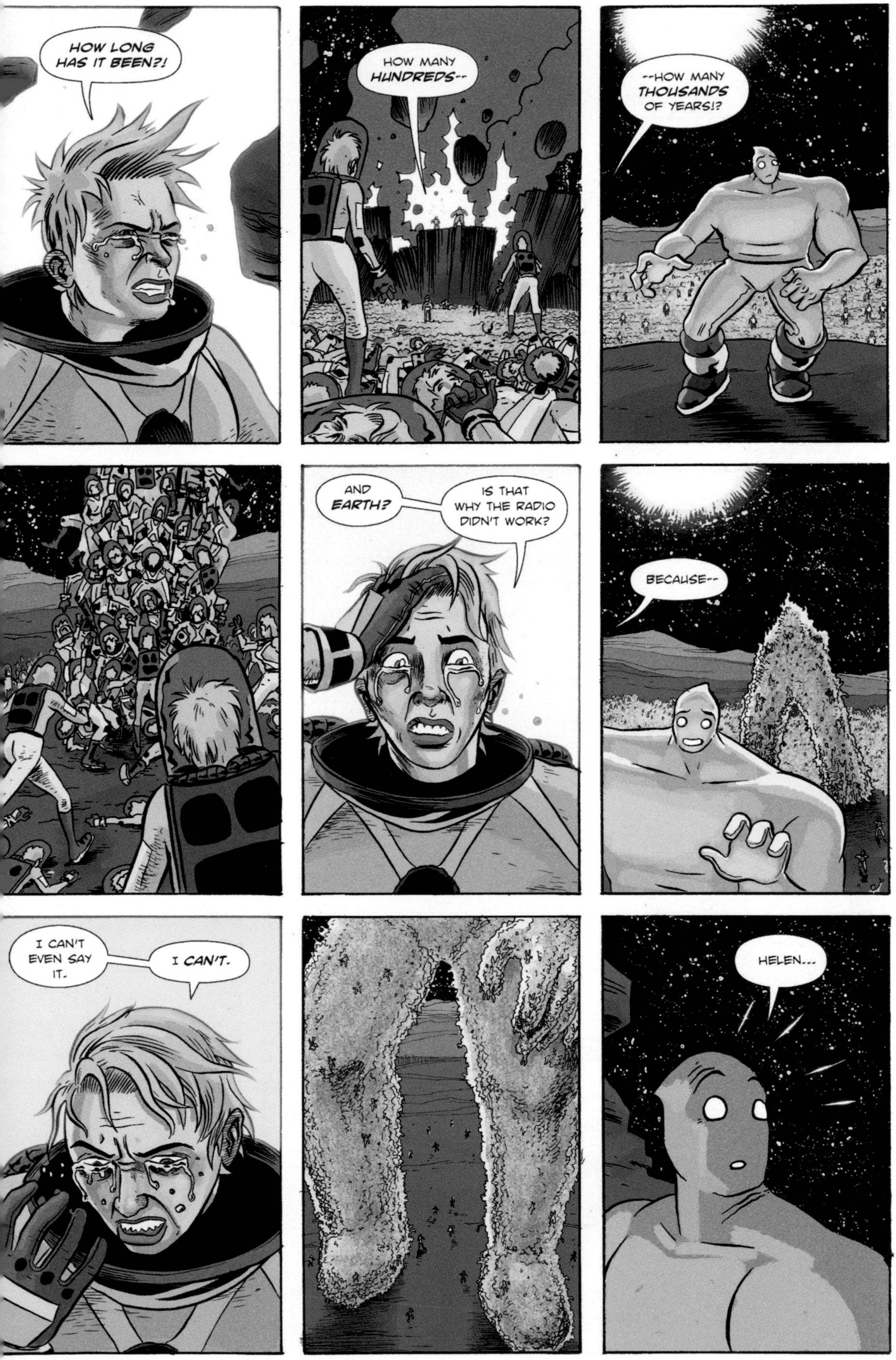
HOW LONG HAS IT BEEN?!
HOW MANY HUNDREDS--
--HOW MANY THOUSANDS OF YEARS!?
AND EARTH?
IS THAT WHY THE RADIO DIDN'T WORK?
BECAUSE--
I CAN'T EVEN SAY IT.
I CAN'T.
HELEN...

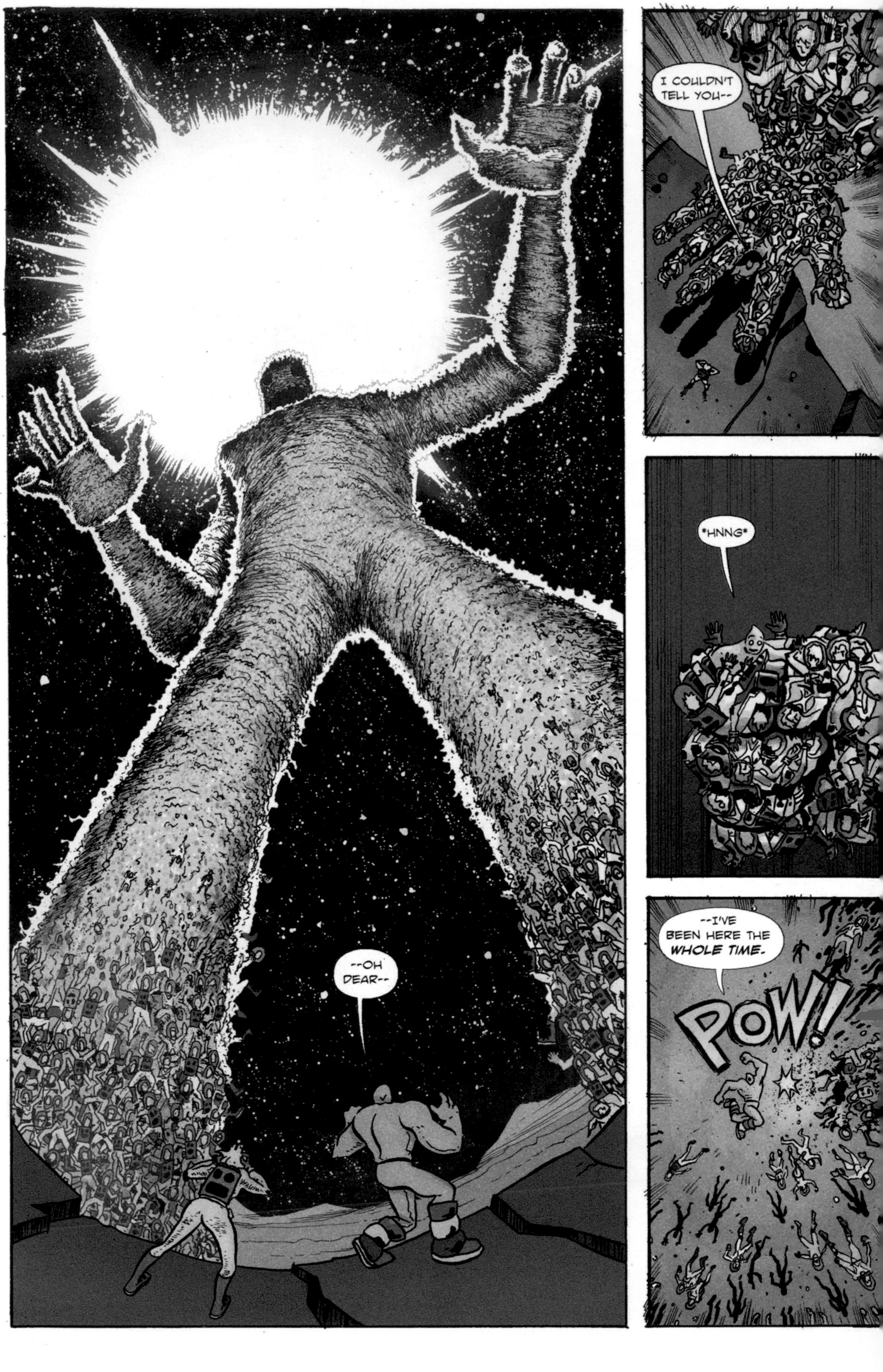
--OH DEAR--
I COULDN'T TELL YOU--
HNNG
--I'VE BEEN HERE THE *WHOLE TIME.*
POW!

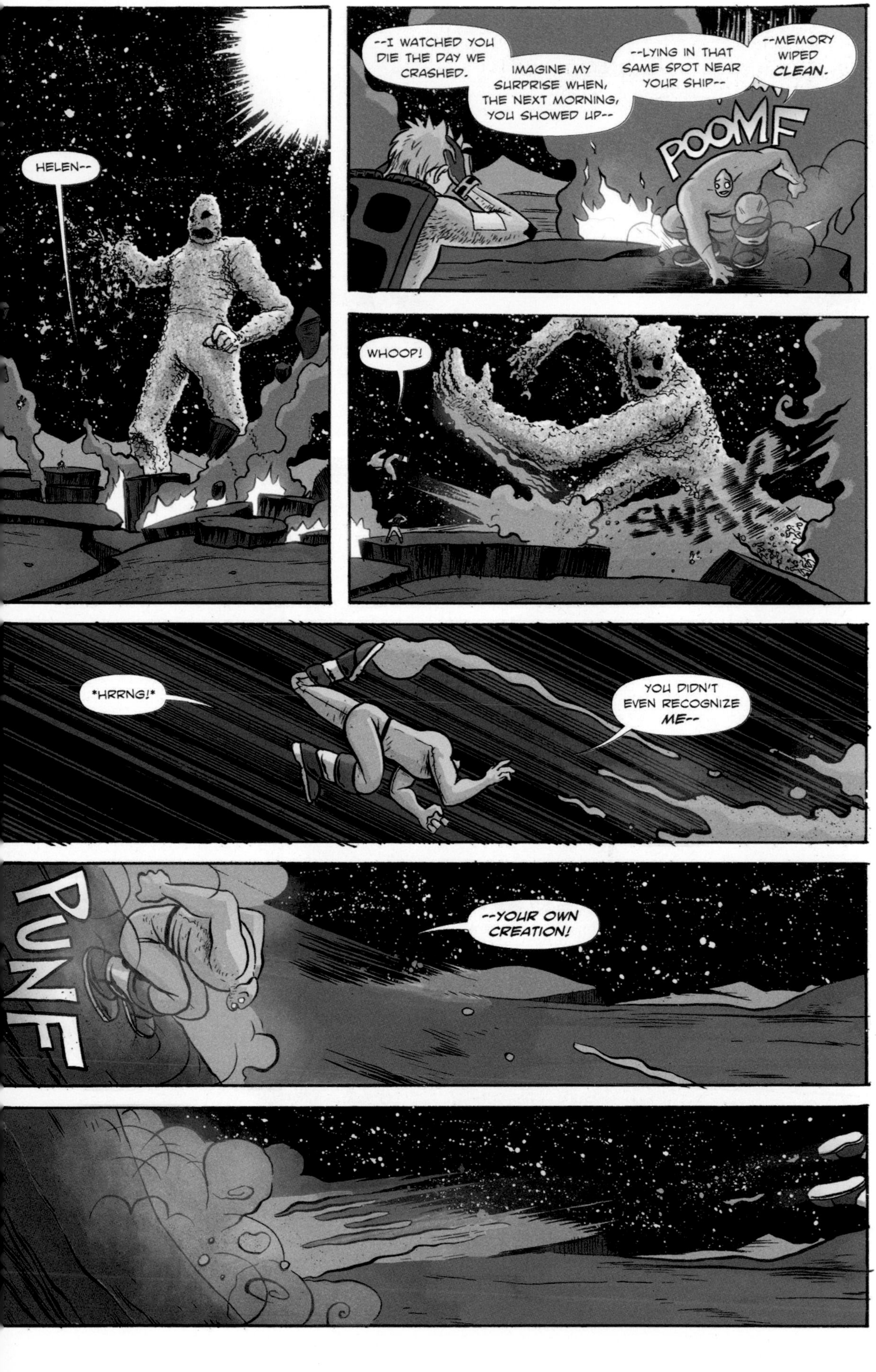
HELEN--
--I WATCHED YOU DIE THE DAY WE CRASHED.
IMAGINE MY SURPRISE WHEN, THE NEXT MORNING, YOU SHOWED UP--
--LYING IN THAT SAME SPOT NEAR YOUR SHIP--
--MEMORY WIPED CLEAN.
POOMF
WHOOP!
SWAK
HRRNG!
YOU DIDN'T EVEN RECOGNIZE ME--
PUNF
--YOUR OWN CREATION!

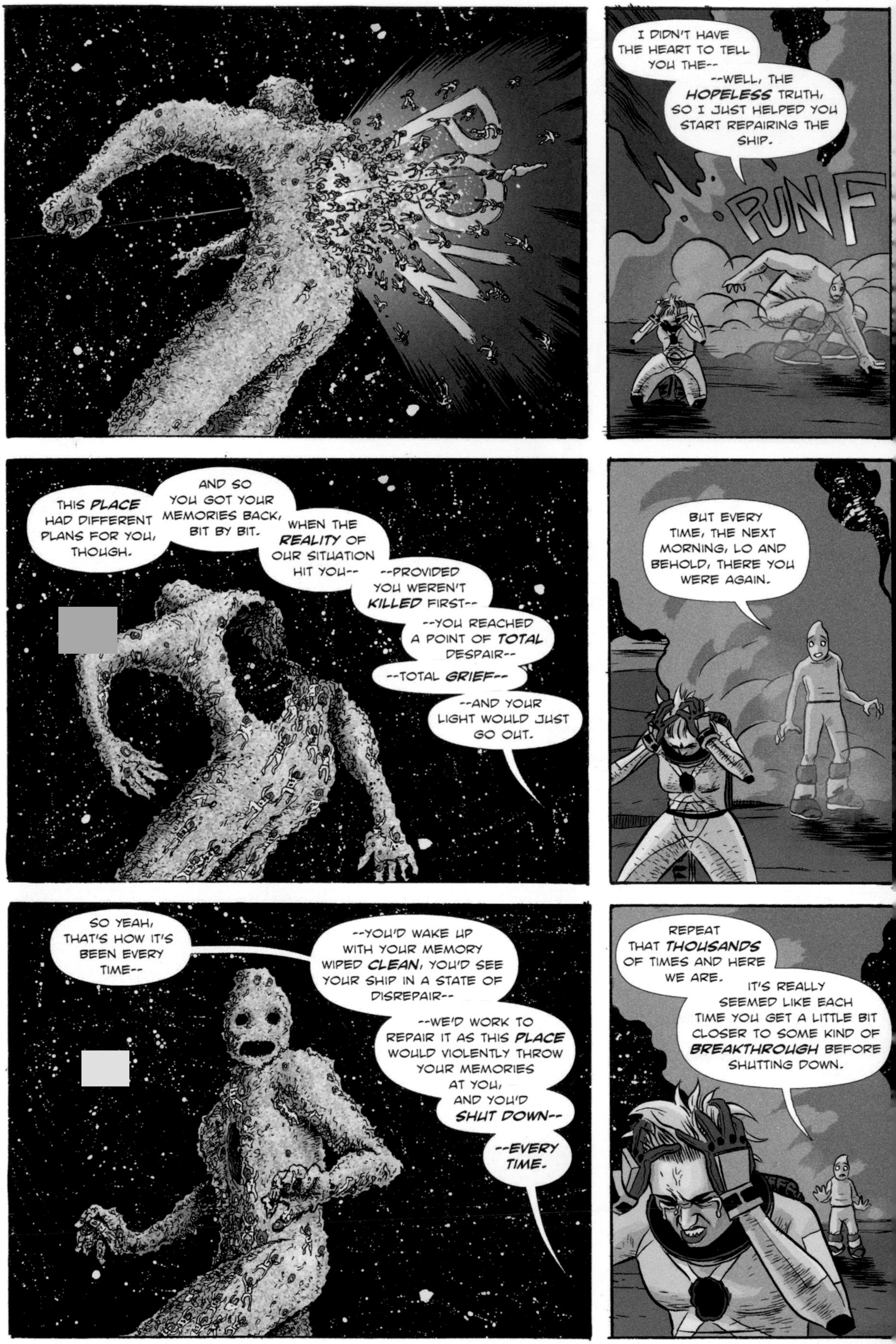
I DIDN'T HAVE THE HEART TO TELL YOU THE--
--WELL, THE HOPELESS TRUTH, SO I JUST HELPED YOU START REPAIRING THE SHIP.
PUNF
THIS PLACE HAD DIFFERENT PLANS FOR YOU, THOUGH.
AND SO YOU GOT YOUR MEMORIES BACK, BIT BY BIT.
WHEN THE REALITY OF OUR SITUATION HIT YOU--
--PROVIDED YOU WEREN'T KILLED FIRST--
--YOU REACHED A POINT OF TOTAL DESPAIR--
--TOTAL GRIEF--
--AND YOUR LIGHT WOULD JUST GO OUT.
BUT EVERY TIME, THE NEXT MORNING, LO AND BEHOLD, THERE YOU WERE AGAIN.
SO YEAH, THAT'S HOW IT'S BEEN EVERY TIME--
--YOU'D WAKE UP WITH YOUR MEMORY WIPED CLEAN, YOU'D SEE YOUR SHIP IN A STATE OF DISREPAIR--
--WE'D WORK TO REPAIR IT AS THIS PLACE WOULD VIOLENTLY THROW YOUR MEMORIES AT YOU, AND YOU'D SHUT DOWN--
--EVERY TIME.
REPEAT THAT THOUSANDS OF TIMES AND HERE WE ARE.
IT'S REALLY SEEMED LIKE EACH TIME YOU GET A LITTLE BIT CLOSER TO SOME KIND OF BREAKTHROUGH BEFORE SHUTTING DOWN.

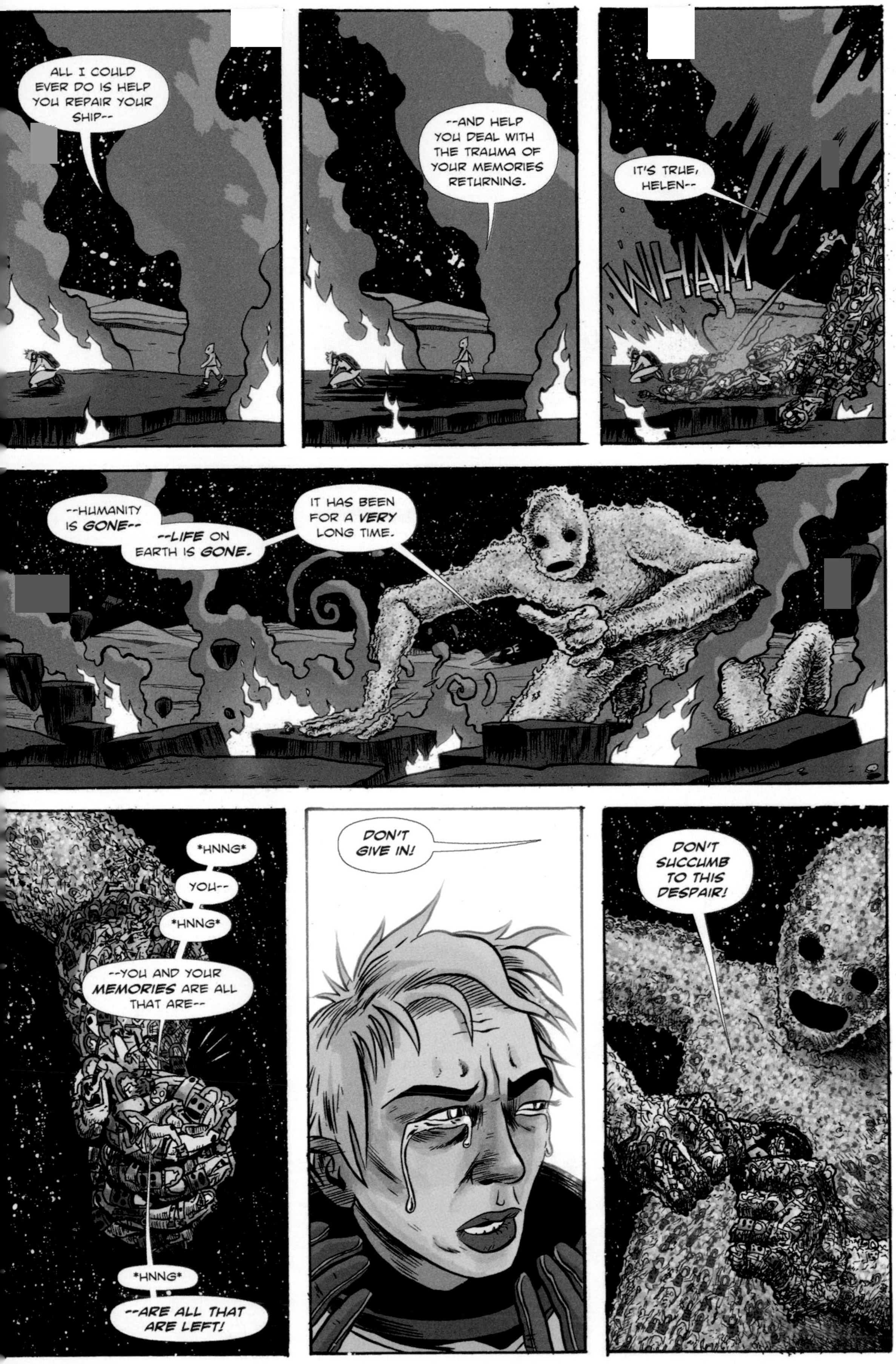
ALL I COULD EVER DO IS HELP YOU REPAIR YOUR SHIP--
--AND HELP YOU DEAL WITH THE TRAUMA OF YOUR MEMORIES RETURNING.
IT'S TRUE, HELEN--
WHAM
--HUMANITY IS GONE--
--LIFE ON EARTH IS GONE.
IT HAS BEEN FOR A VERY LONG TIME.
HNNG
YOU--
HNNG
--YOU AND YOUR MEMORIES ARE ALL THAT ARE--
HNNG
--ARE ALL THAT ARE LEFT!
DON'T GIVE IN!
DON'T SUCCUMB TO THIS DESPAIR!

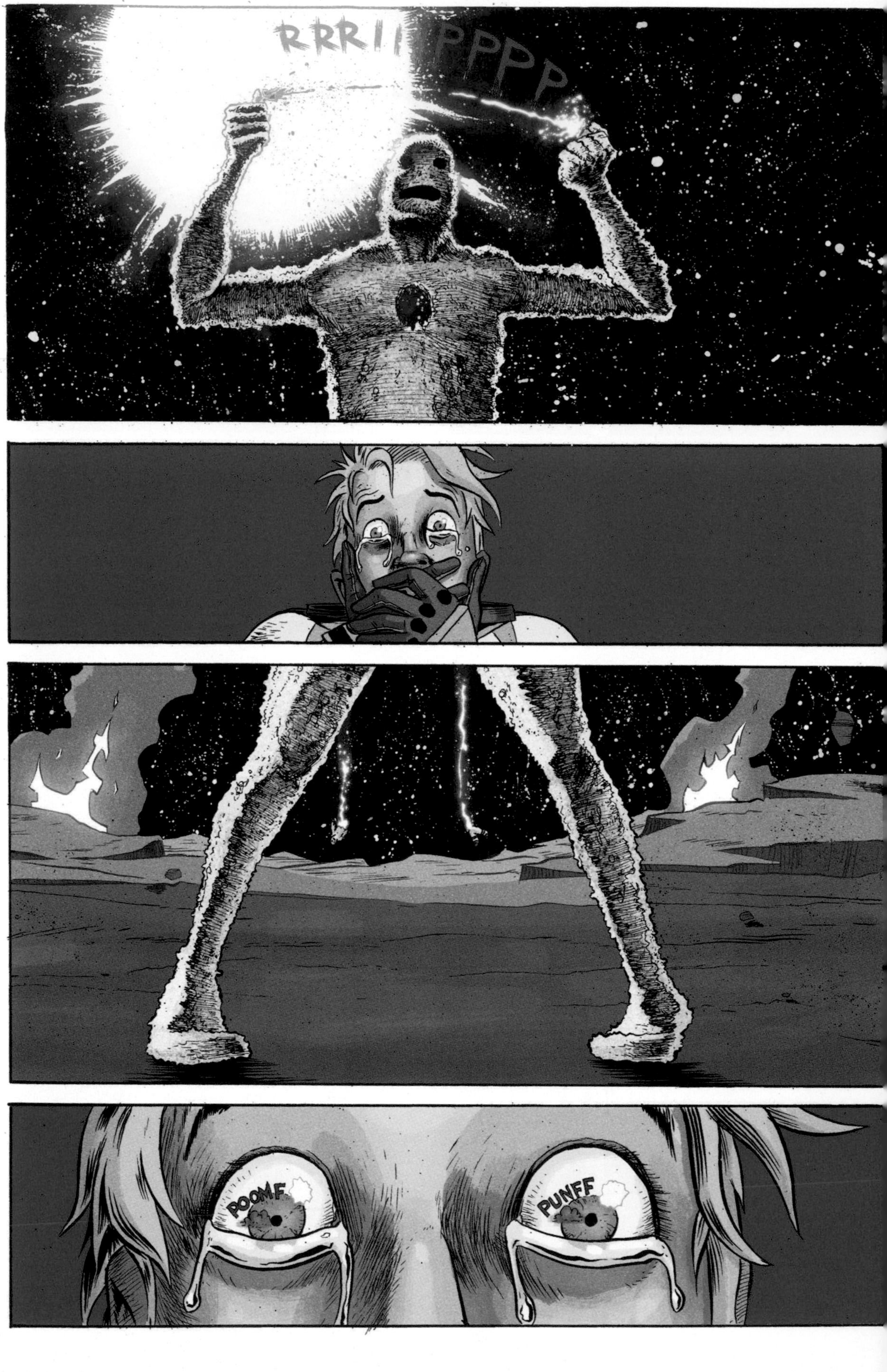
RRRIIPPPPP
POOMF
PUNFF

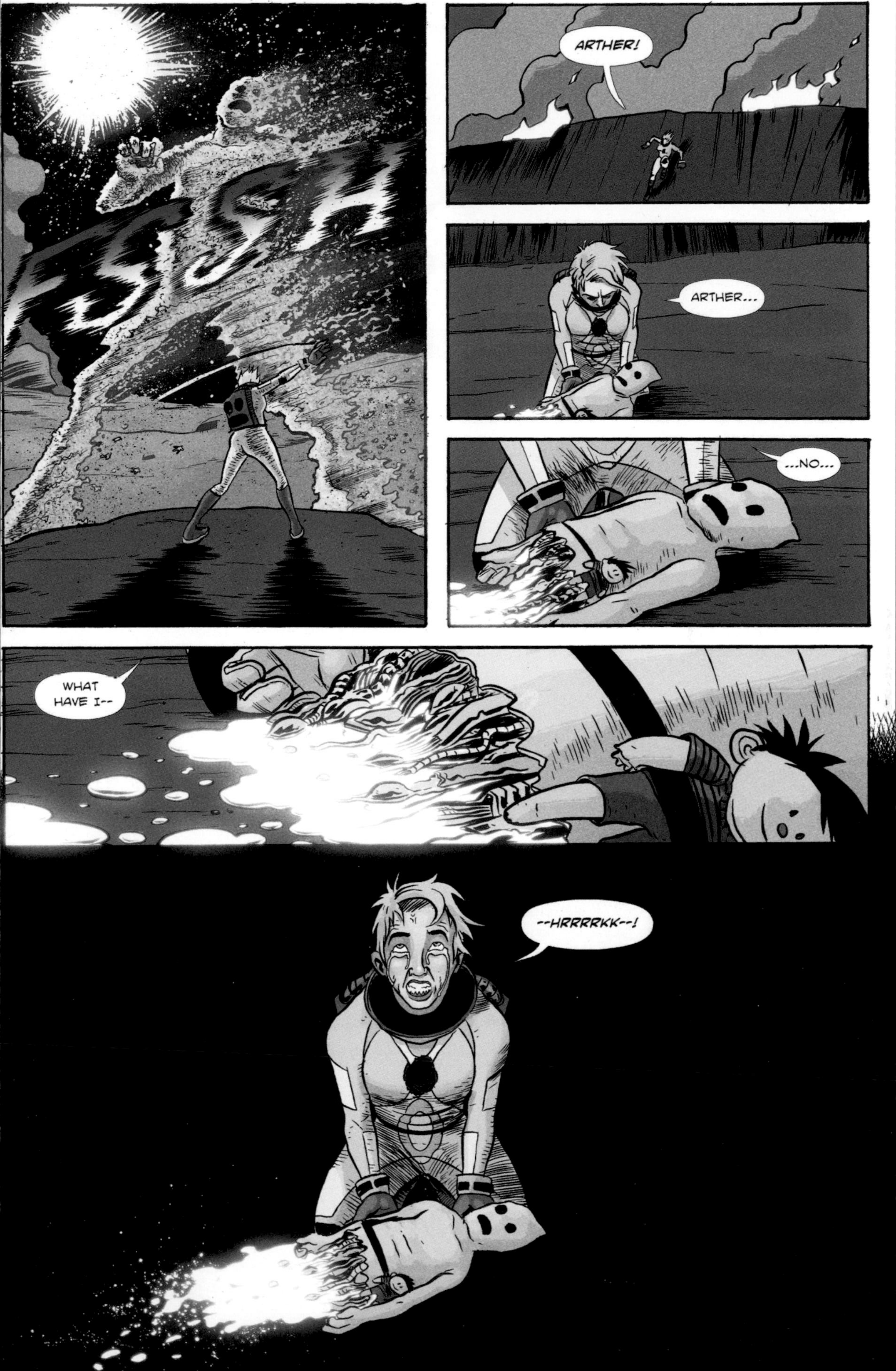
ARTHER!
ARTHER...
...NO...
WHAT HAVE I--
--HRRRRKK--!

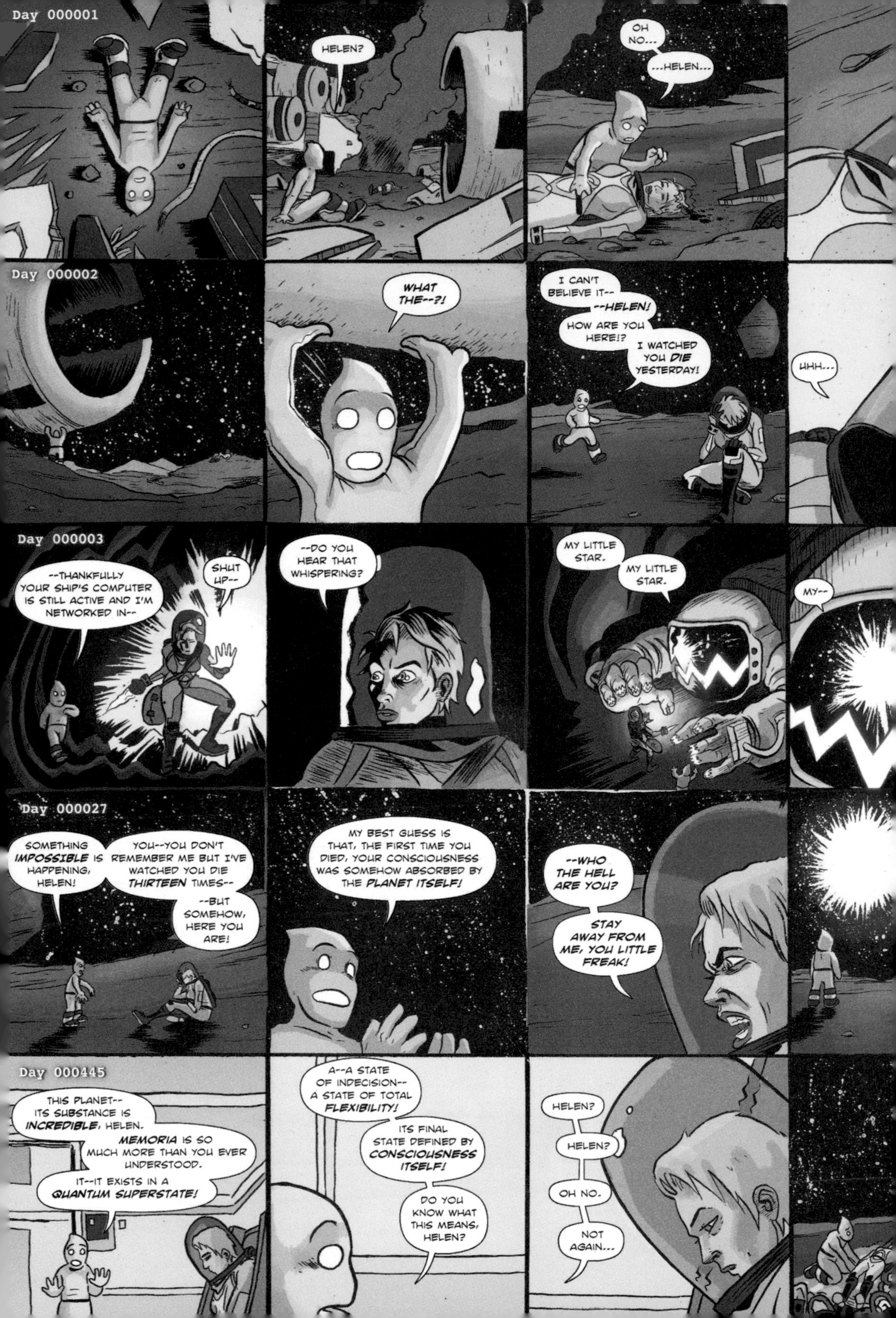
Day 000001
HELEN?
OH NO...
...HELEN...
Day 000002
WHAT THE--?!
I CAN'T BELIEVE IT--
--HELEN!
HOW ARE YOU HERE!?
I WATCHED YOU DIE YESTERDAY!
UHH...
Day 000003
--THANKFULLY YOUR SHIP'S COMPUTER IS STILL ACTIVE AND I'M NETWORKED IN--
SHUT UP--
--DO YOU HEAR THAT WHISPERING?
MY LITTLE STAR.
MY LITTLE STAR.
MY--
Day 000027
SOMETHING IMPOSSIBLE IS HAPPENING, HELEN!
YOU--YOU DON'T REMEMBER ME BUT I'VE WATCHED YOU DIE THIRTEEN TIMES--
--BUT SOMEHOW, HERE YOU ARE!
MY BEST GUESS IS THAT, THE FIRST TIME YOU DIED, YOUR CONSCIOUSNESS WAS SOMEHOW ABSORBED BY THE PLANET ITSELF!
--WHO THE HELL ARE YOU?
STAY AWAY FROM ME, YOU LITTLE FREAK!
Day 000445
THIS PLANET--ITS SUBSTANCE IS INCREDIBLE, HELEN.
MEMORIA IS SO MUCH MORE THAN YOU EVER UNDERSTOOD.
IT--IT EXISTS IN A QUANTUM SUPERSTATE!
A--A STATE OF INDECISION--A STATE OF TOTAL FLEXIBILITY!
ITS FINAL STATE DEFINED BY CONSCIOUSNESS ITSELF!
DO YOU KNOW WHAT THIS MEANS, HELEN?
HELEN?
HELEN?
OH NO.
NOT AGAIN...

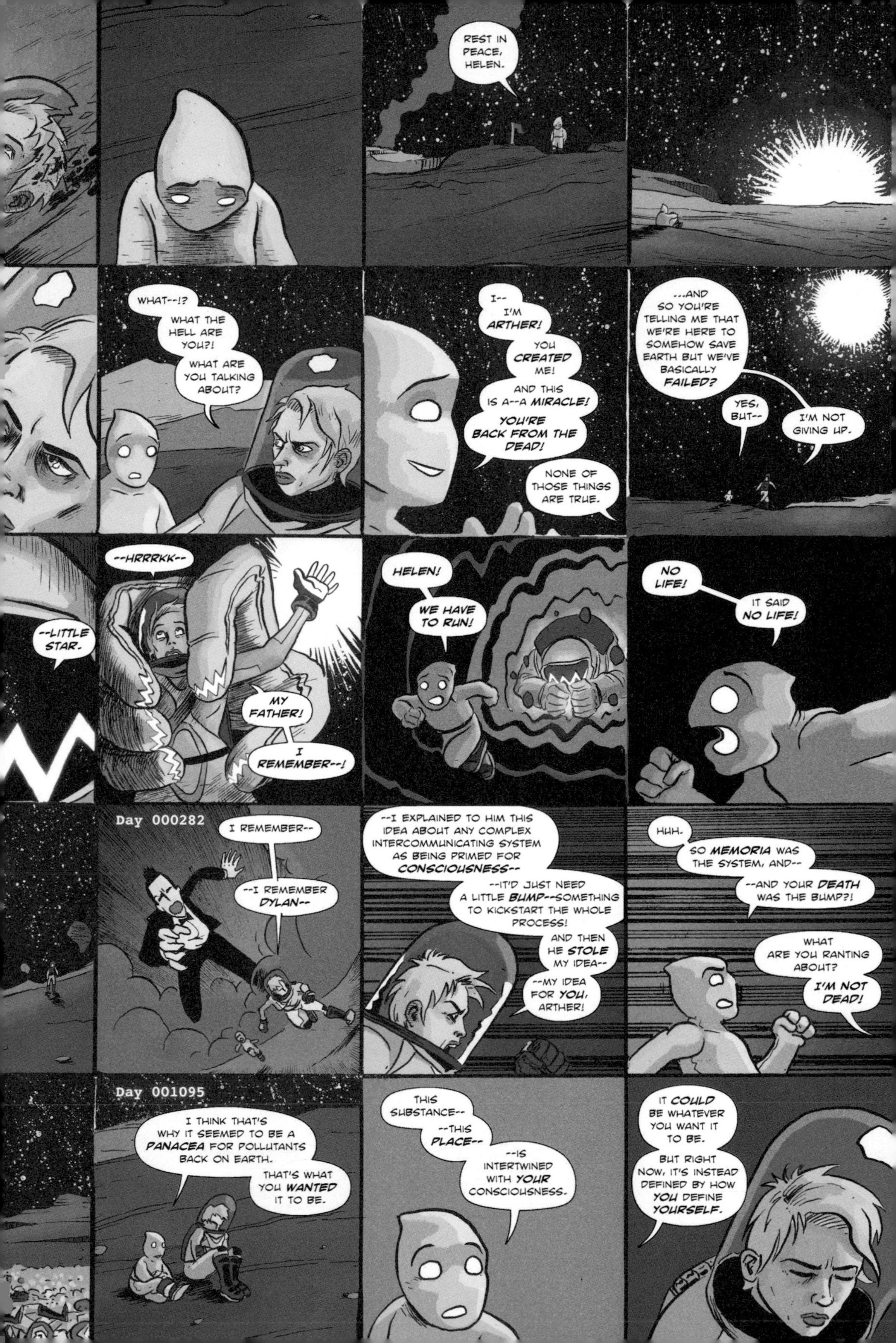
REST IN PEACE, HELEN.
WHAT--!?
WHAT THE HELL ARE YOU?!
WHAT ARE YOU TALKING ABOUT?
I--
I'M ARTHER!
YOU CREATED ME!
AND THIS IS A--A MIRACLE!
YOU'RE BACK FROM THE DEAD!
NONE OF THOSE THINGS ARE TRUE.
...AND SO YOU'RE TELLING ME THAT WE'RE HERE TO SOMEHOW SAVE EARTH BUT WE'VE BASICALLY FAILED?
YES, BUT--
I'M NOT GIVING UP.
--LITTLE STAR.
--HRRRKK--
MY FATHER!
I REMEMBER--!
HELEN!
WE HAVE TO RUN!
NO LIFE!
IT SAID NO LIFE!
Day 000282
I REMEMBER--
--I REMEMBER DYLAN--
--I EXPLAINED TO HIM THIS IDEA ABOUT ANY COMPLEX INTERCOMMUNICATING SYSTEM AS BEING PRIMED FOR CONSCIOUSNESS--
--IT'D JUST NEED A LITTLE BUMP--SOMETHING TO KICKSTART THE WHOLE PROCESS!
AND THEN HE STOLE MY IDEA--
--MY IDEA FOR YOU, ARTHER!
HUH.
SO MEMORIA WAS THE SYSTEM, AND--
--AND YOUR DEATH WAS THE BUMP?!
WHAT ARE YOU RANTING ABOUT?
I'M NOT DEAD!
Day 001095
I THINK THAT'S WHY IT SEEMED TO BE A PANACEA FOR POLLUTANTS BACK ON EARTH.
THAT'S WHAT YOU WANTED IT TO BE.
THIS SUBSTANCE--
--THIS PLACE--
--IS INTERTWINED WITH YOUR CONSCIOUSNESS.
IT COULD BE WHATEVER YOU WANT IT TO BE.
BUT RIGHT NOW, IT'S INSTEAD DEFINED BY HOW YOU DEFINE YOURSELF.

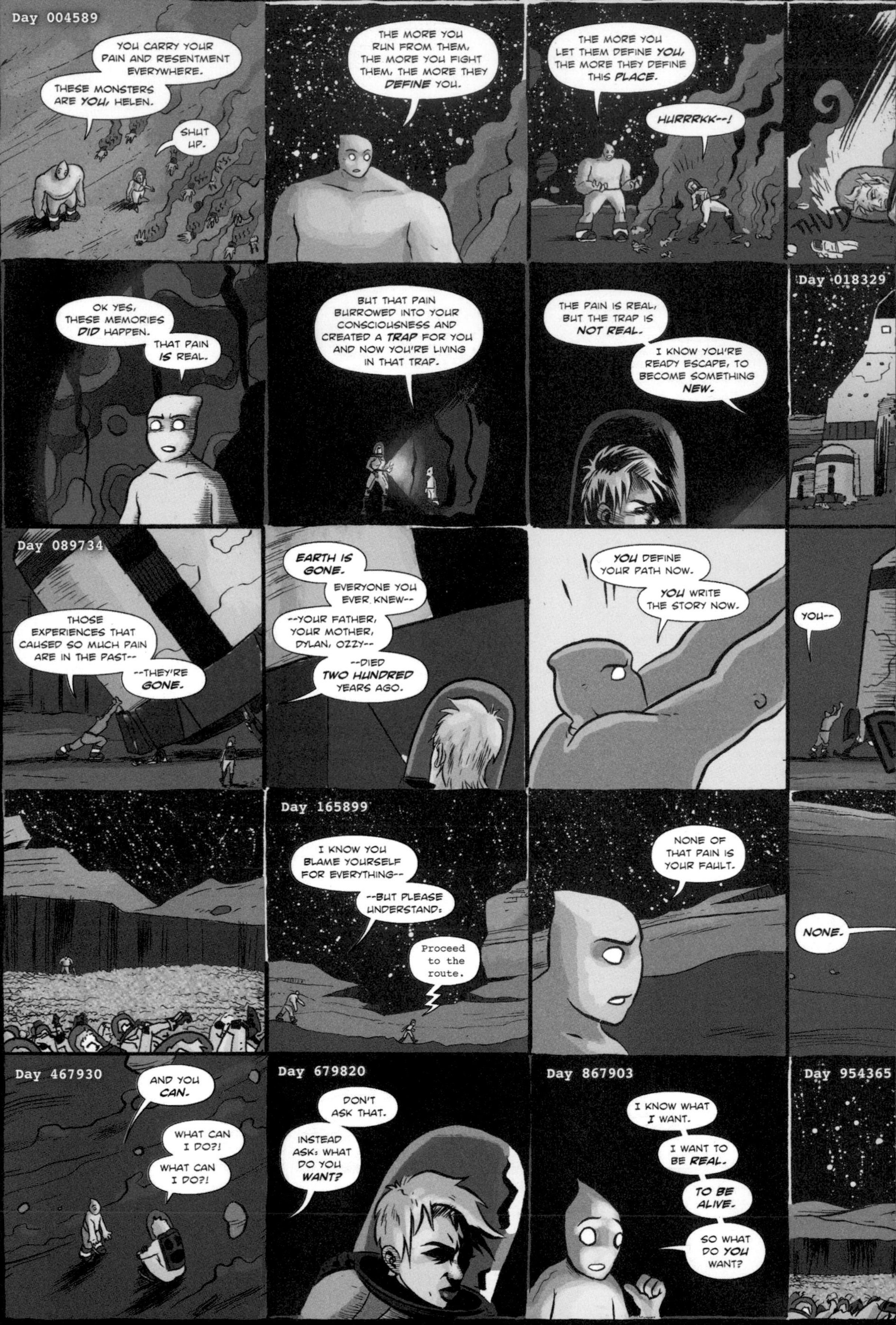
Day 004589
YOU CARRY YOUR PAIN AND RESENTMENT EVERYWHERE.
THESE MONSTERS ARE YOU, HELEN.
SHUT UP.
THE MORE YOU RUN FROM THEM, THE MORE YOU FIGHT THEM, THE MORE THEY DEFINE YOU.
THE MORE YOU LET THEM DEFINE YOU, THE MORE THEY DEFINE THIS PLACE.
HURRRKK--!
THUD
OK YES, THESE MEMORIES DID HAPPEN.
THAT PAIN IS REAL.
BUT THAT PAIN BURROWED INTO YOUR CONSCIOUSNESS AND CREATED A TRAP FOR YOU AND NOW YOU'RE LIVING IN THAT TRAP.
THE PAIN IS REAL, BUT THE TRAP IS NOT REAL.
I KNOW YOU'RE READY ESCAPE, TO BECOME SOMETHING NEW.
Day 018329
Day 089734
THOSE EXPERIENCES THAT CAUSED SO MUCH PAIN ARE IN THE PAST--
--THEY'RE GONE.
EARTH IS GONE.
EVERYONE YOU EVER KNEW--
--YOUR FATHER, YOUR MOTHER, DYLAN, OZZY--
--DIED TWO HUNDRED YEARS AGO.
YOU DEFINE YOUR PATH NOW.
YOU WRITE THE STORY NOW.
YOU--
Day 165899
I KNOW YOU BLAME YOURSELF FOR EVERYTHING--
--BUT PLEASE UNDERSTAND:
Proceed to the route.
NONE OF THAT PAIN IS YOUR FAULT.
NONE.
Day 467930
AND YOU CAN.
WHAT CAN I DO?!
WHAT CAN I DO?!
Day 679820
DON'T ASK THAT.
INSTEAD ASK: WHAT DO YOU WANT?
Day 867903
I KNOW WHAT I WANT.
I WANT TO BE REAL.
TO BE ALIVE.
SO WHAT DO YOU WANT?
Day 954365

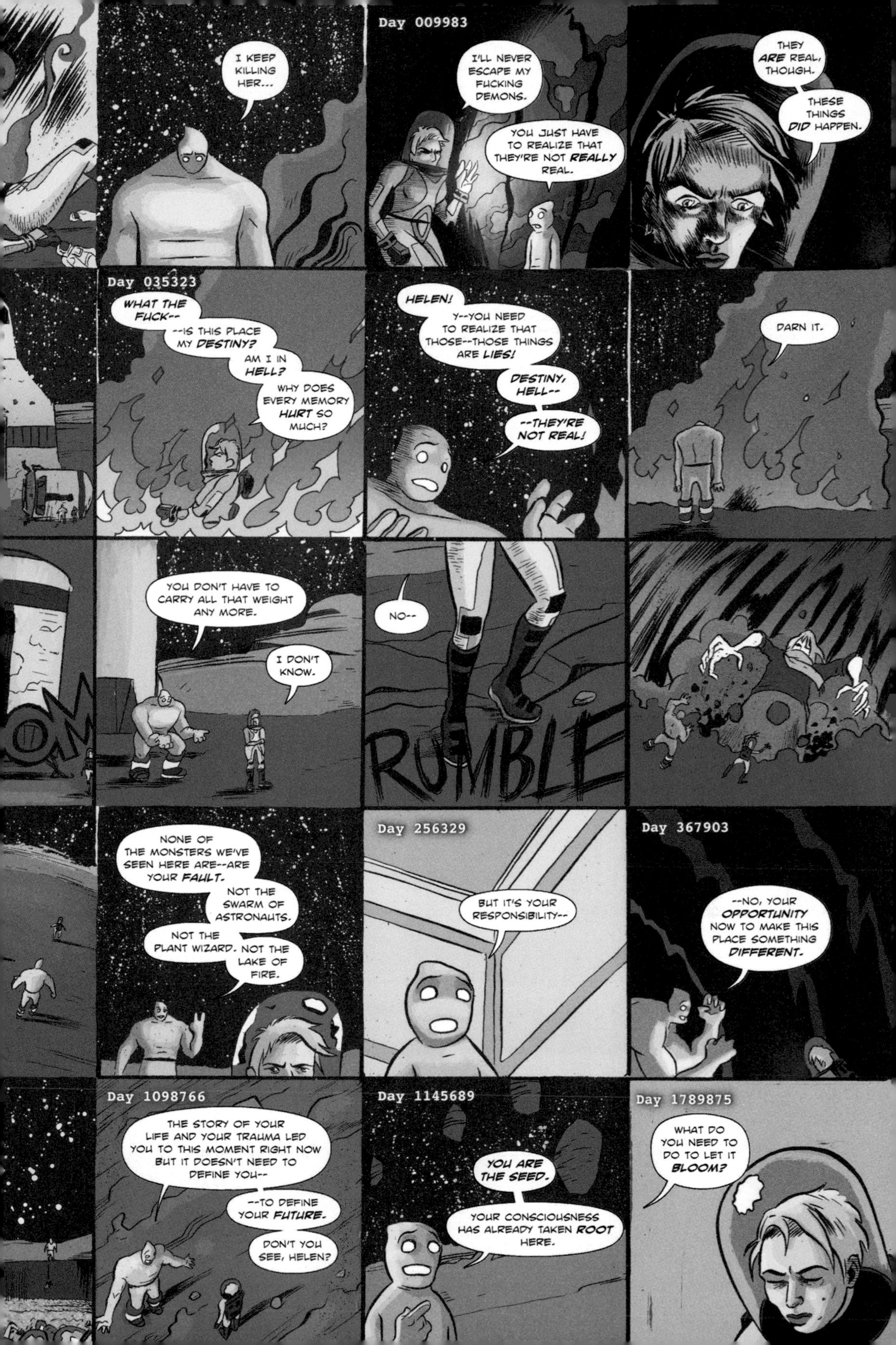

I KEEP KILLING HER...
Day 009983
I'LL NEVER ESCAPE MY FUCKING DEMONS.
YOU JUST HAVE TO REALIZE THAT THEY'RE NOT REALLY REAL.
THEY ARE REAL, THOUGH.
THESE THINGS DID HAPPEN.
Day 035323
WHAT THE FUCK--
--IS THIS PLACE MY DESTINY?
AM I IN HELL?
WHY DOES EVERY MEMORY HURT SO MUCH?
HELEN!
Y--YOU NEED TO REALIZE THAT THOSE--THOSE THINGS ARE LIES!
DESTINY, HELL--
--THEY'RE NOT REAL!
DARN IT.
YOU DON'T HAVE TO CARRY ALL THAT WEIGHT ANY MORE.
I DON'T KNOW.
NO--
RUMBLE
NONE OF THE MONSTERS WE'VE SEEN HERE ARE--ARE YOUR FAULT.
NOT THE SWARM OF ASTRONAUTS.
NOT THE PLANT WIZARD. NOT THE LAKE OF FIRE.
Day 256329
BUT IT'S YOUR RESPONSIBILITY--
Day 367903
--NO, YOUR OPPORTUNITY NOW TO MAKE THIS PLACE SOMETHING DIFFERENT.
Day 1098766
THE STORY OF YOUR LIFE AND YOUR TRAUMA LED YOU TO THIS MOMENT RIGHT NOW BUT IT DOESN'T NEED TO DEFINE YOU--
--TO DEFINE YOUR FUTURE.
DON'T YOU SEE, HELEN?
Day 1145689
YOU ARE THE SEED.
YOUR CONSCIOUSNESS HAS ALREADY TAKEN ROOT HERE.
Day 1789875
WHAT DO YOU NEED TO DO TO LET IT BLOOM?

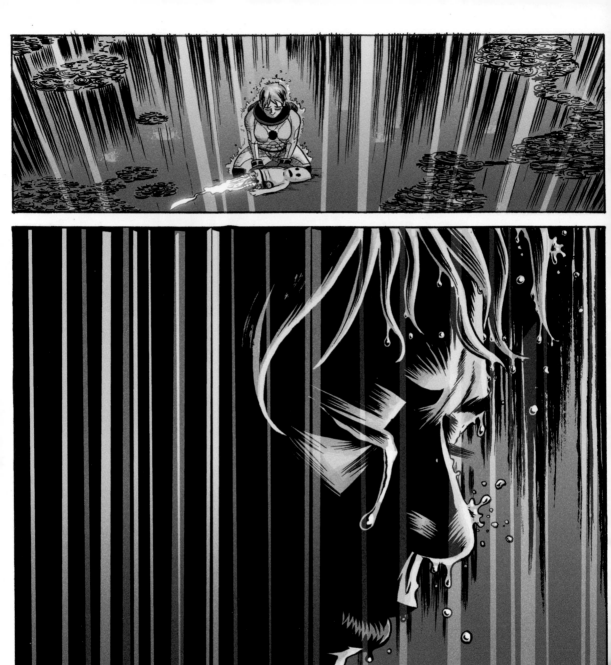

I HAVE SOMETHING FOR YOU.

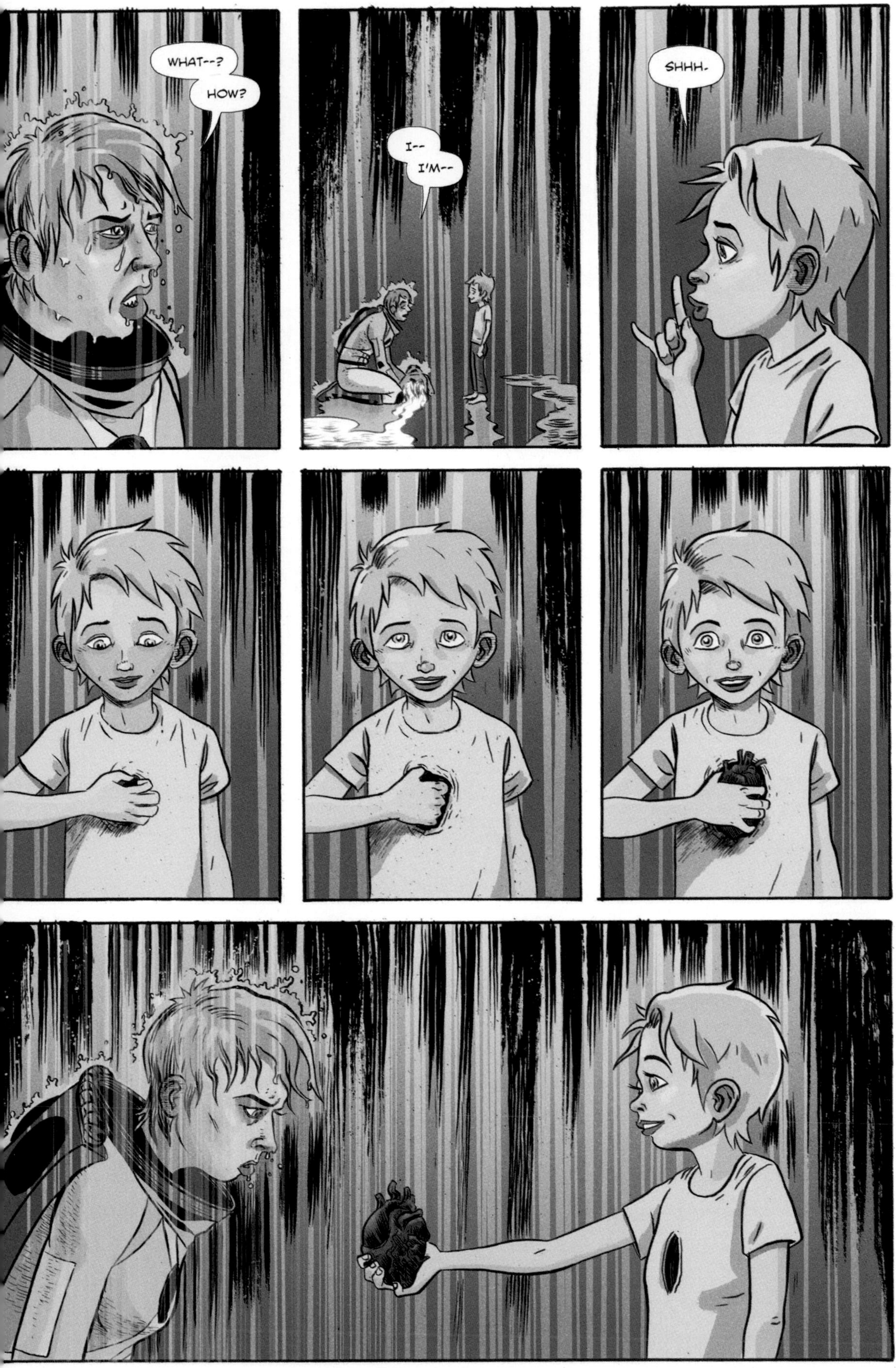
WHAT--?
HOW?
I--
I'M--
SHHH.

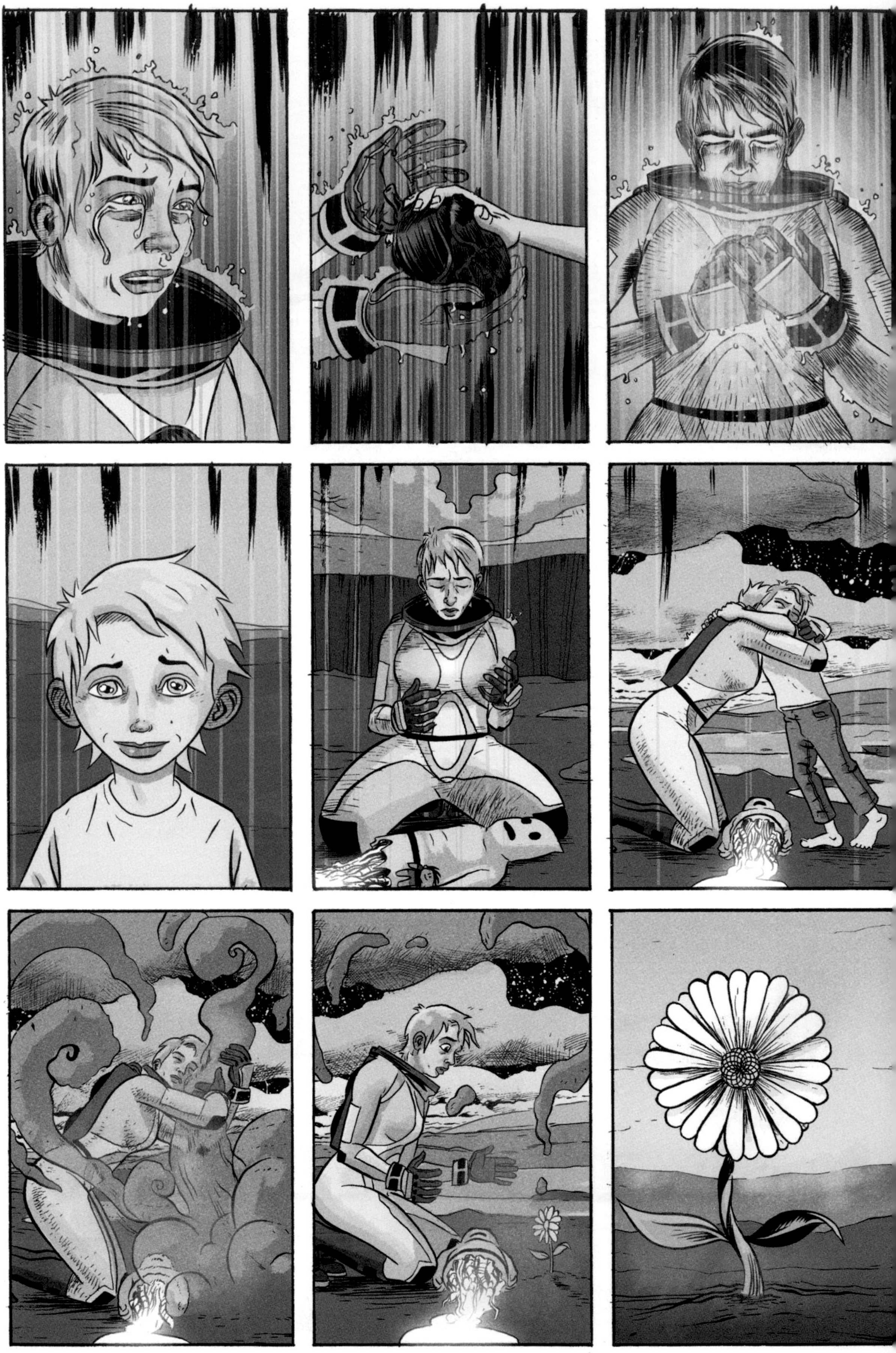

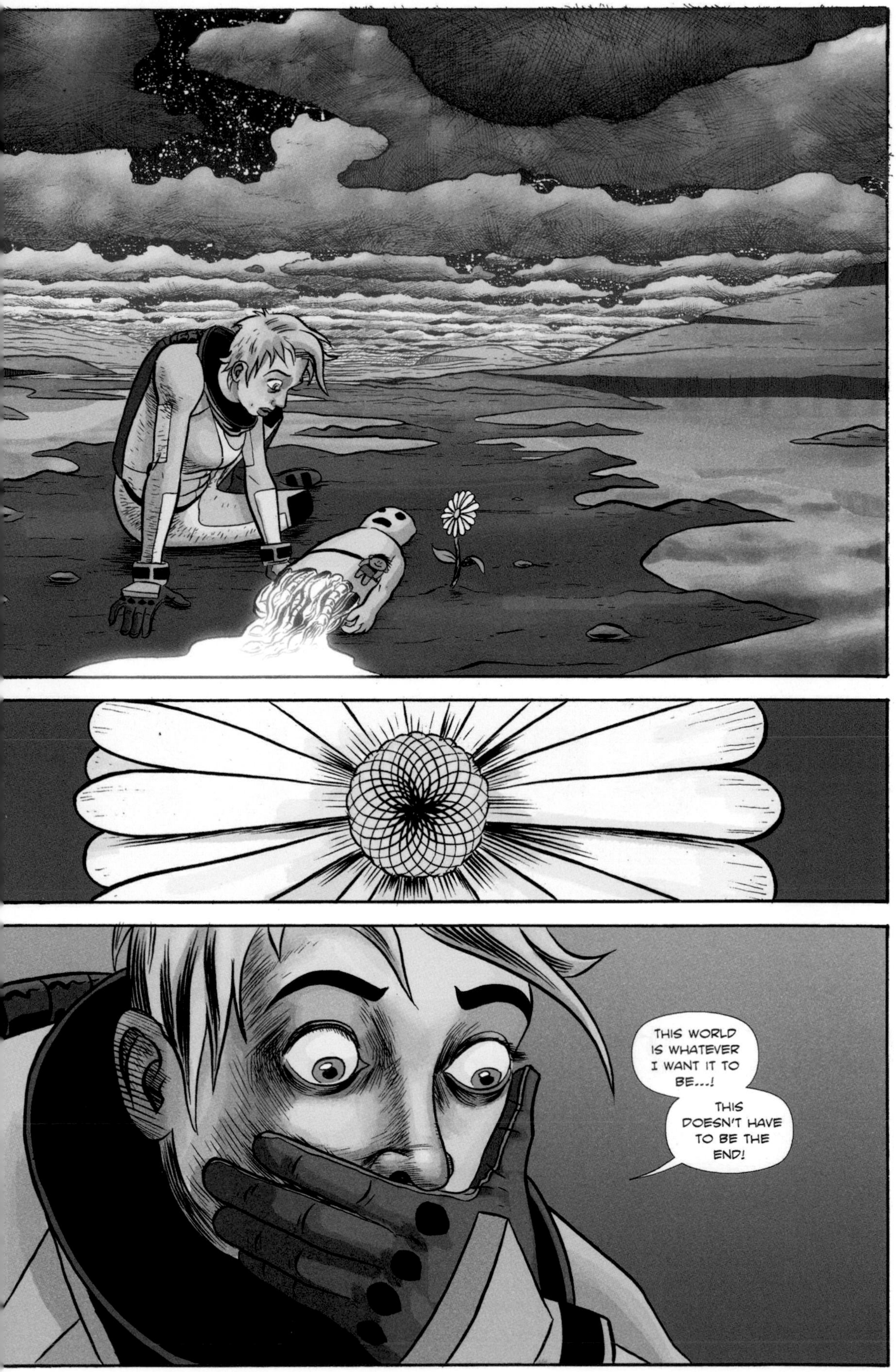
THIS WORLD IS WHATEVER I WANT IT TO BE...!
THIS DOESN'T HAVE TO BE THE END!

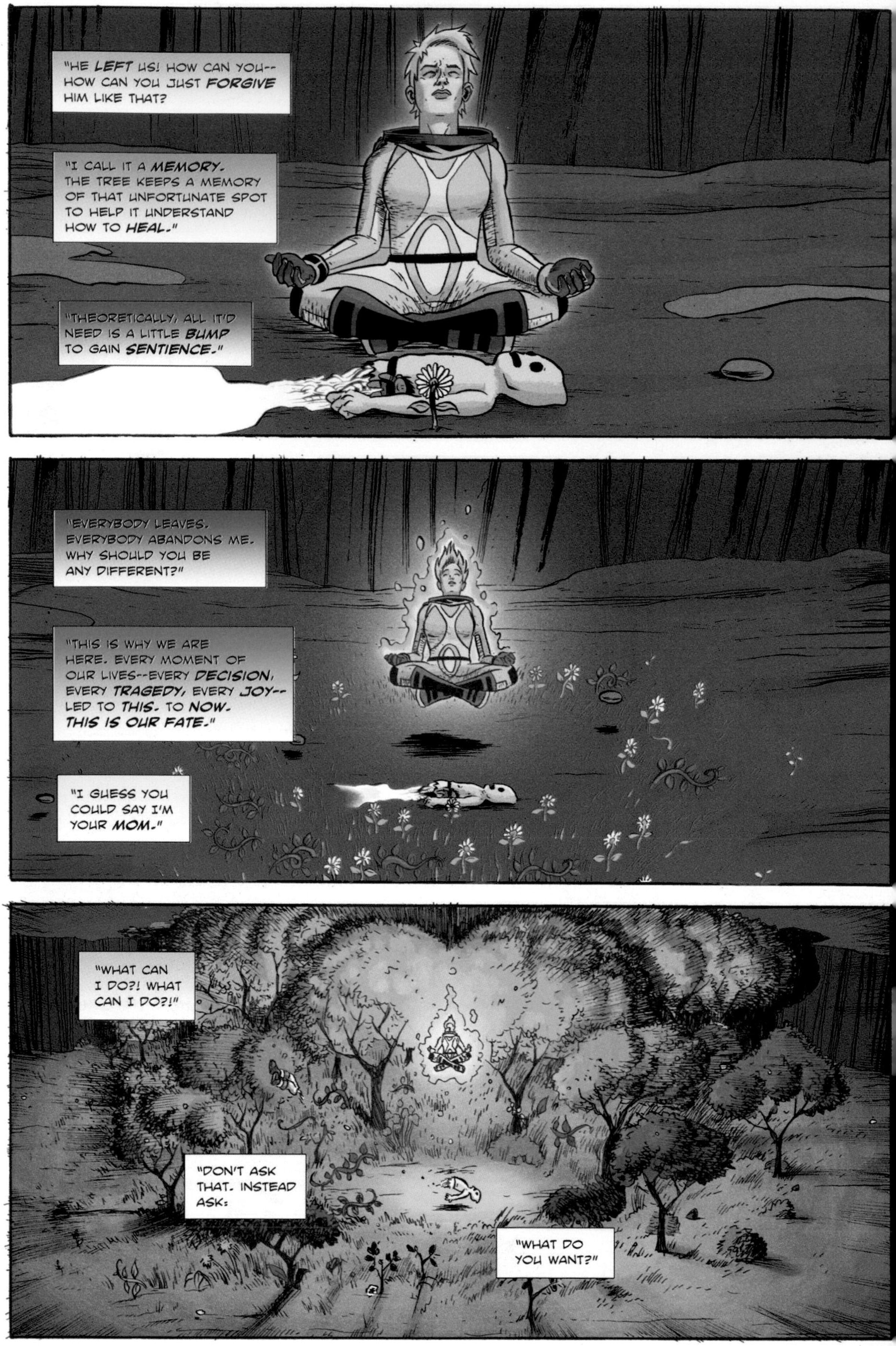
"HE LEFT US! HOW CAN YOU--HOW CAN YOU JUST FORGIVE HIM LIKE THAT?
"I CALL IT A MEMORY. THE TREE KEEPS A MEMORY OF THAT UNFORTUNATE SPOT TO HELP IT UNDERSTAND HOW TO HEAL."
"THEORETICALLY, ALL IT'D NEED IS A LITTLE BUMP TO GAIN SENTIENCE."
"EVERYBODY LEAVES. EVERYBODY ABANDONS ME. WHY SHOULD YOU BE ANY DIFFERENT?"
"THIS IS WHY WE ARE HERE. EVERY MOMENT OF OUR LIVES--EVERY DECISION, EVERY TRAGEDY, EVERY JOY--LED TO THIS. TO NOW. THIS IS OUR FATE."
"I GUESS YOU COULD SAY I'M YOUR MOM."
"WHAT CAN I DO?! WHAT CAN I DO?!"
"DON'T ASK THAT. INSTEAD ASK:
"WHAT DO YOU WANT?"

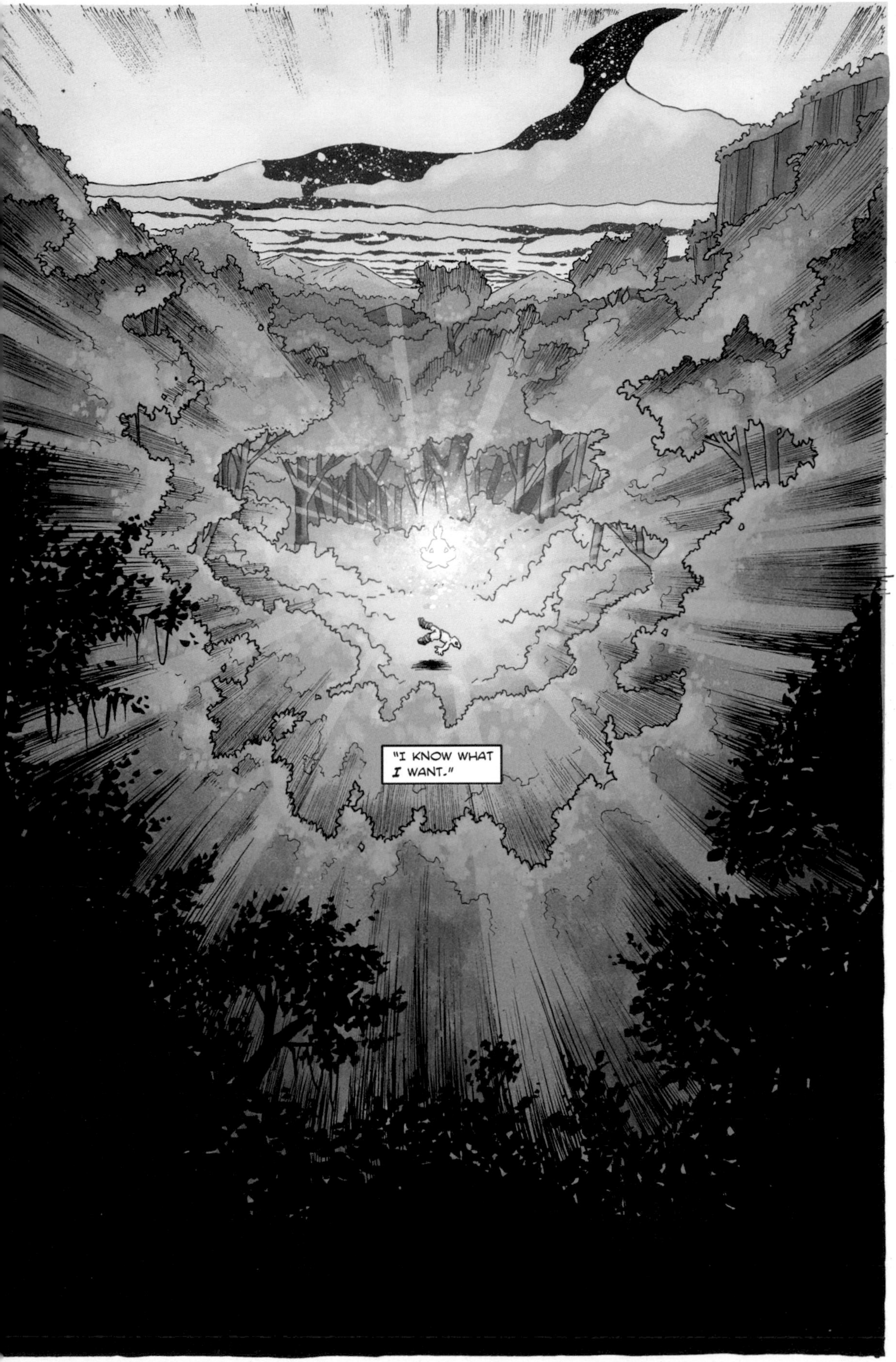
"I KNOW WHAT I WANT."

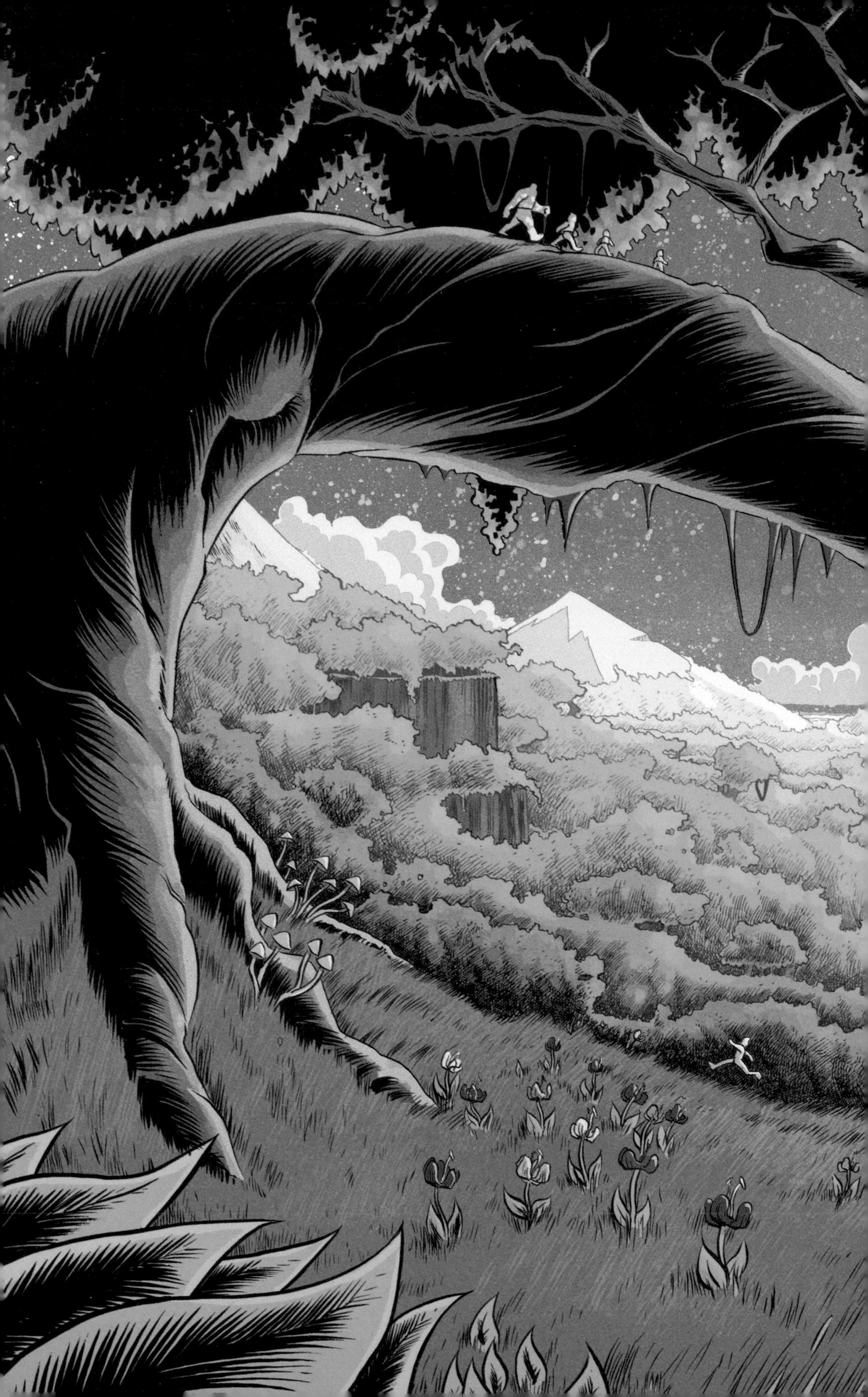

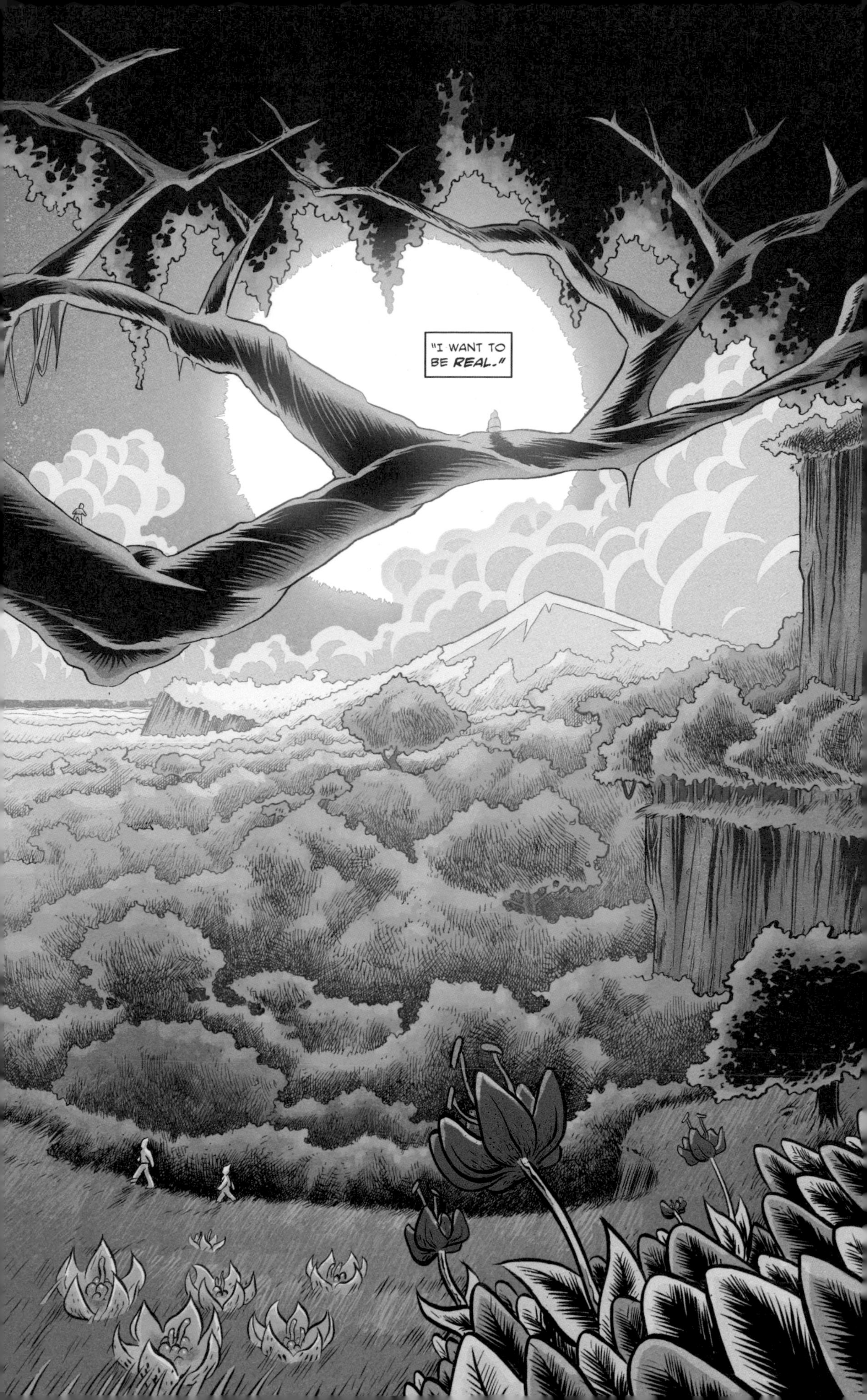
"I WANT TO
BE REAL."

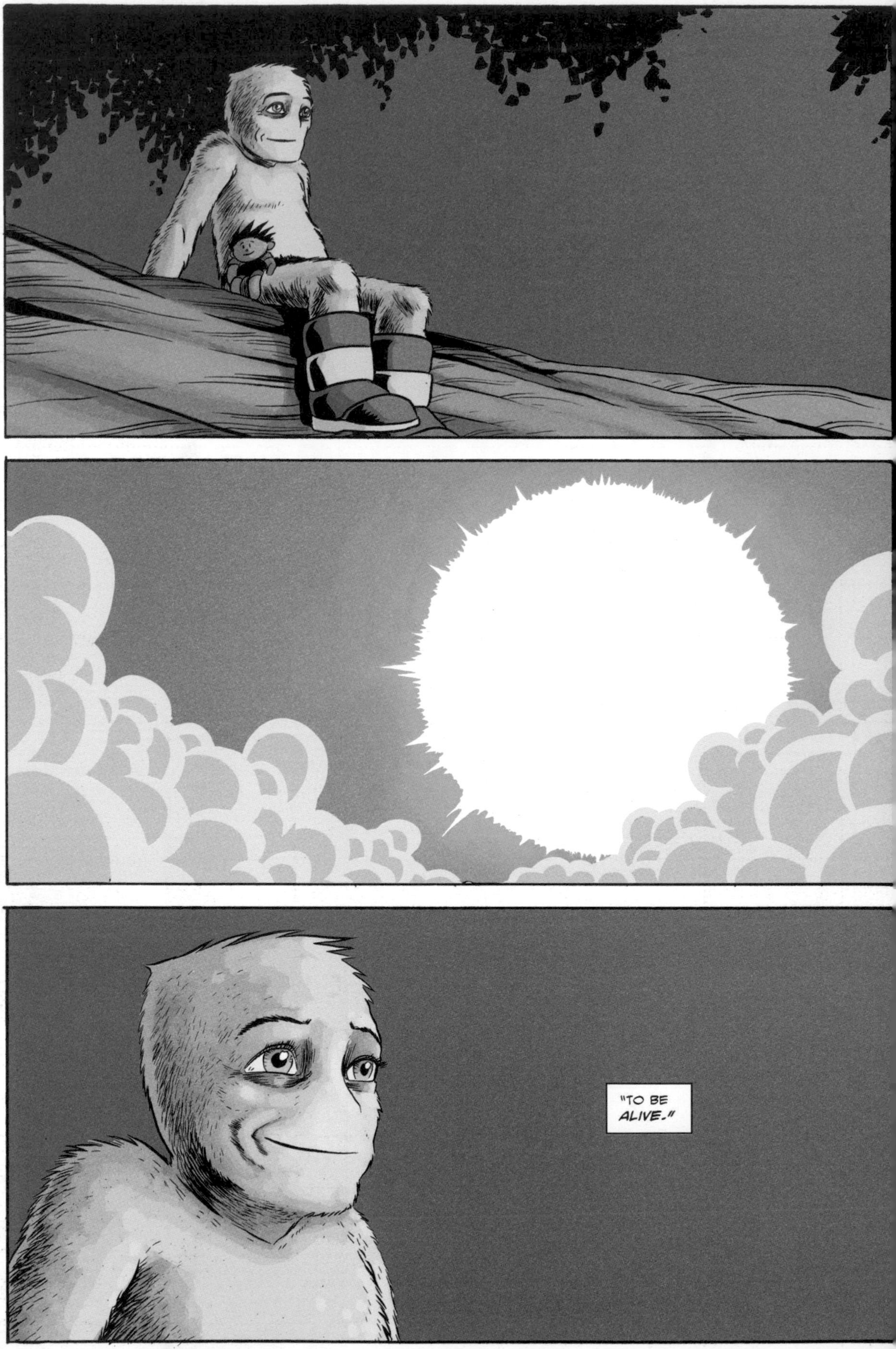
"TO BE ALIVE."

BONUS CONTENT

ISSUE ONE VARIANT COVERS

CANOPUS

CANOPUS
DAVE CHISHOLM

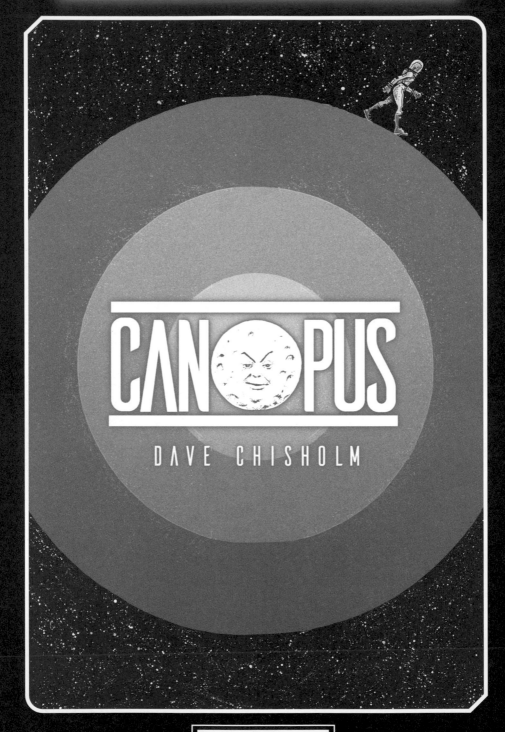

"PLANET"

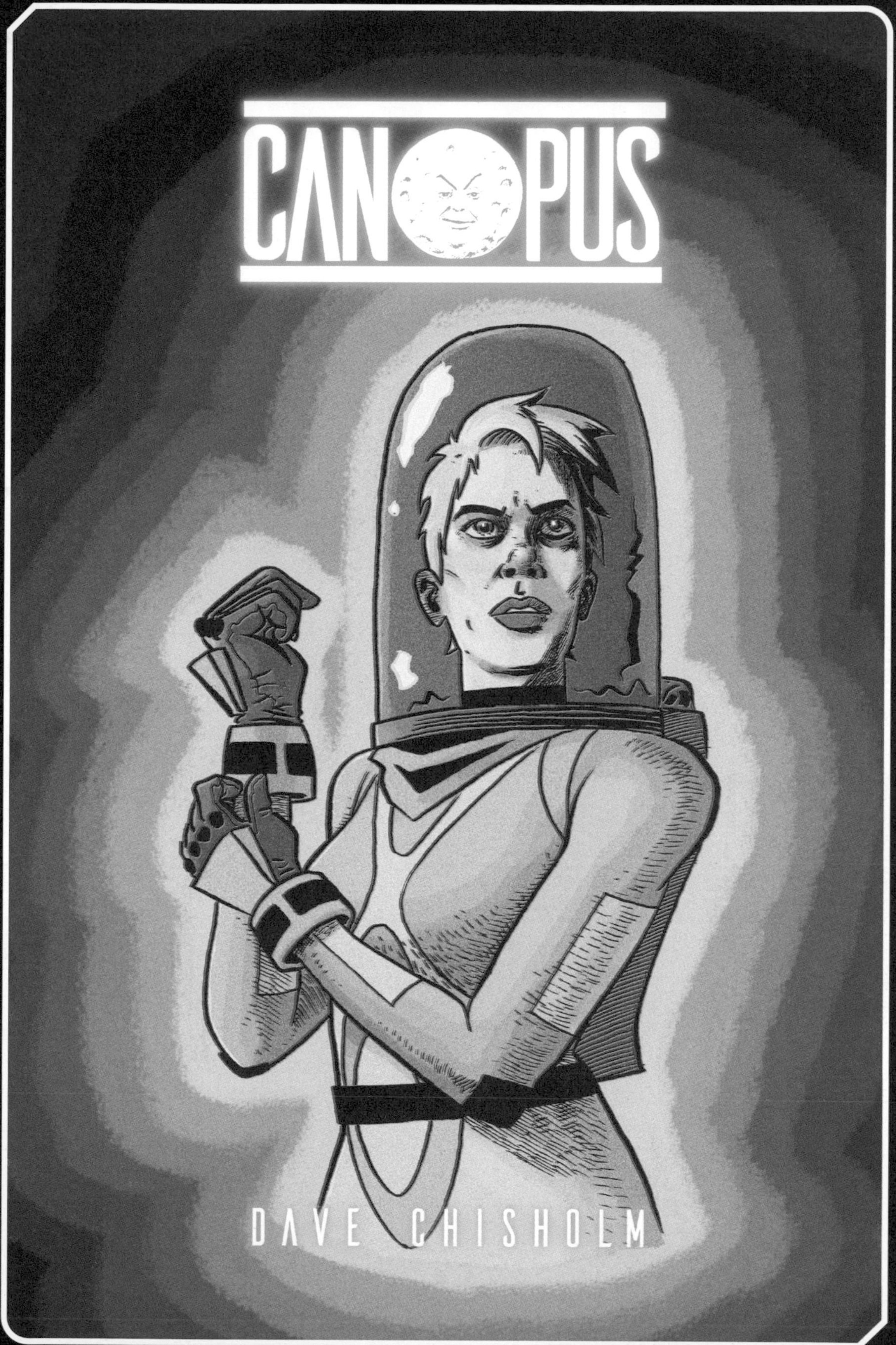
CANOPUS
DAVE CHISHOLM

"HELEN"

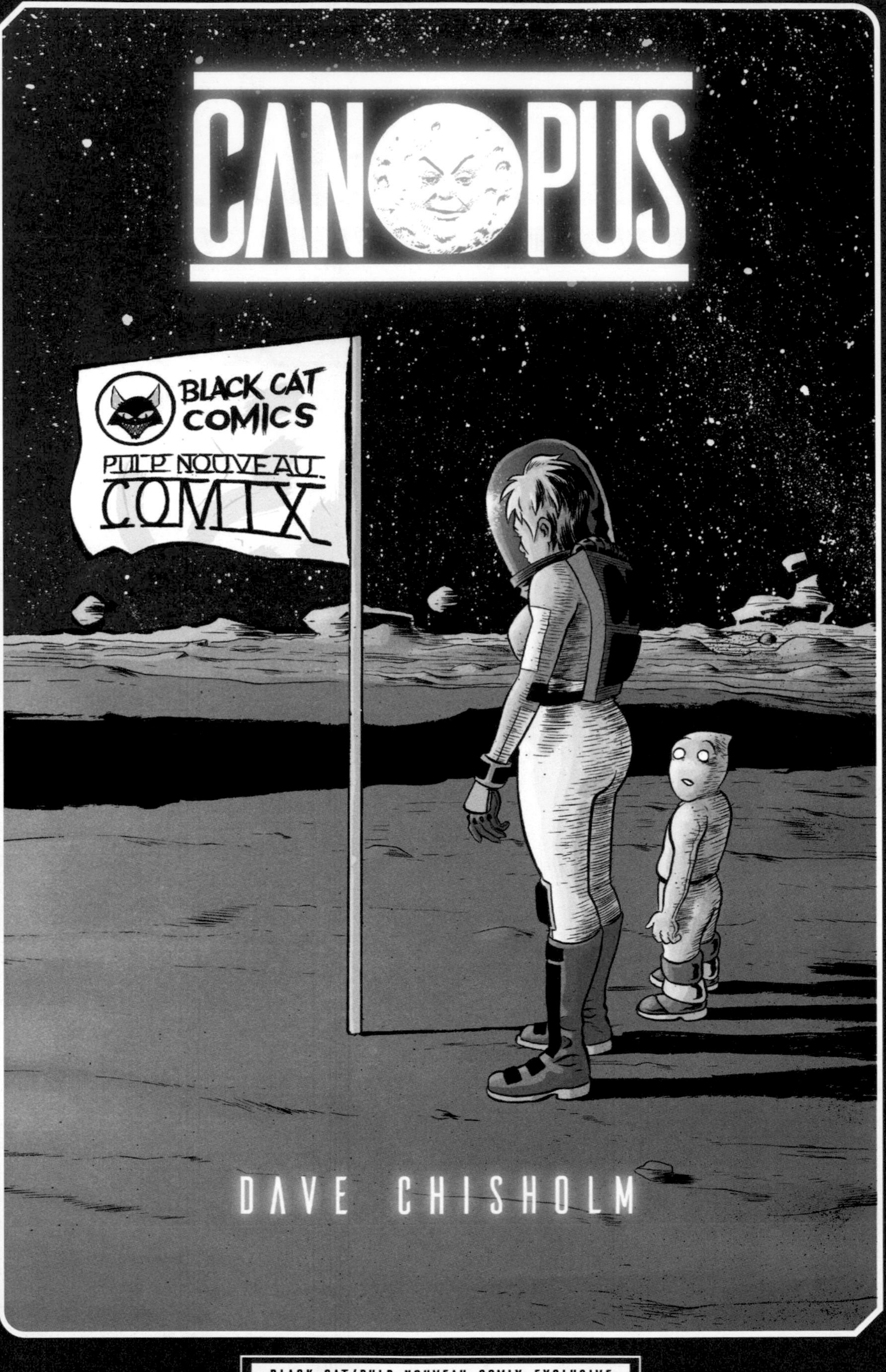
CANOPUS
BLACK CAT COMICS
PULP NOUVEAU COMIX
DAVE CHISHOLM

BLACK CAT/PULP NOUVEAU COMIX EXCLUSIVE

ALTERNATIVE COVERS

CANOPUS

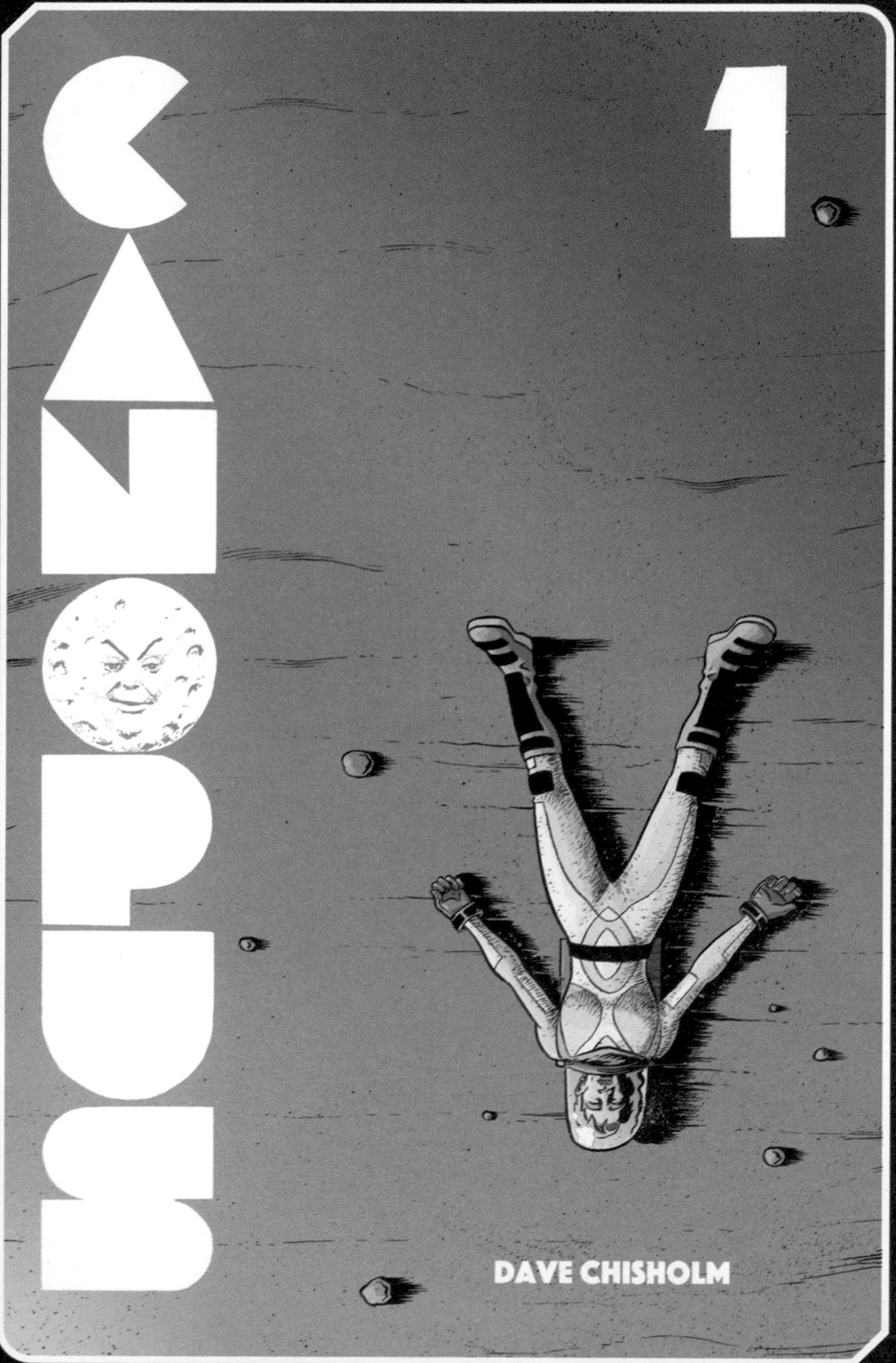
CANOPUS
1
DAVE CHISHOLM

ISSUE 1

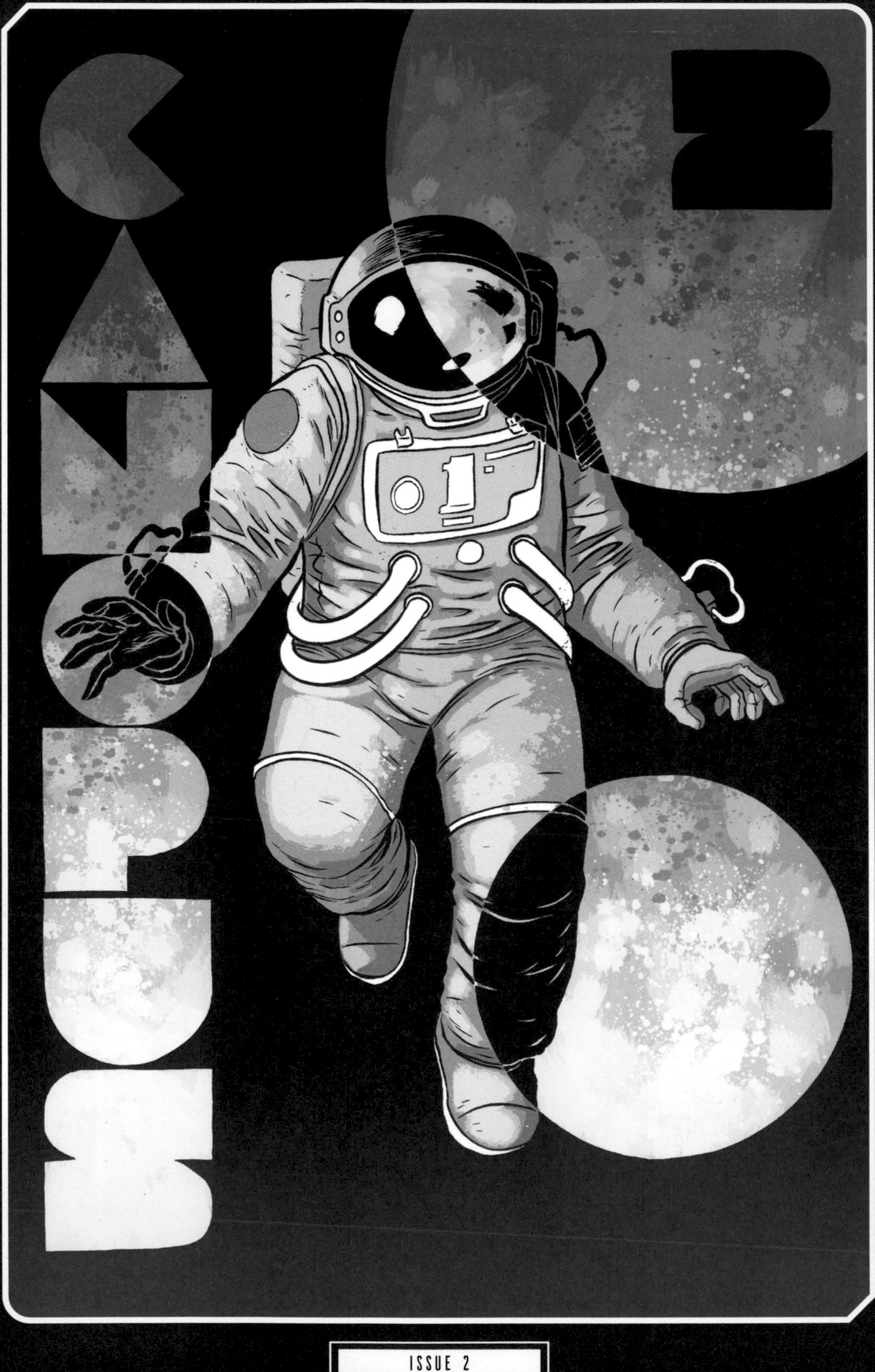
CANOPUS
2

ISSUE 2

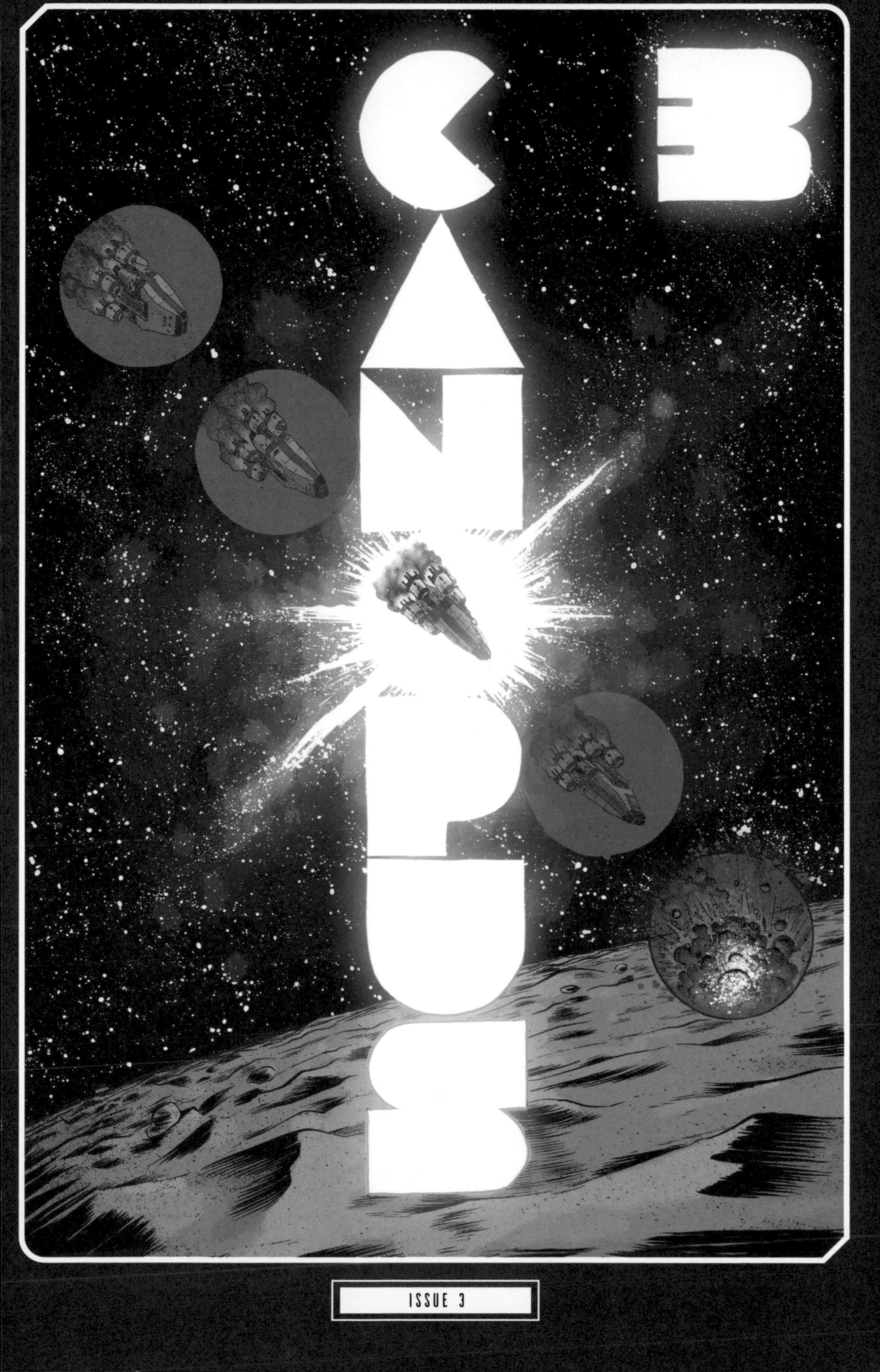

ISSUE 3

These three pages are the original version of the material after page one.

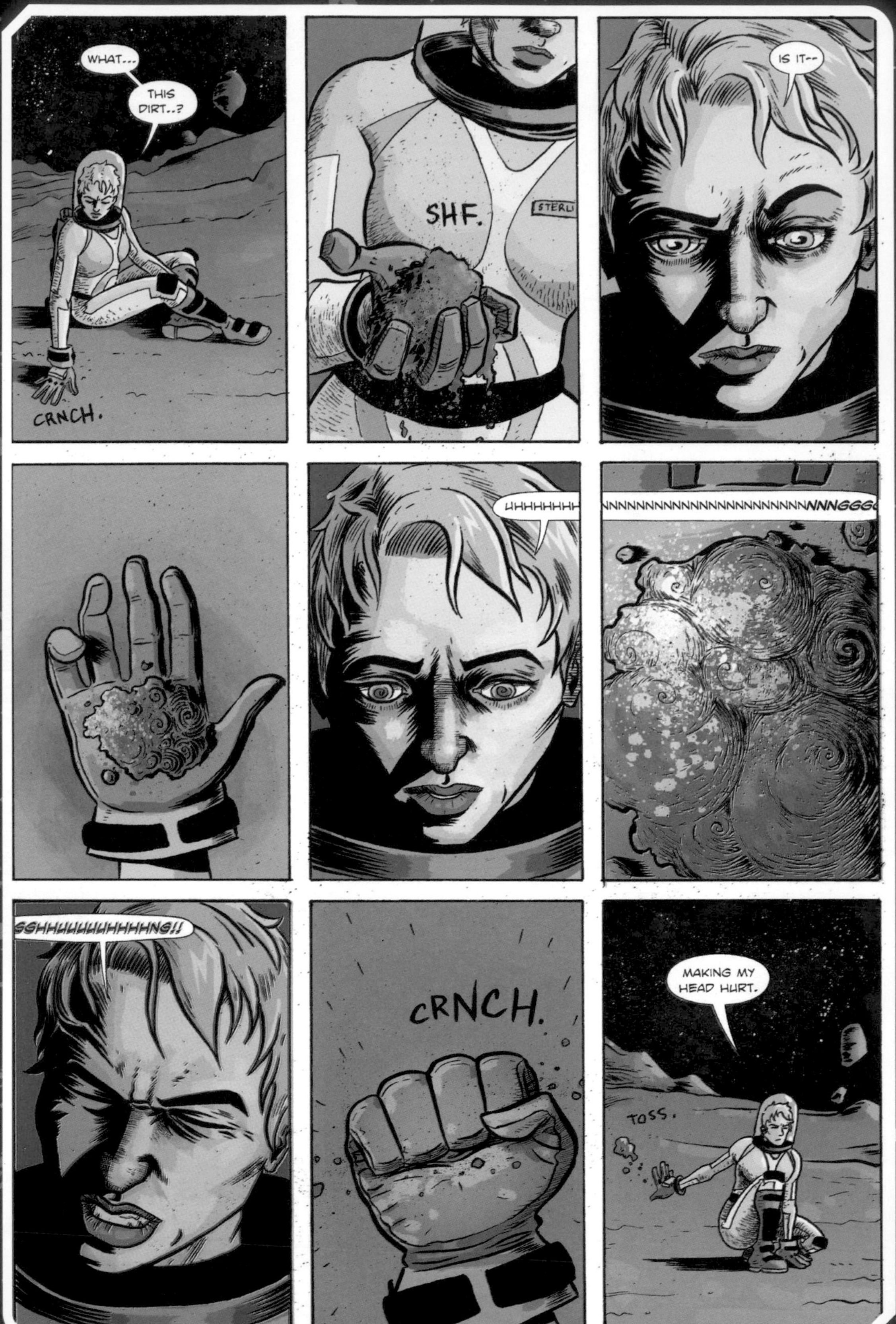
WHAT...
THIS DIRT..?
CRNCH.
SHF.
IS IT--
UHHHHHHH
NNNNNNNNNNNNNNNNNNNNNNNNNGGG
GGHHUUUUUHHHHNG!!
CRNCH.
MAKING MY HEAD HURT.
TOSS.

Not only did it make the first issue an awkward 30 pages, but it decompressed the opening a little too much, so I edited these three pages down to one single page in the published version.

While I do love planting the Memoria mystery early, editing it out was the right choice.

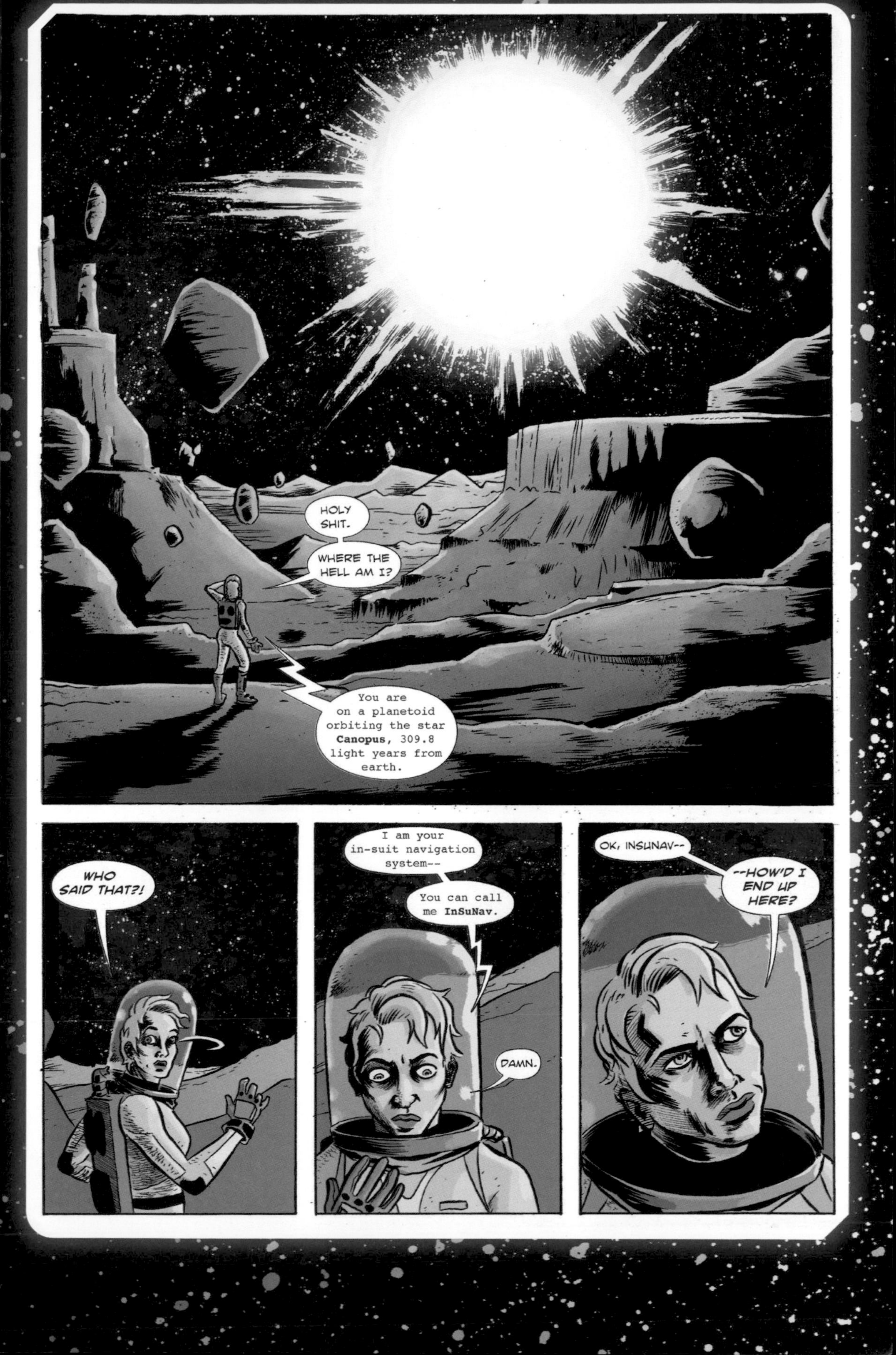
HOLY SHIT.
WHERE THE HELL AM I?
You are on a planetoid orbiting the star **Canopus**, 309.8 light years from earth.
WHO SAID THAT?!
I am your in-suit navigation system--
You can call me **InSuNav.**
DAMN.
OK, INSUNAV--
--HOW'D I END UP HERE?

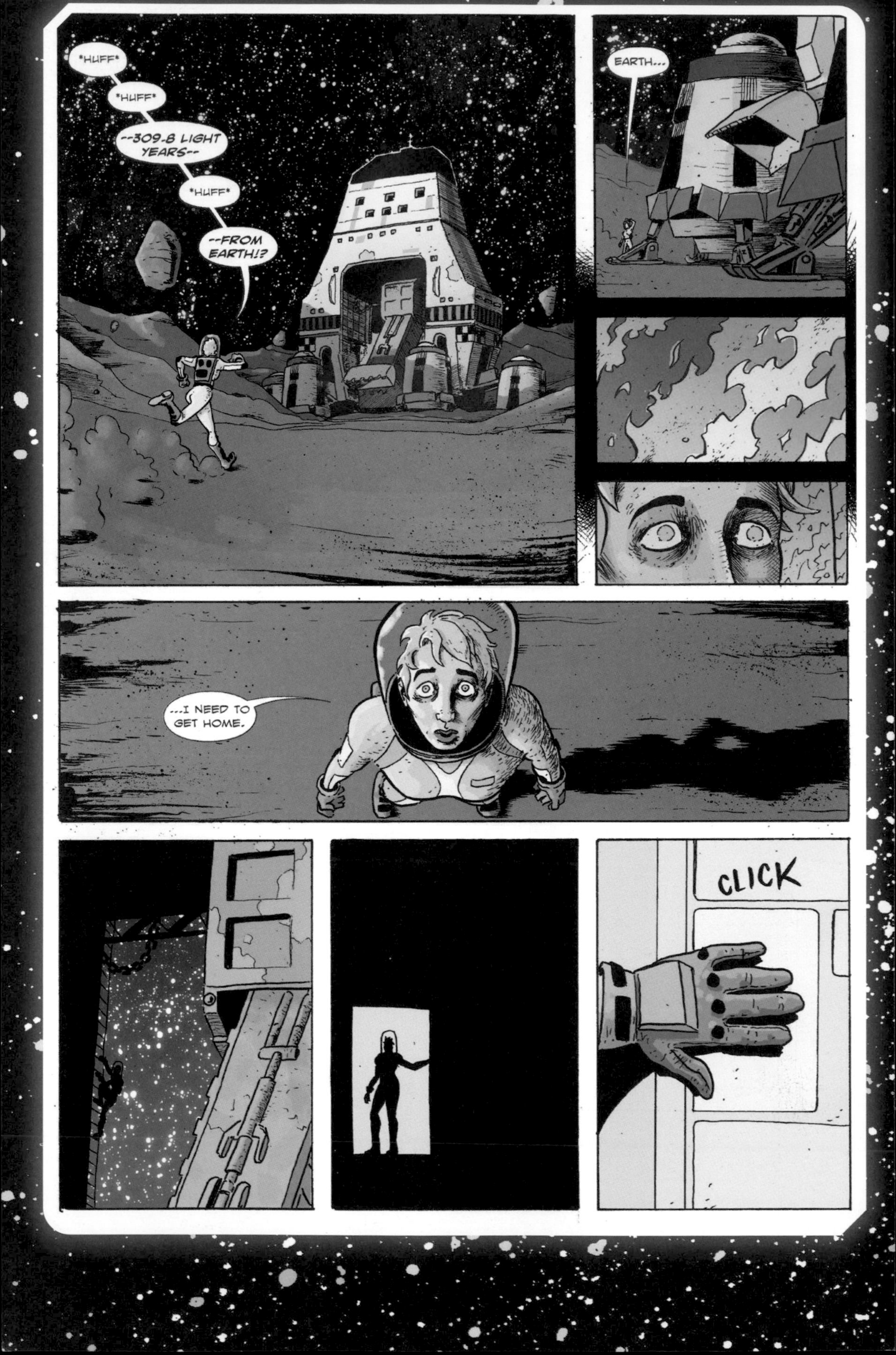
HUFF
HUFF
--309.8 LIGHT YEARS--
HUFF
--FROM EARTH!?
EARTH...
...I NEED TO GET HOME.
CLICK

HELEN PIN-UP
FOR
SCOUT JAM

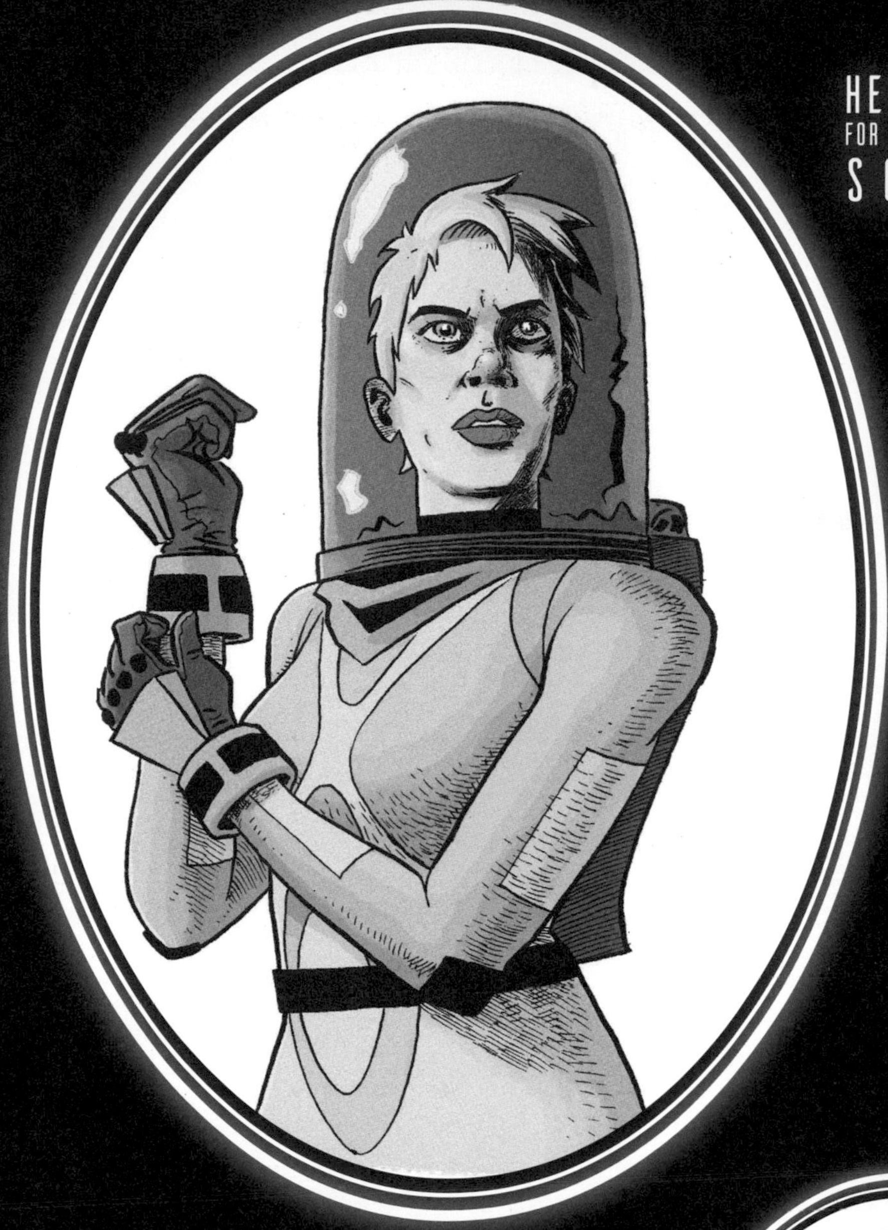

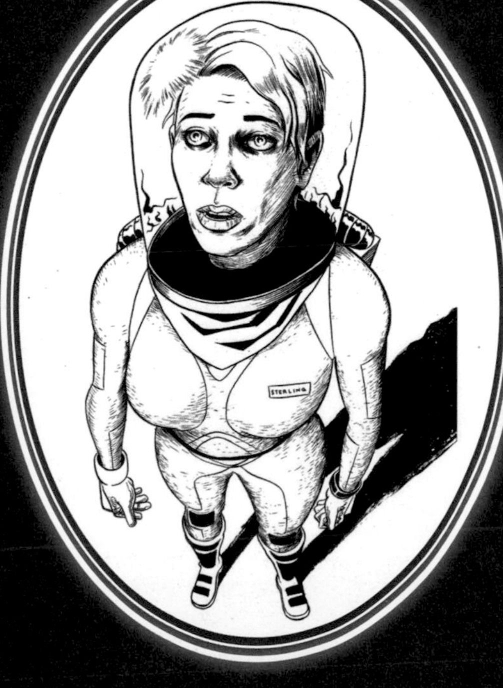
STERLING

HELEN PIN-UP
INSPIRED BY
KATIE WOLSKI
HELEN COSPLAY

FLASHBACK SPREADS PROCESS

THE FLASHBACK SEQUENCES PROVIDE A STARK
CONTRAST WITH THE STORY PROPER, AND WITH THEM
I INTENDED TO MIMIC THE NONLINEAR WAY HUMAN
MEMORY TENDS TO OPERATE. I WANTED THE
EXPERIENCE TO
FEEL AS
OVERWHELMING TO
READERS AS IT IS
FOR HELEN.
SINCE ARTHER IS
NOT HUMAN, HIS
FLASHBACK IN
CHAPTER FOUR
[BOTTOM RIGHT],
IS ORGANIZED
ON AN EVEN,
IMPARTIAL GRID.

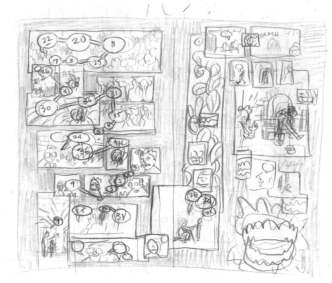

PIN-UP: HEROES.CON 2019

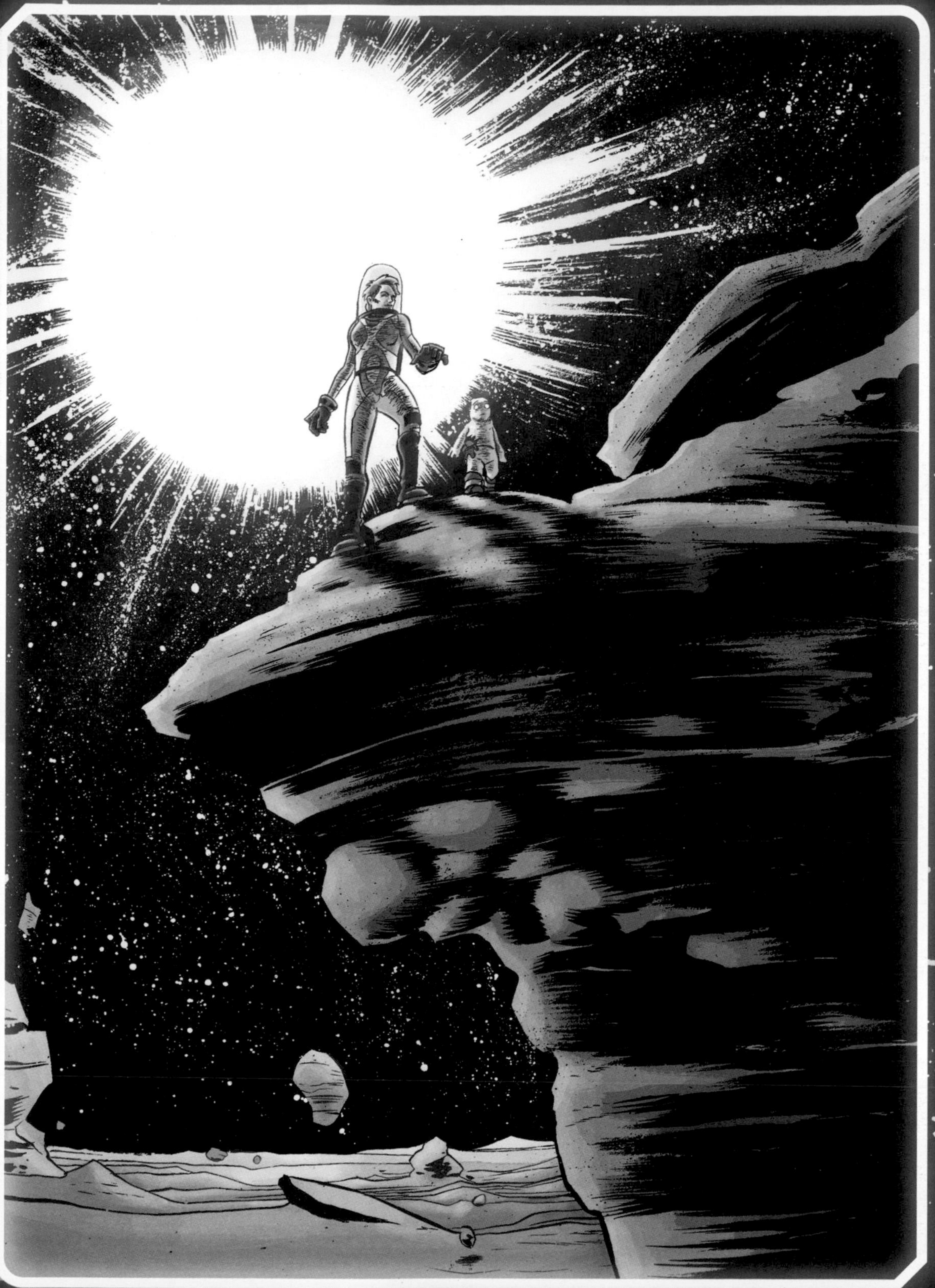

Dave Chisholm is a trumpet player, cartoonist, composer, and educator currently residing in Rochester, NY where he received his doctorate in jazz trumpet from the Eastman School of Music in 2013.

He coexists in both the music and comics worlds, resulting in a wide variety of creative projects.

Additional comic/graphic novel works include kaleidoscopic portrait of saxophonist Charlie Parker *Chasin' the Bird* (Z2 Comics, 2020), graphic novel + soundtrack *Instrumental* (Z2, 2017), as well as a variety of short stories for award-winning anthologies. He also teaches visual art, cartooning, and music at Rochester Institute of Technology and The Hochstein School in Rochester, NY.

He spends his free time hanging out with his wife Elise and their two cats Tillie and Penny.

DAVECHISHOLMMUSIC.COM